£37.50

NB

R

00

D1144797

Heritage Interpretation
Volume 1

Heritage Interpretation

Volume 1
The Natural and Built Environment

Edited by
David L. Uzzell

Belhaven Press
A division of Pinter Publishers
London and New York

First published in Great Britain in 1989 by
Belhaven Press (a division of Pinter Publishers)
25 Floral Street, London WC2E 9DS

Belhaven Press in association with the Centre for Environmental Interpretation and the
Society for the Interpretation of Britain's Heritage.

British Library Cataloguing in Publication Data

A CIP catalogue record for this book is available from the British Library

ISBN 1 85293 077 2 (Volume 1 only)
ISBN 1 85293 078 0 (Volume 2 only)

Library of Congress Cataloging-in-Publication Data

Heritage interpretation / edited by David L. Uzzell.
   p.   cm.
   Includes indexes.
   Contents: v. 1. The natural and built environment – v. 2. The
visitor experience.
   ISBN 1-85293-077-2 (v. 1). – ISBN 1-85293-078-0 (v. 2)
   1. Historic sites – Interpretive programs. 2. Parks – Interpretive
programs. 3. Tourist trade. I. Uzzell, David.
CC135.H46   1989
363.6'8 – dc20   89-6668
            CIP

Filmset by Mayhew Typesetting, Bristol, England
Printed and bound in Great Britain by Biddles Ltd.

Contents

Volume 1: The Natural and Built Environment

List of Figures viii

List of Tables x

List of Contributors xi

Preface xiv
John Foster

1 Introduction: The Natural and Built Environment 1
David L. Uzzell

2 Heritage: An Interpretation 15
Robert Hewison

3 Interpreting the Built and Historic Environment 24
Peter Rumble

4 The Hot Interpretation of War and Conflict 33
David L. Uzzell

5 Opening Doors on the Past 48
Merlin Waterson

6 Heritage: A Post-Modernist Perspective 57
Peter Fowler

7 How the Ship of Interpretation was Blown Off Course in the Tempest: Some Philosophical Thoughts 64
Don Aldridge

8 Looking for the Future Through the Past 88
Marc Laenen

9 Is an Archaeological Site Important to Science or to the Public, and is there a Difference?   96
Hester Davis

10 The Eternal Triangle: Archaeologist, Builder and Public   100
Marion Meek

11 Interpreting the Historic Scene: The Power of Imagination in Creating a Sense of Historic Place   107
Bruce Craig

12 Is There an 'Excluded Past' in Education?   113
Peter Stone and Robert Mackenzie

13 Interpreting the Countryside and the Natural Environment   121
Adrian Phillips

14 Nature Interpretation: A Threat to the Countryside   132
Kenneth R. Olwig

15 Interpretation in Australian National Parks and Reserves: Status, Evaluation and Prospects   142
Elizabeth A. Beckmann

16 Interpreting Cross-Cultural Sites   153
Astrida Upitis

17 The Birth of Interpretation in Spain   161
Jorge Morales

18 Interpretation: A Key to Tourism and Conservation Expansion in Developing Countries   165
David Sayers

19 Interpreting the United Kingdom's Marine Environment   170
Susan Gubbay

20 Interpretation, Participation and National Park Planning   179
Timothy O'Riordan, Ann Shadrake and Christopher Wood

21 Interpreters in the Community: A Discussion Paper   190
Gillian Binks

22 Towards a Co-ordinated Approach to Interpretation Training in Britain   201
Geoffrey Lord and Graham Barrow

23 Training Interpreters   209
William J. Lewis

24 Romantic Interpretation: A Look at Training Techniques   214
John Wagoner

25 For the Dedicated Interpreter of Many Years: Renewal, Invention
   and Creativity   220
   John Brooks

26 Development Training and its Significance in Training Interpreters 224
   James Carter

27 Where Arts, Imagination and Environment Meet   229
   Jan Dungey

   Index   232

   Contents for Volume 2   236

List of Figures

3.1 Tilbury Fort Armada Exhibition, 1988   28
3.2 Participants take lunch at the Tilbury Fort Armada Exhibition   30
4.1 Oradour-sur-Glane: before the Second World War   37
4.2 Oradour-sur-Glane: the village was totally destroyed after the
     massacre   37
4.3 Removing the remains of the women and children after the
     massacre in Oradour-sur-Glane   39
4.4 One of the victims of the massacre   39
4.5 Oradour-sur-Glane today: a place of remembrance and a tourist
     attraction   40
4.6 Re-enacting the English Civil War at Kenilworth Castle   45
5.1 The Long Gallery, Blickling Hall, Norfolk   51
5.2 Blickling Hall at night   52
5.3 Peter The Great Room, Blickling Hall, Norfolk   53
10.1 Londonderry Walls with attached houses removed, presented as
     'perfect'   101
10.2 Clough Castle with stone tower near collapse in 1980   102
10.3 Clough Castle interior in 1980   103
10.4 Clough Castle – over-restored or not enough?   104
10.5 Grey Abbey in 1874   105
10.6 Grey Abbey as restored in the early 20th century with honest,
     but obtrusive flying buttresses   106
12.1 Stonehenge: a world heritage site   118
19.1 Stages in promoting marine conservation at coastal sites   171
19.2 Objectives for groups contacted by coastal wardens   172
19.3 Messages wardens should try to promote   174
19.4 Pro-forma for considering aspects of using a particular technique
     (in this case an underwater nature trail)   177
20.1 Tilden's model of interpretation   178
20.2 Tilden's model applied to the research project   180

20.3 Tilden's model extended as the basis of the current interpretive
      project   182
20.4 Principal interests involved in the Yorkshire Dales National Park
      interpretive project   183
20.5 Basic format for third (choices) stage of the interpretive packages 188
24.1 Romantic interpretation   218

List of Tables

7.1 Site interpretation and environmental education for schools 66
7.2 Nature conservation attitudes 74
15.1 Australian national park management organizations, and specific staffing/funding levels for interpretive services 144
19.1 Suitability of various techniques for promoting themes 176
22.1 Suggested areas of training required by different groups of staff involved in planning, managing and delivering interpretive services 203
22.2 A suggested syllabus for training in the philosophy and practice of interpretation 205

List of Contributors

Don Aldridge
Interpretive Planner, Ian White Associates, 20 Royal Crescent, Glasgow G3 7SL, UK.

Graham Barrow
Centre for Environmental Interpretation, Bellhouse Building, Lower Ormond Street, Manchester M15 6BX, UK.

Elizabeth A. Beckmann
Department of Ecosystem Management, University of New England, Armidale, NSW 2351, Australia.

Gillian Binks
Centre for Environmental Interpretation, Bellhouse Building, Lower Ormond Street, Manchester M15 6BX, UK.

John H. Brooks
Museum Educator, Clark Art Institute, Box 8, Williamstown, Mass. 01267, USA.

James Carter
Centre for Environmental Interpretation, Bellhouse Building, Lower Ormond Street, Manchester M15 6BX, UK.

Bruce Craig
Cultural Resources Coordinator, National Parks and Conservation Association, 1015 Thirty-First Street, N.W., Washington, DC 20007, USA.

Dr Hester A. Davis
State Archaeologist, Arkansas Archaeological Society, P.O. Box 1249, Fayetteville, Arkansas, USA 72702.

Jan Dungey
The Company of Imagination, 8 Earsham Street, Bungay, Suffolk NR35 1AG, UK.

John Foster, CBE
Birchover, Ferntower Road, Crieff, Perthshire PH7 3DH, UK.

Professor Peter J. Fowler
Department of Archaeology, University of Newcastle upon Tyne, Newcastle upon Tyne NE1 7RU, UK.

Dr Susan Gubbay
Marine Site Protection Officer, Marine Conservation Society, 4 Gloucester Road, Ross on Wye HR8 5BU, UK.

Robert Hewison
82 Fetter Lane, London EC4 1EQ, UK.

Marc Laenen
Director, Open Air Museum, Bokrijk, Belgium.

Professor William J. Lewis
Professor of Sociology, University of Vermont, 31 South Prospect Street, Burlington, Vermont 05405, USA.

Geoffrey Lord
Secretary, Carnegie UK Trust, Comely Park House, Dunfermline KY12 7EJ, UK.

Robert MacKenzie
Training Manager, National Association of Citizens Advice Bureaux, 115 Pentonville Road, London N1, UK.

Marion Meek
Department of the Environment Northern Ireland, 66 Balmoral Avenue, Belfast BT9 6NV, N. Ireland.

Jorge F. Morales
Interpretation Consultant, SEEDA, C O Monardes 7 40A, 41004 Sevilla, Spain.

Dr Kenneth R. Olwig
Associate Professor, Danmarks Laererhojskole, Geografisk Institut, Emdrupvej 101, Copenhagen NV, 2400 Denmark.

Professor Timothy O'Riordan
School of Environmental Sciences, University of East Anglia, Norwich NR4 7TJ, UK.

Adrian Phillips
Director, Countryside Commission, John Dower House, Crescent Place, Cheltenham, Gloucestershire GL50 3RA, UK.

Peter Rumble
Chief Executive, English Heritage, Fortress House, 23 Savile Row, London W1X 2HE, UK.

C. David Sayers
David Sayers Travel, The Garden, Lissington, Nr. Lincoln LN3 SAE, UK.

Ann Shadrake
School of Environmental Sciences, University of East Anglia, Norwich, UK.

Dr Peter G. Stone
English Heritage, Fortress House, 25 Savile Row, London W1X 2HE, UK.

Astrida A. Upitis
Senior Project Officer, Australian National Parks Wildlife Service, 5 Baines Place, Lyneham Act 2602, Australia.

Dr David L. Uzzell
Department of Psychology, University of Surrey, Guildford, Surrey GU2 5XH, UK.

John J. Wagoner
Chief Park Interpreter, Mammoth Cave National Park, Kentucky 42259, USA.

Dr Christopher Wood
Yorkshire Dales National Park, Hebden Road, Grassington, Skipton, North Yorkshire BD23 5LB, UK.

Preface

The Second World Congress on Heritage Presentation which took place at Warwick, England, in September 1988 was a worthy successor to the pioneer effort of Dr John Lunn and his colleagues who staged the First World Congress at Banff, Canada, three years previously. Over 350 participants from 20 countries were present at Warwick and together took part in some 12 major plenary and half plenary sessions, 44 workshops and a variety of useful study tours.

The Congress was three years in the planning. This task was undertaken by a fifteen-strong Organizing Committee representing a wide range of interests, including environmental, tourist, recreational and academic, supported by a further group of international advisers drawn from twenty-two countries around the world.

The breadth of material contained in the keynote and other papers and discussed in the workshops amply demonstrated that interpreters worldwide are now well aware that theirs is no narrow profession tied only to the special interests of conservation, important though these are in their own right. They recognize that interpretation is now part and parcel of the leisure and tourist scene, with all the tremendous opportunities that provides to help more and more people to understand the vital importance of protecting their environment as we move into the 1990s and towards a new century. Interpreters are rapidly learning the value of promotion and marketing techniques to the success of their work.

It was noteworthy at the Congress, and is self-evident in both volumes of this book, that interpreters have become much less self-conscious about the word 'interpretation' and are now paying less attention to definitions and more to improving the effectiveness of interpretation as a tool for presenting heritage and explaining the importance of conservation to a wider public.

I believe this Second World Congress to have been a significant landmark in the development of interpretation. The two volumes of this book, in my view, reflect the advanced state of the art of interpretation and the breadth of the concerns which motivate interpreters. The wide range of contributions amply demonstrates that interpretation has become an important profession in its own right, with its own corpus of theory and philosophy and a lively awareness of the changing environmental and institutional scene since its early days in the 1950s and 1960s.

This book is not simply a record of the proceedings at the Congress. Rather it is a distillation of the best of the many broadly based contributions which gave the occasion its distinctive character and which, along with the work of other writers on the subject, will make a valuable addition to the range of knowledge about interpretation already on record. That it should appear less than a year after the event is a remarkable achievement and we must all be greatly indebted to its editor, Dr David Uzzell, his editorial board and the publishers for their hard work in bringing the book together and getting it out so promptly.

I would like to take this opportunity to express my warm thanks, as Chairman of the Congress, to my two Vice-Chairmen, Graham Barrow and Professor Terence Lee, and to the other members of the Organizing Committee who gave so freely of their time and energies in preparing for the event, in chairing sessions and undertaking a hundred and one other essential tasks at Warwick.

In conclusion, I wish also to record my thanks to the promoting organizations, namely the Centre for Environmental Interpretation and the Society for the Interpretation of Britain's Heritage, and to their associate, the University of Surrey. Without the initiative of these bodies and their constant support from the outset there would have been no congress and this book could never have been published.

John Foster   March 1989
Chairman, Second World
Congress on Heritage Presentation
and Interpretation, 1988

1

Introduction: The Natural and Built Environment

David L. Uzzell

Heritage Interpretation: Volumes I and II draws on papers delivered at the Second World Congress on Heritage Presentation and Interpretation at the University of Warwick in September 1988. However, this book is not a 'proceedings' of the congress, as all the papers have been carefully selected from those presented, and revised for inclusion. The two volumes of *Heritage Interpretation* attempt to provide a comprehensive 'state of the art' review of current interpretive philosophy, theory, practice and research.

Volume I comprises papers which examine the interpretation of both the natural and built environment, and the role and nature of training in interpretation. The first volume also includes a number of the specially invited keynote papers at the congress, which address the status and philosophy of heritage interpretation as we are about to enter the last decade of the twentieth century and critically analyse the current direction of heritage interpretation and what has come to be termed the 'heritage industry'. As Aldridge writes at the beginning of his paper 'some of the best recent contributions to the subject have come from critics of interpretation and of the so called "heritage industry"' (Chapter 7). The papers in the first half of Volume I have been ordered to put the critics and leading actors of the heritage industry on the same stage side by side. This has not been done as part of an implicit Marxist methodology of contrasting thesis with antithesis with the ultimate intention of arriving at synthesis, although should this be the outcome then perhaps so much the better. Their contiguity reflects the fact that Rumble (Chapter 3) and Waterson (Chapter 5) attempt to answer some of Hewison's (Chapter 2) criticisms of the current philosophy of heritage management and presentation, and in the process raise further issues which Uzzell (Chapter 4), Fowler (Chapter 6) and Laenen (Chapter 8) confront from alternative and critical perspectives.

The papers in Volume II, under the collective theme of 'The Visitor Experience', focus on the promotion, marketing and funding of interpretation; current research on visitors and the effectiveness of interpretive provision; identifying and responding to the needs of visitors and the infrastructural facilities and services required to complement interpretive facilities. The second volume also includes a number of the invited keynote papers at the congress.

Landmarks in the Development of Interpretation

A crucial landmark on the historiographical map of the subject is Tilden's (1957) *Interpreting Our Heritage*. We could look further back to the first interpretive programmes. Aldridge (1975) cites the pioneering work of the Goethes who in 1919 guided visitors around Lake Tahoe in California. Aldridge takes us back even further to the efforts of a British schoolteacher, T.C. Horsfall who, a century ago, conducted parties of Manchester inner city schoolchildren into the surrounding countryside. Likewise, Adrian Phillips reminds us (Chapter 13) of the pioneering work of Hazelius who created the Nordiska Museum in Stockholm in 1886 and the first open air museum at Skansen in 1891. Stimulated by the Great Exhibitions in London and Paris earlier in the nineteenth century, it was the Scandinavian open air museums which inspired the establishment of reconstructed Colonial Williamsburg and its progeny throughout the rest of the world. There was a parallel development of interpretation in the US national parks around the turn of this century by those who had the responsibility of conserving not only some of the most beautiful places in the world, but places which had a national cultural and ideological significance (Runte, 1979).

We could continue to reference the history of interpretation back still further, and no doubt find earlier examples of the activities described above. After all, storytelling and the passing on of shared histories to succeeding generations can be seen as part of the interpretive tradition of making the significant meaningful, instilling appreciation, enhancing understanding and encouraging conservation in its broadest sense. However, all this serves to demonstrate is that interpretation, far from being a new phenomenon, is one of the oldest practices for cultural transference in existence.

In more recent times we have seen the formation of the Association of Interpretive Naturalists and the Society for the Interpretation of Britain's Heritage and the other national bodies throughout the world concerned with promoting good interpretation. There have also been important and well attended conferences, not least of which have been the First and Second World Congresses. While all these events are part of the pedigree of interpretation, they also represent significant milestones in its development. Tilden's book is seminal because he attempted to provide a coherent philosophy and codify best practice guidelines based on his many years experience of interpreting the US national parks. However, by the time Tilden was writing in 1957, interpretation had become a 'service' supplied by government agencies or the public sector. This is not to say that the role of enterprising individuals such as latter-day Horsfalls and Goethes ceased to exist; it is just that interpretation had started to become accepted, at least in the United States, as part of most enlightened organizations' goals and objectives.

Creating the Heritage

It has been a notable feature of recent years that interpretation as a practice has been adopted (some would say hijacked) by the tourism, leisure and public relations industries. Interpretation has been regarded as a novel way of pepping up tired tourist attractions and giving them a value-added component; it has even been used as a way of selling everyday commercial products such as pottery, glassware or whisky, viz, the whisky trails that lead the tourist from one distillery to another around the glens of Scotland, which have been justified by attaching the word 'heritage' to the enterprise. Some would argue that this is entirely appropriate: the whisky industry in Scotland is an important part of Scottish culture and heritage. But we should have no illusions as to the motivation.

This has been taken a stage further with the manufacturing of heritage. There is a recent development within nature conservation called 'creative conservation'. In essence, this means that wildlife habitats are created from what seem to be unpromising, typically polluted or derelict, urban sites. Old building sites and other wasteland are carefully restored, landscaped, planted and managed to provide an ecologically rich habitat for wildlife to establish itself and flourish. This might be seen as a means by which natural processes are speeded up. It is rather more contentious to suggest that what Fowler (Chapter 6) has termed 'post-modernist heritage' can be treated in the same fashion. It is perhaps noteworthy that both Fowler and Hewison (Chapter 2) discuss heritage in the context of post-modernism, with Hewison quoting Jameson's definition of post-modernism as 'flatness or depthlessness, a new kind of superficiality in the most literal sense' (Jameson, 1984). Both Fowler and Hewison raise serious and worrying questions concerning the enthusiasm exemplified by many to promote this product we call 'heritage' as it has led to the creation of phoney heritage, or what Fowler refers to as 'antiquing'. Artefacts, large and small, are 'antiqued' to give a heritage appearance; in some cases their 'soul is antiqued' in order to give the illusion that the presented heritage is significant historically as well as simply being old. It is precisely this myth-making that leads Hewison to argue that our heritage is in danger, not so much from external pressures (e.g. developers and agricultural over-production) although it would be foolish to discount these obvious and real forces, but from within – from the heritage industry itself – due to the abandonment or compromising of the values of stewardship, scholarship and sense of identity wherein lies the true worth of the heritage.

Peter Rumble, the Chief Executive of English Heritage, puts up a spirited defence to the critics of the heritage industry. After the initial refutations that the public's current obsession with the heritage is symbolic of an economically declining and culturally moribund society, Rumble points to the economics of running an organization responsible for a large proportion of the nation's built heritage. English Heritage, like other organizations, is operating in a highly competitive market and visitors' needs and wants are ignored at one's commercial peril. This philosophy has to be balanced against the demands of historical accuracy and authenticity. This balancing act is perhaps most difficult in the case of historical re-enactments. While Rumble argues that compromises inevitably happen and questions whether it does actually matter, both Fowler and Uzzell (Chapter 4) point to the philosophical difficulties inherent in the idea of reconstructing the past. This theme is taken further by Uzzell who argues that versions of the past re-created in historical re-enactments are invariably and often unavoidably treated in a mythical and sanitized way. History is made supposedly benign and inoffensive by the passage of time that separates us from the history being re-enacted.

'Nothing so practical as good theory . . .'

One criticism which has been levelled at interpretive writings is that they are often descriptive, uncritical and lacking any particular disciplinary or theoretical perspective. Such accusations cannot be levelled at many of the chapters in this book. Aldridge, for example, takes the reader through a number of philosophies from social Darwinism to hermeneutics by way of regional ethnology, determinism and human ecology to demonstrate how these have informed both the conservation movement and interpretation this century. The practitioner is always quick to denigrate theory and philosophy as navel-gazing exercises which do little to help with the day to day practicalities of 'doing interpretation'. Kurt Lewin, an American social psychologist, once wrote that 'there is nothing so practical as good theory', and Aldridge has demonstrated, not for the first time, in his provocative essay that an understanding of theory is essential for although it will 'not solve ecological problems . . . it can help to clarify issues, define terms, identify mysticism and expose mumbo-jumbo or "eco-talk" for what it is'.

Uzzell (Chapter 4) draws from cognitive psychology the concept of 'hot cognitions' when he asserts that interpretation usually fails to address the affective dimension of the human response. Most cognitions and decision-making, however cool and objective we try to be, contain an emotional and affective component: Uzzell argues for 'hot interpretation'. Accordingly, interpretation of some of the most crucial issues which dominate contemporary society as we approach the twenty-first century – war and conflict, pollution, the destruction of the countryside and wildlife – should be interpreted rationally and intelligently, but also with feeling and passion. He uses as case studies the interpretation of contemporary East–West conflict in West

Berlin, the Second and First World Wars in England, Belgium, France and Portugal, and a massacre in twelfth-century York. Concluding, he writes:

> We are deceiving ourselves if we think that when we stand in front of a case of medals, or guns or photographs of mutilated bodies we are looking at the past. We are looking also at the present and the future. If interpretation is to be a source of social good then it must recognize the continuity of history and alert us to the future through the past. Interpretation should be interesting, engaging, enjoyable, informative and entertaining. But now and again it has to be shocking, moving and provide a cathartic experience.

Claude Levi-Strauss (1970) drew a distinction between the 'raw' and the 'cooked', and the translation of nature into culture. Society requires food to be cooked for it to be acceptable. By analogy in the media, images of nature are 'cooked' in culture to become more acceptable and part of a recognizable symbolic system. In the process of cooking, nature becomes natural and improved (Williamson, 1978).

Olwig (Chapter 14) cites the example of an interpreter who refused to recognize and accept, in response to a question from a visitor, that a cow was part of nature. The interpreter wanted to talk about lapwings, even though the grazing cow, the lapwing and the farmer's mowing regime are locked together in a critical ecological chain. The interpreter's failure to countenance cows and lapwings as part of the same natural domain, leaves Olwig to pose a number of philosophical questions, such as can the natural be cultural and how natural is natural? Olwig shows that these philosophical considerations are critical to our perception and understanding of places and wildlife as artefacts of nature and culture, how it is through an integration of such natural/cultural interpretation that effective action can take place, for example, by influencing agricultural policy and changing society's values concerning ecology and wildlife conservation.

The Professionalization of Interpretation

The setting up of professional bodies and holding national and international conferences reflects the professionalization of interpretation. This is a good thing as it increases expectation of the highest standards and the development of new and more effective techniques. However, there is a danger with all professionalization that it can lead to a division between providers and consumers, those who have the approved skills and those who do not, those who are 'interpreters' and those who are not, those who are accepted by the professional gate-keepers and through some *rite de passage* become a member of the in-group, and those who remain at the margin. Interpretation has not reached this stage yet, but should it, there are a number of important implications which should be borne in mind.

In the first place, the establishment of a profession invariably implies the acceptance of an orthodoxy, an appropriate way of doing things. Central to interpreters' concerns is the significance and uniqueness of place. Each place is special and requires particular approaches and applications of techniques for its interpretation. There is already some evidence to suggest that once a need for interpretation has been identified by an organization, a formulary response ensues in terms of buying in the latest or most fashionable approach or technology. To a certain extent, visitor centres fell into this category a few years ago. The need for interpretation was almost immediately equated with a need for a visitor centre or what Jorge Morales (Chapter 17) calls 'visitor centre fever'. Rather than reflecting the interpretive needs of the site or the audience for whom the interpretation is intended, the visitor centre fulfilled organizational goals which could be totally independent of conservation, education and even recreational objectives. Visitor centres were seen as symbols of an organization's virility and modernity, similar to industrial corporations' obsession with occupying high-rise offices and developing countries' desire to have their own airline.

Adrian Phillips (Chapter 13) identifies a number of important trends which have characterized the development of interpretation in Britain: its wide acceptance as a practice; its extension into other areas, such as industrial social history; the growing professionalism and expertise in the area; and the wide range of bodies which engage in interpretation for the public – no longer just the public sector but also the private and voluntary sectors; interpretation's beneficial interaction with the tourism industry; and its role in the economic regeneration and diversification of industrially declining areas and areas of agricultural overproduction.

Some may question, however, Phillips' later assertion that a sizeable part of the countryside visiting public is now relatively well informed about conservation and the countryside. Higher car ownership and accessibility (for some) may have exposed a greater proportion of the population to the countryside, but more vicarious contact through television or other media, while it may be a precondition is not necessarily a determinant of awareness. Although awareness levels undoubtedly have been raised we need to know more, through evaluation and assessment, about the public's perception and understanding of the natural and cultural heritage if interpretive programmes are to be effective. Interpretation should start where the visitor is, not where interpreters think the visitor is or should be. This is a message which comes across strongly in the chapters on research in Volume II.

The uniqueness of place and the individual response that is required to interpret effectively, meaningfully and enjoyably to the public means that planning and design solutions should reflect local environmental, organizational and cultural circumstances. Imposing stock solutions that work in one setting or organization may not be appropriate in another. This applies not only to the application of interpretive approaches and techniques in museums and national parks, battlefield sites and art galleries, but equally to countries as a whole. The type of highly sophisticated technological developments which we are now witnessing in the developed West may be totally inappropriate in the Third World. For this reason alone, there can be no such thing as a standardized approach to interpretation. There is a danger, however, that Third World countries will become 'disenfranchised' because they have neither the technological resources nor the skills to implement the kind of interpretation visitors in Europe, the United States and Australasia are beginning to expect. Yet the need to get across the conservation message is clearly no less important in these countries. Therefore, approaches and techniques will have to be developed by interpreters working in these settings which reflect local requirements, resources and messages.

Interpretation and Cross-Cultural Sensitivity

While many papers in these two volumes address the issue of raising the level of awareness and instilling pro-conservation attitudes, this is usually at an implicit level. Astrida Upitis (Chapter 16) addresses directly what she identifies as a challenge for interpreters. The difficulty at Aboriginal sites is to help visitors go behind a superficial encounter of another culture and lifestyle, to an appreciation of their attitude and world view. This is not easy when Aboriginal people's detailed knowledge of the land and the significance it holds for them has come from a lifetime of learning. Visitors to Aboriginal sites are there for a very short time . . .' The challenge for interpreters is to move beyond the superficial where everyone seems to be aware but does not have much in the way of knowledge and understanding to establishing 'cross-cultural common ground'. But Upitis goes beyond making a plea for a more complete understanding and knowledge to emerge out of our cross-cultural encounters. Quite the opposite, she argues; some aspects of cultural knowledge should *not* be communicated.

Cross-cultural interpretation poses political questions, such as who has control over cultural sites and whose interpretation of the past and present is to be conveyed so that sites are not themed or altered either for interpretive effect or propaganda purposes to support particular ideological or political positions as MacKenzie and Stone (Chapter 12) have found happens in the educational curriculum.

Indeed, what knowledge can be shared with the visitor, as there are strict cultural rules and norms amongst Aborigines as to rights of access to their culture? Visitors may assume that having paid their entrance fee they have a right to expect all features of Aboriginal life and culture to be revealed, recognizing no distinction between public and private knowledge. But, as Upitis notes, there are some subjects which arguably are not appropriate topics for public discussion.

The argument that interpreters should be sensitive to native cultures and different value systems and world views is echoed by Hester Davis (Chapter 9) in relation to the 'reburial issue'. This concerns the display of photographs of prehistoric human burials and remains which causes offence to native cultures. It is not difficult to see how minority or outgroups in society become victims of intrusive voyeurism. It is most likely to occur in the case of cross-cultural contact where inter-group differences can lead to the outgroup being devalued for a variety of social, historical and cultural reasons with the consequence that they and their ancestors are treated as depersonalized objects. The tourist dollar/pound/yen is perceived to buy ownership and the right to see all. Native American Indians and Aboriginal Australians are challenging this assumption. There is an important lesson to be learnt by interpreters for the future here, because it is not difficult to foresee the same problem occurring as tourism and interpretation services develop in the Third World (Weightman, 1987).

Intrusive insensitivity has long been a feature of international tourism, ranging from visitors peering through the windows of sixteenth-century cottages in English Cotswolds' villages through to a blatant disregard of the sacred sites and burial places of native American Indians. The desire to know on the part of tourists has to be balanced be a desire to tell on the part of the host culture. Interpreters also have a key role in enabling this dialogue to occur while ensuring cultural honesty, integrity and sensitivity.

The need for culturally sensitive approaches is also addressed in Sayers' (Chapter 18) paper on the relationship between tourism, conservation and interpretation in the Third World. He points out that it seems that 'all the world's interpreters are comfortably based in the developed world, far from where planet earth now needs them, in the front line of the ravaged environments of the Third World'. Political pressure to change land management practices and conserve the natural environment in the Third World seem to have had a limited impact although there are signs of an awareness of the problems and the need for change. Using case studies from Madagascar, the Andaman Islands, Nepal and South Korea, Sayers argues that although tourism is often criticized for its negative impact on the natural environment and local cultures (Consumers' Association of Penang, 1985; Cohen, 1978), the combination of tourism and interpretation offers important opportunities for making an impact on resource protection and wildlife conservation.

There is generally felt to be little need these days for environmentalists and conservationists to justify their actions, certainly in terms of the scientific work which underlies conservation as it affects the natural world. This is also increasingly so for those who are charged with presenting and interpreting the natural world to the public. The built environment does not perhaps have this status yet and, as Hester Davis points out, 'in the United States, archaeologists have for so long only talked to each other'. Davis goes on to highlight the difficulties faced by archaeologists in communicating the meaning and significance of their work to non-experts, either because they use jargon or because they talk about those things in which *they* think the public will be interested. This problem is not, however, unique to archaeologists. Sensitivity and integrity are recurring themes, especially in the context of the cultural heritage. A further aspect of this concerns the integrity of the archaeological heritage in the face of the conflicting needs and interests of conservationists, interpreters and visitors, as Meek demonstrates (Chapter 10).

Giving Interpretation Away

We should be giving interpretation away. By this I mean that interpreters should be giving away the tools and skills of interpretation to enable Everyman to become his or her own interpreter. This can have several meanings. Firstly, there is a danger that the more sophisticated we make our interpretive techniques, the more passive and unquestioning the audience becomes. The visitor sits back and waits to be entertained and interpreted at by banks of tape slide projectors or computers. The development of first person interpretation techniques is perhaps an encouraging sign that imagination has not lost out yet to technology, although as both Wagoner (Chapter 24) and Craig (Chapter 11) argue, interpreters could do much more to unleash visitors' imagination.

Secondly, we should be encouraging people to become interpreters themselves. When we interpret a site, inherent in the interpretation should be the communication of those skills which enable the interpretation in the first place. It is not sufficient simply to interpret a site for visitors: surely we want visitors to be able to generalize from what they have learnt at one site to another site, so that they can interpret those other sites themselves. Tilden was at pains to point out in his second principle that 'information as such is not interpretation. Interpretation is revelation based on information.' Yet so much interpretation is simply information: interpreters should be giving away the skills of revelation.

Establishing interpretation in any country is not simply a question of getting it recognized by statute or by professionals in cognate fields, or even by adequate funding. One can do all those things, but it still takes time to acquire experience and understanding, as Morales (Chapter 17) demonstrates with reference to the development of interpretation in Spain. While Morales places considerable emphasis on training, he also highlights the importance of personal contact between interpreters and the need for opportunities to exchange experiences. We should be concerned that interpretation does not become the preserve of the affluent West. If interpretation is to assume a major international force, then its approaches must be seen to be relevant to those working in Asia, Africa and Latin America as much as Europe and North America. We must also give interpretation away to those responsible for conserving and interpreting the natural and cultural heritage in these countries: but giving interpretation away does not mean imposing our will and technologies.

Interpretation at Sea

Marine interpretation has not received as much attention as other forms of interpretation such as in national parks or at historic sites. This might be expected, although Sharpe (1976) discussed the various opportunities open to marine interpreters more than a decade ago. Susan Gubbay (Chapter 19) describes the attempts at marine interpretation in Britain. It is clear that marine interpretation quantitatively and qualitatively has a long way to go this side of the Atlantic. The cold waters of Britain's coastline provides one excuse and the declaration, only recently, of the UK's first marine nature reserve is another. However, there are two papers in this book which examine this subject, and it is interesting to note the difference between Raymond Tabata's account (Volume II) of the type of experiences for marine interpretation offered in Hawaii and that described by Gubbay.

At West Edmonton Mall in Canada, the owners have added to their 'seaworld' three submarines (more than the Canadian Navy possess) so that visitors to the largest shopping mall in the world can now explore marine life in the comfort of a themed environment. It is a sad reflection of our society that such facilities are provided in a totally artificial environment when the natural world can offer so much more. On the other hand, some might argue that such a development is a truly democratic one. It takes wildlife and inter-pretation to the people and provides interpretation where the people are, thereby heightening awareness of conservation issues and reaching an audience that otherwise might not be reached.

The failure to understand that the presentation and interpretation of sites to the public should be seen as a functional part of an organization's respon-sibilities for overall resource management is exemplified in Beckman's paper (Chapter 15). National parks serve as both recreational and conservational reserves: this inevitably determines management and interpretation strategies, and leads to conflicts in terms of resource allocation, the consequences of which will be familiar to many. Reviewing the status and nature of inter-pretation in national parks in Australia, Beckman reports on conditions which can be readily found in other parts of the world.

Where Interpretation and Participation Meet

At the beginning of the 1970s public participation in the planning process was highly fashionable throughout Europe and North America amongst those local authorities who wished to appear, if not be, highly democratic and responsive to the public's concerns and aspirations for their environ-ment. The postwar years witnessed a major transformation of our cities and some of that change was seen to be for the worse. Familiar places, homes and communities were destroyed in the name of development and improvement.

Public participation was seen as a means of involving the public in the planning process, giving them a role and enabling planning agencies to understand something of the sense of place felt by residents. Unfortunately within the space of ten years public participation changed from being *de rigueur* to a *bête noire*. Both planners and the public became disillusioned with both the process and the outcomes as it seemed not to deliver on either count.

Various reasons have been suggested for this but research at the time clearly demonstrated that communication programmes, even at an elementary level, were not all that they might have been. The public's ability to read and understand maps, for example, was overestimated with the result that the public was not able even to begin to participate, because there was no common language between public and planners (Stringer, 1982). There is a lesson here for interpreters: how often do interpretive designers assume that the public can read maps? To someone who has worked both in the area of planning participation and in interpretation, it seems to me that interpretation offers urban, countryside and regional planners an extensive array of tools to assist in generating a meaningful dialogue with communities. At an instrumental level, interpreters could provide a range of techniques that would more effectively communicate the meaning and significance of places to the inhabitants and to the planners. At a more fundamental level, interpretation offers not only the opportunity to communicate alternative perspectives on the past (which unfortunately it rarely does at historic sites even now), but also to anticipate the consequences of planning actions and indeed alternative futures for the communities affected.

There have been some isolated examples of the application of participatory techniques to aid the interpretive planning process, but the project spearheaded by Timothy O'Riordan, Ann Shadrake (University of East Anglia) and Chris Wood (Yorkshire Dales National Park) in the Yorkshire Dales National Park (Chapter 20) which seeks to involve the moors community in the planning of the agricultural landscape of the future, probably represents the most exciting and comprehensive initiative to date. They contend that 'interpretation can play a vital role in laying out various landscape futures so as to enable those most interested, involved and motivated to participate in the design of the national park landscape of tomorrow'. Their project is particularly interesting in that it has not only established a comprehensive programme of interpretation in order to involve the public, but has built in an evaluation process in order to monitor the outcomes and their effectiveness.

Action is meant to be a consequence of interpretive programmes, yet rarely are visitors informed in unambiguous ways about what they can do to promote or assist, for example, countryside conservation. A further significant feature of the O'Riordan project is that participation presupposes some form of response or action. Therefore, aligning interpretation alongside participation in countryside planning can be mutually beneficial to both planners (interested in encouraging participation) and interpreters (in encouraging action).

In essence, this approach draws on a community-based model of interpretation in that the interpretation presupposes community involvement and co-operation. The discussion paper by Gillian Binks (Chapter 21) focuses on the role of interpreters in the community and the opportunities that exist for communities and community organizations to play a more active role in interpretation, so that they not only become consumers, but also providers, of interpretation. This paper provides a useful bridge between the participatory orientation of O'Riordan's paper and the following papers which concentrate on training needs and opportunities.

Training

A survey undertaken in England in the late 1970s revealed that over 50 per cent of those practitioners who called themselves interpreters had not attended a training course on the subject. Partly this was a reflection of the fact that there were far fewer courses in existence at this time, and partly because it was probably seen as something that many professionals could do given a little practice. It is also probably not unfair to suggest that interpretation in the 1970s was much more in the grasp of the graphic design professionals: interpretation by and large meant leaflets and exhibition panels.

The last ten years have seen a proliferation of interpretation techniques, along with a parallel acceptance of the research findings that 'books on the walls' are often not only boring, but ineffective in getting a message across. In short, people do not read them. There are now many excellent courses which emphasize the importance of interpretive planning, knowing who the visitors are, their interests and knowledge, and encouraging interpretive techniques appropriate to the audience, situation and interpretive subject matter. These range, to take a number of examples from Britain, from one-day training courses and seminars (e.g. those run by the Society for the Interpretation of Britain's Heritage), short courses and workshops (e.g. those organized by the Centre for Environmental Interpretation at Manchester Polytechnic; the Peak National Park at Losehill Hall), interpretation taught as part of other courses and degrees (e.g. MSc in Environmental Psychology at the University of Surrey) through to postgraduate and diploma courses lasting a year (e.g. Diploma in Heritage Interpretation at St Mary's College, Twickenham). The national environmental agencies have also recognized the need for the co-ordination of courses in order to ensure high standards and a curriculum to meet their needs. The Centre for Environmental Interpretation has played a key role in achieving this objective.

Geoffrey Lord and Graham Barrow (Chapter 22) have attempted the difficult task of reviewing the whole field of training provision in Britain. However, it is quite clear that their conclusions are relevant to interpretation and interpretive planners in many countries. Their paper is partly aimed at identifying the shortcomings in the field at present, such as the failure of many employers to recognize that training is of equal value to employers as well as employees. But the value of the paper lies in its prescriptive advice for the development of interpretive education and training as a whole, and the potential constraints on its advancement.

While Lord and Barrow paint the overall picture, Lewis (Chapter 23), Wagoner (Chapter 24), Brooks (Chapter 25), Carter (Chapter 26) and Dungey (Chapter 27) attempt to supply the individual pieces of the jigsaw. Each describes gaps in current training provision and outlines the imaginative and creative programmes with which they are associated as they attempt to rectify these shortcomings. It is especially interesting to see ideas and techniques developed in other disciplines imported into interpretive training, whether it is the use and development of staff training, poetry and creative writing, drama or interpersonal skills. But what is lacking in these papers is any evaluation that these techniques are demonstrably better than conventional techniques. One has little doubt that they are, but one wants to know *in what way* they are better and why? Which aspects of the cognitive, affective and behavioural domain do they address and with what effect?

Reference was made at the beginning of this introductory chapter to landmarks in the development of heritage interpretation. The First World Congress on Heritage Presentation and Interpretation held at Banff, Canada in 1985 was such a landmark. History will reveal whether the Second World Congress held in Warwick, England in 1988 deserves similar landmark status. If some of the issues in this book are addressed then maybe it will.

Acknowledgements

The task of editing and preparing this book was undertaken by an Editorial Board comprising Graham Barrow, Gillian Binks, Malcolm McBratney, Dr Roger Miles, Ian Parkin and Dr David Uzzell, who were originally responsible for organizing the six theme groups of the congress. I am very grateful to all of them for their hard work over an exceptionally short period of time to ensure that this book would be published within a year of the Second World Congress. I would also like to express my sincere gratitude to Mrs Rosalind Gilbert for undertaking a great deal of the administration and typing that a project such as this requires. The speed of publication to ensure that the book is, rather than was, the 'state of the art' is also dependent upon a highly professional publishing staff who at one and the same time know when to 'crack the whip' but who are also sensitive to the pressure of work faced by editors. Iain Stevenson, Patrick Armstrong and Sara Wilbourne of Belhaven Press fulfilled this role admirably.

References

Aldridge, D. (1975) *Guide to Countryside Interpretation, Part I: Principles of Countryside Interpretation and Interpretive Planning*, HMSO, London.

Cohen, E. (1978) 'The impact of tourism on the physical environment', *Annals of Tourism Research*, 5 (2), 215–37.

Consumers' Association of Penang (1985) *See the Third World While it Lasts*, Consumers' Association of Penang, Penang, Malaysia.

Jameson, F. (1984) 'Post-modernism, or the cultural logic of late capitalism', *New Left Review*, 146, 53–92.

Levi-Strauss, C. (1970) *The Raw and the Cooked*, Jonathan Cape, London.

Runte, A. (1979) *National Parks, The American Experiment*, University of Nebraska Press, Lincoln, Nebraska.

Sharpe, G. (1976) *Interpreting the Environment*, 2nd edition, Wiley, London.

Stringer, P. (1982) 'Towards a participatory psychology', in P. Stringer (ed.) *Confronting Social Issues, Volume II*, Academic Press, London.

Tilden, F. (1957) *Interpreting Our Heritage*, University of North Carolina Press, Chapel Hill.

Weightman, B. A. (1987) 'Third World tour landscapes', *Annals of Tourism Research*, 14 (2), 227–39.

Williamson, J. (1978) *Decoding Advertisements*, Marion Boyars, London.

2

Heritage: An Interpretation

Robert Hewison

Although the word *Heritage* has been in existence for a long time, its usage in the present context is relatively recent, and is subject to a variety of presentations and interpretations; from the patriotic, as in the case of the Historic Buildings and Monuments Commission for England adopting the title, English Heritage, to the ironic, as in the title of my own study, *The Heritage Industry* (Hewison, 1987).

Dictionary definitions tend to be deceptively straightforward: 'that which is inherited, one's inherited lot, the condition of one's birth, anything transmitted from ancestors or past ages.' For we know that in practice the word has acquired fresh layers of association and meaning. My favourite definition – which, considering its source, carries considerable authority – was offered by none other than the Chairman of the National Heritage Memorial Fund, Lord Charteris, who when asked what the word meant, simply replied, 'Anything you want.' Did he mean, I wondered, that the word means anything you choose it to mean, or that you can have anything you want, provided you attach the word heritage to it?

It might be hoped that, now that the 'heritage' is the subject of considerable legislation, it would be possible to find some closer definition there. An important moment in the international growth of the heritage movement – and though my own comments in this field have been confined to the United Kingdom, it is a movement that touches both the developed and underdeveloped world – was the United Nations Convention concerning the Protection of the World Cultural and Natural Heritage, adopted in 1972, and which came into force in 1975.

Article One states that 'for the purposes of this Convention, the following shall be considered as 'cultural heritage':

monuments: architectural works, works of monumental sculpture and painting, elements or structures of an archaeological nature, inscriptions, cave dwellings and combinations of features, which are of outstanding universal value from the point of view of history, art or science;

groups of buildings: groups of separate or connected buildings which, because of their architecture, their homogeneity or their place in the landscape, are of outstanding universal value from the point of view of history, art or science;

sites: works of man or the combined works of nature and of man, and areas including archaeological sites which are of outstanding universal value from the historical, aesthetic, ethnological or anthropological points of view.

Article Two states, in similar terms, what should be defined as 'natural heritage'.

Article Three is commendably brief, but fundamental: 'It is for each State party to this Convention to identify and delineate the different properties situated on its territory mentioned in Articles 1 and 2 above.' In other words, within broad parameters, heritage means 'anything you want'. Internationally, the Elgin Marbles are an example of what different nations differently delineate as 'their' heritage.

This legislative generality has been followed in the United Kingdom, which has two National Heritage Acts (1980; 1983). These Acts prescribe what can be undertaken in the name of the concept that gives the legislation its title, without ever defining that concept.

In fairness, the 1980 Act talks about 'providing financial assistance for the acquisition of land, buildings and objects of outstanding historic and other interest' and of materials 'of outstanding scenic, historic, aesthetic, architectural or scientific interest', but these qualities of scenic, (historic, aesthetic etc.) interest are only to be judged so 'in the opinion of the Trustees', and as the Chief Trustee, Lord Charteris has told us, that means 'anything you want'.

The first National Heritage conference, held in 1983, did however produce a useful definition of 'heritage': 'That which a past generation has preserved and handed on to the present and which a significant group of the population wishes to hand on to the future.'[1] But this statement begs several questions. To begin with, it ignores the economic and commercial uses to which the so-called heritage is being put *in the present*. Secondly, it ignores the extent to which heritage – rather like the current meanings attached to the word – is an entirely contemporary creation. Thirdly, who constitutes the 'significant group' which, out of the vast flux of past time, selects that which is to be treated as (in a slightly different sense) significant?

Yet the 1983 definition is useful in that it narrows the meaning down from its dictionary sense 'that which we have inherited' to something which is the subject of cultural choice. And as in many matters of cultural choice, that choice is practically demonstrated by the decision to spend money on something, or by trying to get others to spend it for us. Thus the National Heritage Memorial Fund stated quite categorically in its first report, for 1980–1, that it would let the heritage 'define itself. We awaited requests for assistance from those who believed they had a part of the national heritage worth saving.'[2]

Such self-definitions can be bizarre. A traveller in Australia who visits Woomera will discover a brightly painted collection of rockets and bombs described as a 'heritage centre'.

In practice, the definition of heritage is the product of conflicting interests in our culture, and its real meaning is the job of cultural critics to decipher. Clearly there is a difference between the desire to preserve woodlands and historic houses on the grounds that they represent 'our heritage', a public resource, and the construction of brand new houses on the subsequently razed woodlands under the billboard 'Heritage Homes', or the redevelopment of county towns by a property developer called Rosehaugh Heritage plc.

In Britain, a lot of what we defend as 'our heritage' is in fact 'my heritage', though many owners choose to justify their private ownership by denying it. A reporter for *The Guardian* was told by a country house owner recently:

You have to understand, I am the custodian of a heritage. I do not feel this estate really belongs to me at all. It is only in my keeping to hand on in as good, or in better condition, and so on down the generations. That is the duty that comes with primogeniture. (*The Guardian* 2 June, 1988)

This sounds noble and appealing, but our 'custodian' would be quick to assert to whom the estate belonged if you tried to take it away from him.

If we return to the United Nations World Heritage Convention, we can see that we are concerned with a variety of material objects which are deemed to have 'outstanding universal value'. It is the valorization of these material objects which distinguishes them from all the others that constitute the physical world. These objects are from the past, and hold value because they represent the past in the present. In turn, they call for the exercise of certain disciplines which we regard as valuable in our culture: firstly, the value of stewardship, which is concerned to preserve these objects to the best of our ability. It is a value which we have encountered, in what might be called a privatized form, in the country house owner. Secondly, there is the value of scholarship, which seeks not simply to preserve these objects, but to enlarge our understanding of them, in terms of both of their original significance, and of interpreting that significance in a contemporary context.

These are positive values. And beyond that, this past-in-the-present has another cultural value, much harder to define. This is as a source of location, and hence identity. You don't know who you are if you don't know where you have been. This is a matter that concerns individuals, and concerns nations. Heritage is a source and vehicle for myth. The word myth is as dangerous and difficult to handle as the word heritage. You will appreciate that if I describe something as a myth, that does not necessarily mean that it is untrue. Simply, that it is true in a special sense, in that it has truth for a great many people, and this general belief gives it a contemporary validity. It may contain elements that are unhistorical, or ahistorical, but it adds up to a cultural truth. It may indeed contain a great deal of historically accurate and factually testable material, but this is transformed into a touchstone of national, local, even individual, identity.

But these positive values – stewardship, scholarship, identity – are under threat. The heritage, I contend, is indeed in danger – but not from external threats such as decay or redevelopment, nor even, it would appear any more, from economic recession. The danger is internal, the enemy is within, and it is carrying out a massive subversion of those very 'outstanding universal values' which I have tried briefly to describe. The danger to the heritage is: the Heritage Industry.

It is ironic that while those of a *Marxisant* persuasion have difficulty in convincing people that heritage and the arts are a form of cultural production, the chiefly non-*Marxisant* bureaucracy that manages them thinks more and more in terms of culture as 'product'. Product that is offered to 'consumers', for whose purchasing power the various aspects of the heritage are increasingly in 'competition'. The language of the market structures present thinking about the function and future of the heritage, as indeed it does nearly all discussion of contemporary cultural activity. It is notable that at English Heritage, 'Interpretation' is part of the marketing division. Another example may be seen in Sir Roy Strong's speech at a press conference to relaunch the Victoria and Albert Museum in October 1985. It was helpfully titled 'Towards a more consumer-orientated V & A', and it was during this speech that Sir Roy remarked: 'The V & A could be the Laura Ashley of the 1990s' (Strong, 1985).

This image is more telling than one might at first think. It reveals the probably repressed thought that the ersatz images of the past presented by a Laura Ashley catalogue might be more appealing than the galleries of the V & A. But the plight of the V & A, a great national museum and a resource of stewardship and scholarship, might usefully be taken to represent that of 'our' heritage.

The V & A finds itself, willy-nilly, 'in competition'. Technologically, it is in competition with other forms of communication, both in terms of other media such as film and television, and within its own field, where systems of display have so changed that we may even encounter actors performing in a completely reconstructed environment. Spatial relationships have also changed. As the term 'open air museum' implies, visitors now enter an entirely three-dimensional space, where a visit becomes a 'day out', one of a number of leisure options where museums compete with sporting events, the seaside, funfairs and so forth, for the necessary number of visitors to justify their existence.

But the idea that museums like the V & A − and this applies to ancient monuments and other forms of the built heritage as well − are changing in response to shifting demands from their potential users, though true, is too simple an explanation.

They are being *made* to change as a result of economic pressures, which are the result of political decisions. Traditionally, ever since the British Museum Act of 1753, the great national museums have been a public responsibility, supported by general taxation, and this model was followed by the local museums established from the mid-nineteenth century onwards. In both museum types, access was free in that there was no individual payment at the point of entry or, as we would now say, at the point of consumption.

This principle, at local and national level, is now moribund thanks to government policy. Museums are being forced into the market place. If they remain free at the point of entry they must do more to justify their existence by the volume of visitors passing through their doors and, inside, they must do more to exploit the opportunities for the sale of souvenirs, refreshments and so forth.

The most immediate competitors of national and local authority museums are the so-called independent museums, which have sprung up in large numbers, and which account for the paradoxical growth in the number of museums at a time of funding restraint. The Association of Independent Museums estimates that there are at least 1,250 institutions in the independent sector.

They are termed independent because, although in a few cases they are commercial operations, in most they are non-profit distributing companies or charities under the control of independent trustees. Yet their independence from public sector finance is an illusion. While the national museums complain of the lack of capital for conservation, improvements or purchases, the public sources of finance for independent museums include the area councils funded by the Museums and Galleries Commission; local authorities; the government's urban programmes; the European Community Regional Fund; the English Tourist Board; the National Heritage Memorial Fund and government supplements to business sponsorship, while, at least until recently, unskilled labour has been available via the Manpower Services Commission. The report by the Policy Studies Institute on the *Economic Importance of the Arts* shows that non-national, non-local authority museums gain 53 per cent of their income from public funds (Myerscough, 1988).

The true 'independence' of these museums of recent foundation is their independence from the traditional educational and social-welfare motivations which launched the original museum movement in the nineteenth century. They perceive themselves as part of the leisure and tourism industry, and so have no inhibitions about charging, which they have to do anyway, since they have a pressing need for revenue. 'Entertainment' becomes an overriding factor in their presentation, and they have to be ruthless in extracting revenue from the visitor. The need to satisfy business sponsors that they can draw the crowds is a contributory factor.

The ultimate logic of the new type of museum is the museum that has no collection, the Heritage Centre, where the original purpose of having a museum, i.e. to preserve and interpret in a scholarly manner a significant number of objects, has been almost entirely displaced by the desire to give the visitor some kind of more or less pleasurable 'experience'. The significant finds from the archaeological dig that produced the Jorvik Viking Centre could be displayed on the top of a single table – but that is not the attraction that draws the visitors, any more than the industrial bric-à-brac and domestic bygones of Wigan Pier.

The real paradox of the 'consumer orientation' that is being forced on museums of whatever type of foundation is not simply that concepts of education have been supplanted by concepts of consumption, but that museums – and the rest of the heritage – in addition to being objects of consumption, are also units of production. A new museum is not only one of the convenient ways of re-using a redundant building like a mill or factory. It is treated as a form of investment to regenerate the local economy that has decayed as a result of the closure of that mill or factory. That is why it is relatively easy to obtain the capital funds and public support to set up a new museum. The economic calculations are interesting: museum projects are a useful means of cleaning up a derelict environment prior to business and commercial investment in the area, and the relative costs of job creation are impressive: while the cost of creating a job in manufacturing is calculated as £32,000, and in mechanical engineering £300,000, the cost of creating a job in tourism is a mere £4,000 (Lumley, 1988, p. 22 n. 38).

If, then, the whole thrust of museum policies is towards treating them as objects of consumption and production, the meaning of Sir Roy Strong's remark becomes clear: the V & A *will* be the Laura Ashley of the 1990s because there will be no difference between them. A museum or heritage site will have become just another commodity. Laura Ashley and the V & A will simply be competitors in the same vast cultural market place.

But if museums are centres of production, what is it they produce? To those of a *Marxisant* persuasion, the answer is that they are manufacturers of social and cultural meaning. And the commodity that they produce has been described in a number of different ways:

In 1967 the Situationist Guy Debord called this commodity *Spectacle*;
In 1975 Umberto Eco called it *Hyperreality*;
In 1984 Fredric Jameson called it *Historicism*.

The Situationist argument, as presented in Guy Debord's *La Société du Spectacle* (1967), is repeated in Jameson's essay, 'Post-modernism, or the cultural logic of late capitalism'. Jameson writes that the latest stage of capitalism has been a massive internal expansion, the invasion and restructuring of whole areas of private life, leisure and personal expression. This invasion, I suggest, includes the restructuring and commodification of private memory itself, something that is very evident in the new folk and industrial museums which seek to reproduce 'the way we were', and where individual memories are erased by the collectively reconstructed image of a period or way of life.

In his essay, 'Travels in hyperreality', Umberto Eco describes this restructuring in terms of a deliberate replacement. His examples are taken from the extraordinary Disney Worlds, waxworks and museums to be found in the United States. In Austin, Texas, he visits the Lyndon B. Johnson Library, which includes a full-scale model of the Presidential Oval Office, 'using the same materials, the same colours, but with everything obviously more polished, shinier, protected against deterioration.' The result is that:

The 'completely real' becomes identified with the 'completely fake'. Absolute unreality is offered as real presence. The aim of the reconstructed Oval Office is to supply a 'sign' that will then be forgotten as such: the sign aims to be the thing, to abolish the distinction of the reference, the mechanism of replacement. Not the image of the thing, but its plaster cast. Its double, in other words. (Eco, 1986)

Fredric Jameson attempts to describe not hyperreality, but what he calls 'post-modernist hyperspace', which he associates with 'flatness or depthlessness, a new kind of superficiality in the most literal sense' (Jameson, 1984, p. 60). His chief concern is with contemporary art and architecture, but this depthlessness also applies to the past. 'Historicism', he writes, 'effaces history' (Jameson, 1984, p. 65). Past styles are ransacked at random for an idea of the past which exists entirely in the present. Thus:

It is for such objects that we may reserve Plato's conception of the 'simulacrum' – the identical copy for which no original has ever existed. Appropriately enough, the culture of the simulacrum comes to *life* in a society where exchange-value has been generalised to the point at which the very memory of use-value is effaced, a society of which Guy Debord has observed, in an extraordinary phrase, that in it 'the image has become the final form of commodity reification'. (Jameson, 1984, p. 66)

In conformity to post-structuralist linguistic theory he argues, as does Umberto Eco, that the past is effaced by its own image, and we are 'condemned to seek History by way of our own pop images and simulacra of that history, which itself remains forever out of reach' (Jameson, 1984, p. 71).

My own quarrel with the Heritage Industry is the result of empirical observation rather than any great familiarity with post-structuralist linguistic theory, but I see what they mean. For me the effacement of history and the commodification of the past was summed up by the organizer of 'Fire Over England', one of the Armada spectacles of 1988. He told a reporter for *The Times*: 'If you've got something to sell, then package it up and sell it, and what's history if you can't bend it a bit? (*The Times*, 30 January 1988)

History is gradually being bent into something called Heritage, whose commodity values run from tea towels to the country house. My criticism is not simply that it is largely focused on an idealized past whose social values are those of an earlier age of privilege and exploitation that it serves to preserve and bring forward into the present. My objection is that Heritage is gradually effacing History, by substituting an image of the past for its reality. Our actual knowledge and understanding of history is weakening at all levels, from the universities to the primary schools. At a time when the country is obsessed by the past we have a fading sense of continuity and change, which is being replaced by a fragmented and piecemeal idea of the past constructed out of costume dramas on television, re-enactments of civil war battles and misleading celebrations of events such as the Glorious Revolution.

Yet this pastiched and collaged past, once it has received the high gloss of presentation from the new breed of 'heritage managers', succeeds in presenting a curiously unified image, where change, conflict and clashes of interest are neutralized within a single seamless and depthless surface, which merely reflects our contemporary anxiety. If there is any illusion of historical perspective in this image, it is usually the pastoral perspective surveyed from the terrace of a country house.

Museums, ancient monuments, preserved artefacts, indeed history itself, as I am well aware, have always tended to record the achievements and values of the dominant class. All that the new wave of industrial and folk museums has done is to co-opt industrial and agricultural labour experience into the picturesque, bourgeois image of the past. As Horne (1984, p. 111) remarks, in *The Great Museum*, of displays of science and technology: 'What is presented is an industrial revolution without the revolution'. There seem to be no winners – and especially no losers. The open story of history becomes the closed book of heritage, where the cultural values are predominantly white, male and middle class.

These 'outstanding universal values' are, ultimately, commodity values. And that is what is most piquant about Sir Roy Strong's metaphor: the V & A is really a shop. One of the most important areas of every museum now is its shop. New museums are laid out in such a way that a visit to the shop is literally unavoidable, since it represents the only exit, from which you may emerge bearing ersatz items from the past, a history bought off the shelf. Even more striking are the public houses which form parts of the display at places like Ironbridge, or Beamish or Dudley, where costumed attendants sell you 'real ale' (at *real* prices). They are the ultimate site of historical consumption.

The commodity which is the result of the vast system of cultural production, many of whose agencies are represented at this congress, is, I submit, Heritage. Those universal values in the United Nations World Heritage Convention, those values of stewardship, scholarship and cultural identity are now subservient to questions of cash flow and consumer orientation. They are threatened by the ideology that asks, in the terms of the draft subthemes circulated in the preliminary papers for this conference, 'Can the truth be commercially viable?'

My final point is, perhaps, a paradoxical one. The Heritage Industry has got it wrong, even in its own terms. We cannot summon up the past to revive the present, for this obsession with heritage is ultimately entropic. It will lead to a state of inertia, where we are distracted from the present by ever-improving images of the past, and paralysed by the thought of a future which can only, by comparison with these simulacra, be worse than the way we never were.

Notes

1. ref. Heritage Education Trust.
2. ref. NHMF 1980/1.

References

Debord, G. (1967) *La Société du Spectacle*, Buchet/Chastel, Paris.
Eco, U. (1986) *Faith in Fakes*, Secker & Warburg, London.
Hewison, R. (1987) *The Heritage Industry: Britain in a Climate of Decline*, Methuen, London.
Horne, D. (1984) *The Great Museum: the Re-presentation of History*, Pluto Press, London.
Jameson, F. (1984) 'Postmodernism, or the cultural logic of late capitalism', *New Left Review*, 146, 53–92.
Lumley, R. (ed.) (1988) *The Museum Time-Machine*, Routledge, London.
Myerscough, J. (1988) *The Economic Importance of the Arts in Britain*, Policy Studies Institute, London.
National Heritage Act 1980, HMSO, London.
National Heritage Act 1983, HMSO, London.
National Heritage Memorial Fund 1981, *Annual Report, 1980/81*, London.
Strong, R. (1985) 'Towards a more consumer-orientated V & A', typescript press release, V & A, London.

3

Interpreting the Built and Historic Environment

Peter Rumble

Those who attempt to interpret and present the past, at least in England, have a lot to answer for. We have been told that we misrepresent or falsify the past: that we create and foster a soft society which looks back romantically at those days when rustics danced around the maypole before slipping into the woods; we encourage eating, drinking and belching at some mock medieval feast, where participants are more concerned to leer at the low-cut dress of the serving wench that to wrestle with the social, political, economic and technological problems of today; and that we contribute to a long-term economic decline. This is, of course, a garbled version of some of the serious issues which we face when interpreting the past.

It is not my intention to spend much time refuting these arguments, but as they are voiced with increasing frequency it is worthwhile addressing two of them. They relate to the social and economic impact of what we do.

The first argument runs that the current interest in our heritage and the development of the heritage business is unhealthy because it concentrates people's minds on the past, a past which can only be inadequately represented, and that an excessive interest in the past is a symptom of, or contributory factor to, a nation in decline. There is no decisive evidence to support this proposition. One should ask about the nature of that interest. Is it the curiosity of an emerging nation in its past? Is it a search for stability in a fast-changing society? Is it a society in the middle age of its life span contemplating its historical navel? Certainly, there have been periods when an absorption in the past can be linked with a nation's political, moral and economic decline. That is probably true of Venice and of Spain during parts of their history. But one can also select examples to argue the converse. Few people would suggest that the Italian renaissance was not a time of one of the greatest flourishings of art in man's history. It was also a period of the deepest respect for and interest in the classical past. The flowering of French culture in Racine, Corneille and David was again related to the classical past. The same can be said of Augustan Rome. The only conclusion I can draw is that the past can provide either an inspiration for the future or a debilitating, even decadent, yearning for earlier assumed glories. The interest occurs throughout a nation's rise and fall and seems to me to be neither the exclusive cause nor the symptom of either strength or weakness.

Likewise, the argument that a flourishing heritage industry points to economic decline seems to me to be a gross oversimplification. Again, what is the evidence? I suppose that one could stretch an argument and point to the circuses and spectacles of Rome in decline as an analogy with some current interest in historical spectacle, but is there any direct correlation between economic success or decline and the interest in the past? If one looks at Japan, Australia, Great Britain, Germany, the United States or indeed the emerging Third World nations, what pattern exists? There is none. What one can identify is an interest in the past at almost any stage in a nation's history. That interest may come from academic curiosity, nationalistic pride, economic or military threat or a dozen other causes. It may be heightened at periods of either intense growth or decline but it is extraordinarily difficult to point to a causal relationship between the two. If anything, I would see our present interest in the past as a response to greater leisure time or spending power, or both. Of course, greater leisure time for some may come about through economic success or failure.

Let me turn to the more positive aspects of heritage presentation and interpretation and in particular the theme of interpreting the built and historic environment. We are talking about assets of immense historical, cultural and social value. It is the unique nature of those assets which above all should condition the purpose and nature of their interpretation. Consider, for example, the buildings and monuments which we in English Heritage administer. They have an immense time span and variety. They range over a period of some 4,000 years. They include prehistoric sites such as Stonehenge; hill forts such as Maiden Castle; Roman remains such as parts of Hadrian's Wall; Norman and later medieval castles such as Dover Castle and Kenilworth Castle; ecclesiastical ruins such as Whitby Abbey; great historic houses such as Audley End; and factories of the industrial revolution such as Stott Park Bobbin Mill. I could have chosen similar examples from the estate of the National Trust or from the heritage of great cathedrals and churches or from country houses owned by the private sector. It is the nature of these individual assets which should determine the purpose and style of their interpretation. Each illustrates some part of a nation's development in the field of religion, defence, political or social structures, industry and commerce. The purpose of interpretation must be to illustrate that particular aspect, and the style and the media used must respect the monument as part of a continuing evolution of a nation, whether or not we like the ethos or custom it represents.

We will often face the difficult choice of seeing a monument as a component of a much larger canvas, whether it be in the development of monastic life or the development of defences against Napoleonic invasion. The interpreter is concerned to present the story of a particular building or site. One of the greatest difficulties is to know where the story starts and where it finishes. Clearly selectivity is important and in most cases my money would be on telling the story in relation to the individual monument rather than starting the story too far back or with too many sub-plots. I believe that the professional jargon is that one should aim for 'minimum conceptual orientation of the visitor'. If so, I hope to heaven that we do not speak to our visitors as we speak to ourselves.

I sometimes think that the approach which conservationists use to the conservation of our historic buildings can, and indeed should, be used as a model for our approach to their interpretation. That basic approach is still largely built on the philosophy of Morris and Ruskin to 'conserve as found'. We no longer restore 'romantic' castles to make them even more romantic with imaginative embellishments. We don't go in for conjectural reconstructions; we don't go in for imaginative reproductions built on the groundwork or ruins of what remains; we respect what there is. We conduct academic research; we conduct physical research; we record what exists, we examine options, we examine costs; we choose the best option; we do the work; we record it; and we evaluate what is done. I cannot see that any less rigorous approach can be justified for the interpretation of our historic buildings than the way in which we exercise care for their fabric.

So far I have stressed the nature of the assets we are interpreting as the dominating influence, but I doubt whether the public generally distinguishes as sharply as I am doing between monuments of national importance and the 'heritage' business at large. I may not wish our activities to be clubbed together with leisure parks which have historical themes. A Roman feast in a twentieth-century hotel may be good clean fun – or it may not. We have to accept that we compete with such places for visitors, and there are some aspects of their work which we ignore at our peril. These are the qualities of sheer professionalism, whether in presenting a picture to the public, in market research or in commercial evaluation. What is produced may on occasions seem vulgar or meretricious; those marketing the product may be driven mainly by a commercial motive; but, by heavens, the best of them know what they are doing and so should we. If we don't we may fail abysmally in attracting the audience with whom we wish to communicate.

There is a very good commercial reason for saying what I do. Funding and marketing should always be at the back of our minds when discussing interpretation. In the UK, the number of attractions offered to the public increases dramatically year by year. I believe that at least one museum has been opening each week in recent years. The harsh reality is, however, that the numbers of visitors to historic buildings or sites have increased very little over the past ten years. More and more people are slicing at the cake, and anyone involved in interpretation needs expertise in marketing, financing and visitor attitudes if he does not want to stand the risk of landing himself and his colleagues in the bankruptcy court. The able get rich, and the incompetent go bust. Fortunately the assets we interpret are of such permanent value that they have an inbuilt long-term interest and commercial value well beyond that of those attractions which are not based on the existence of an historic building or monument of outstanding cultural interest.

It is also the quality of those buildings which adds a further dimension to our responsibilities in their interpretation. Interpretation has been defined as the attempt to create understanding. I agree, provided that the word 'understanding' is seen to have an active quality. There should be a positive educational element in what we do. We should offer the means of understanding and a springboard for further study. Our historic monuments cover the whole field of human activities and experience. They can provide both a stimulus and a challenge. It is this demanding intellectual content of interpreting historic buildings which I think sets our work apart from the sops of more passive entertainment and in which lies the long-term strength of what we do. Of course, we must decide at the design stage the age group of the audience which is being targeted, but the educational element is one which should run through all our interpretation, whether aimed at the young, the teenager or the adult.

I hope it follows that we have a responsibility to work to the highest standards of scholarship. It is something to which we should aspire whether in the living history presentations we commission, the exhibitions we mount or in the popular souvenir guides we publish. We are gladly following a trend which has been emerging over the past twenty-five to thirty years. If one compares some of the early two-dimensional exhibitions or those at the time of the Festival of Britain in 1951 or some of the television documentaries made two decades ago with today's products one can see just how staggering the advance has been. Even so, the lesson may not have been fully learned. In Britain, we have been marketing the 400th anniversary of the Spanish Armada. The reaction to that event provides a fascinating case study for anyone interested in interpretation. BBC television showed three absorbing programmes looking at the event through the eyes of eminent historians using contemporary documents and also by means of operational research on tides, currents and winds, using the expertise of the Navy and the coastguards. The National Maritime Museum are holding a distinguished exhibition, including tableaux, again seeking to establish the authenticity of historical events. It is very traditional and full of rare and valuable objects. They set a somewhat lower value on the role accorded to Sir Francis Drake than does myth and popular tradition. In so doing they aroused the wrath of Plymouth City Council, who held firmly to the cool determination of Drake to finish his game of bowls before finishing the Spaniards. The publicity achieved was, no doubt, good for both! Plymouth's extensive programme included a re-enactment of the game of bowls, lectures and concerts as well as 'It's an Armada Knockout' – crazy Elizabethan games for all the family on Plymouth's famous Hoe promenade.

The English Heritage exhibition at Tilbury was principally concerned to set

Figure 3.1 Tilbury Fort Armada Exhibitions, 1988

the scene for the Armada, to give the basic story, and generally to stimulate interest in the subject. The use of period-costumed actors was designed to break away from traditional exhibition techniques, and the living history event was aimed at being authentic and attractive at the same time. The centrepiece of the living history display, the demi-culverin, was reconstructed after considerable historical research, and everyone's outfits were carefully made replicas.

Thurrock District Council marked the date of Queen Elizabeth's address to her troops by a pageant. To quote from their brochure:

Once again as in 1588 Queen Elizabeth will travel by Royal barge along the Thames to Tilbury Fort where she will be greeted by the Commander of her army the Earl of Leicester.

Riding on a magnificent grey horse, Queen Elizabeth I will lead her entourage of over 1000 of her loyal subjects across the Fort and on towards Parsonage Common where she will make her first address.

But unlike the event in 1588 this visit to Tilbury will not be a solemn occasion for along with Queen Elizabeth I, her Generals and courtiers, will be jugglers, tumblers and fire eaters all creating the colourful pageantry of a Grand Elizabethan celebration. The events include an Elizabethan fayre with Pig and Ox Roasts; ale tents; Elizabethan side shows; children's rides and fun fair; grand firework display; fire eaters, jugglers, stilt walkers and medieval jousting.

Does it matter? Were the public misled in any of these events or were they perceptive enough to distinguish between the historic representation and the entertainment accretions? Who served the cause of interpretation best in the form it chose? What is the role of myth and popular tradition in interpreting our historical sites? How far should the role of entertainment tip the scales between authenticity and the pulling power of the event? I hope that in most circumstances the two are not incompatible. The quality of the research that went into some of the Spanish Armada events was outstanding. It showed a readiness to explore and present events in a non-jingoistic, non-nationalistic way. The distance of time makes all that much easier for an event like the Armada. Worldwide there seems to be a readiness to explore even the recent events of history in a much more impartial way. In the long run, the responsible, authentic presentation of events will stand the test of time in terms of public interest and commercial viability more than those which aim at an undemanding public response. If that means debunking some of the popular traditions, so be it.

Of course, however high our standards of scholarship, we shall continue to face the challenge of how far we can represent historical truth, particularly in living history presentations, and just how far scholarship can be translated into authenticity of representation.

Although it may be easy enough to enact social progress or the great intellectual debates, we shall continue to be faced with how to represent the inhumanity, the cruelty, the squalor, the filth and stench of some events. In living history presentations these can only be enacted to a limited extent. We can't kill people on the battlefields; we can't have dysentery and disease in medieval re-enactments. Do we debase people's understanding of the past because such events can't be fully reproduced? For example, in Colonial Williamsburg we have some splendidly imaginative insights into eighteenth-century colonial life but, at least until recently and before a wider portrayal

Figure 3.2   Participants take lunch at the Tilbury Fort Armada Exhibition.

of conditions including those of slaves was being tackled, wasn't it all a bit too hygienic or antiseptic? Wasn't there a feeling that at any moment Julie Andrews might pop out singing 'The Hills are Alive with the Sound of Music'? But just how far should we go? Even if we cannot have reality in living history presentations, if we cannot have actual torture, we could, for example, give some very effective portrayals by way of frightening presentations. We choose not to do so. It is, of course, the same debate that erupts every so often over violence on television. We try to show some of the harshness and cruelty of war as well as the glories of men's courage, in, for example, the Queen's Regimental Exhibition at Dover Castle. But the line has to be drawn somewhere. I think that our critics would have a substantial point in saying that we misrepresent history if living history events did not lead on to some fuller study.

Almost any interpretation has to be selective and incomplete. The presentation of a great house will almost inevitably concentrate on the glories of the house, its collection of paintings assembled on the Grand Tour, its furniture, the elegance of its gardens, the glories of the landscape designed by Capability Brown or Kent. The presentation of a Yorkshire mining village will almost inevitably concentrate on the harshness of the life of the miner. Both pictures are incomplete. It matters that they are incomplete but I think the accurate presentation from a single point of view can be justified provided it leads on to a consideration of the totality. What seems to me to be a greater danger in any interpretation based on a selective standpoint is the risk of the personal attitude of the interpreter coming through too strongly, particularly in the use of the past to point to a political lesson for today. We ought to be seeking a passionate detachment from the past, passionate in the story it tells, and passionate in the intention to preserve objectivity in the telling of what may be an intensely subjective story.

On the basis of our experience we take the view that graphic reconstructions of scenes and events from the past are a vital part of the interpretation of our historic buildings, and indeed of modern museums, and that they can transform a visitor's experience. But they work best when integrated with actual fragments of the past, whether buildings, personal items, grave goods, furniture and so on. Without this anchorage, a physical contact with the past is lost. Indeed, in some ways unless an event is linked to the relevant building a vital link may be broken and what is left is good or bad theatre. I am conscious that this argument cannot be pushed too far. The performances of Laurence Olivier in Richard III or Henry V may provide as dramatic inspiration to the past as any performance at a monument. But in that case we are dealing with Shakespeare and Olivier and that somewhat moves the goal posts.

Research

My final point relates to research. The main value of the popular reenactments ought not to be that they are easy crowd-pullers but that they are an introduction to the historical background which people might never approach otherwise. We should be willing to explore many versions of techniques to attract people and to interpret buildings and events, but exhibitions and living history presentations are not ends in themselves. They are avenues for a fuller understanding of the people who lived in the past, and of the buildings, towns or cities which they inhabited. However, the effect of what we do is often judged by the numbers of people who attend events or exhibitions, on the amount people spend, and on their effect on subsequent numbers and income. Too often merit is judged solely in commercial terms. Possibly for many events that is the only way of assessing them, although analyses of the reasons for return visits may help. For events aimed at schoolchildren we do, however, try to get feedback from schools about the level of interest and indeed the quality of work following such enactments. Certainly they appear to enrich the lives of the children at the time and subsequently. The impressions we get are largely anecdotal. Perhaps we and others ought to do more research on the educational impact of the interpretation work we are doing.

I should like to conclude by stressing the respect which should be paid to any historic building in its presentation. It would seem to me extraordinary if we did not treat the interpretation of such buildings with the same care as we do their conservation. In one American textbook on interpretation William Alderson and Shirley Low (1985) concluded their distinguished contribution (as are so many from our American colleagues) with words which are as relevant now as they were then:

Finally, we wish to state our credo that historic sites are a part of the national heritage and that consequently they should be run for the benefit of the public at large. We who work for historical agencies do not own the sites. We are trustees for them. They are ours to restore and manage and interpret because earlier generations saved them for us; so we, in turn, have an obligation to future generations who have an equal claim to that heritage. Our trusteeship places upon us an ethical commitment to accuracy in restoration, truth in interpretation and protection for the next generation . . . We do not meet that obligation just by saving and restoring a historic site. Only when the essential meaning of the site and of the people and events associated with it is communicated to the visitor can we truly say that we have met our responsibilities.

Reference

Alderson, W.T. and Low, S.P. (1985) *Interpretation of Historic Sites*, American Association for State and Local History, Nashville, Tenn.

4

The Hot Interpretation of War and Conflict

David L. Uzzell

It makes no judgement upon the morality of a particular conflict
or the justice of a particular cause
to say that we, as interpreters, face a dilemma
in the interpretation of battlefield sites.

Do our usual preoccupations with the tactics and skill of the soldiers,
the magnitude of their success (or failure),
and the historic significance of what took place
in fact serve to obscure wider questions about war
as a means of resolving differences and
war as a source of great human suffering.

Anthony Fyson
Heritage Interpretation (1982)

A Hot Approach

In our society, a detached, objective and cool approach to the presentation
and assessment of information is highly valued, especially before choices and
decisions are made. Even where such decisions involve significant personal
aspects of our life such as career, marriage and health, a cool and detached
approach is aspired to and valued. Such cool objectivity has to be questioned
though, both in terms of whether it is achievable or even desirable. Whether
we like it or not, when presented with information or choices which
challenge our personal interests, rarely do we stand by as disinterested
observers. Our actions are affected by personal emotions, motivations and
conflicts. And as we all know, emotional investment is not limited to those
issues and decisions that affect us personally. Causes, ideologies and the
interests of the various groups to which we belong can excite similar levels
of affective response, whether it is wildlife conservation, historic building
preservation or the dumping of nuclear waste.

Apart from whether such dispassionate objectivity is possible, there is the equally important question as to whether it is desirable? As Janis and Mann (1979) argue, 'A world dominated by Dr Strangelove and like-minded cost accountants might soon become devoid of acts of affection, conscience, and humanity, as well as passion.'

In contrast to this model of detached, cold, routine problem-solving, Abelson (1963) has called our thinking about vital issues which have an emotional or affective dimension, hot cognitions. This is not to argue that decision-making can be divided into two types: cool and dispassionate, and hot and emotional. Rather, it is to suggest that because we are human and not automatons, issues which involve personal values, beliefs and interests will nevertheless excite a degree of emotional arousal, even though contemplated in a calm and level-headed way.

Interpretation at the Front Line

The salience of this notion of hot cognition was brought home to me on a trip to West Berlin where I visited an interpretive centre adjacent to Checkpoint Charlie on Friedrichstrasse. Das Haus am Checkpoint Charlie, tells the story of the history of the Berlin Wall and the successful and unsuccessful attempts by those in East Berlin to jump, climb, tunnel or fly over it (Hildebrandt, 1983). Das Haus seeks to fulfil its purpose in four ways.

The ground floor comprises an exhibition made up of panels of photographs and text in three languages. All available wall space is crammed with such flatwork. In addition, the exhibition contains many of the escape vehicles and contraptions used to pass over, under or through the wall. An objective and critical analysis of the exhibition would reveal all sorts of shortcomings. The power of the message and the strong human interest story, however, overcomes all the design flaws.

On the first floor, an exhibition of paintings and sculpture attempts to communicate the spirit of the same message. This is no less powerful. Thirdly, Das Haus acts as a documentation centre collecting information about the Wall, its defences and the people who have tried to cross it. In this capacity though, it has defined for itself a wider role, the documentation of violations of human rights in the Eastern Bloc. The organization that runs Das Haus sees itself as having an important function in understanding and interpreting larger processes and forces, and taking a wide spatial and temporal perspective.

Finally, from various windows in Das Haus am Checkpoint Charlie, the visitor overlooks the Wall. The imposing Wall and the stark visual contrast between the urban landscapes of East and West, takes the visitor very quickly from the interpreted message to the reality of two very different political and ideological systems. Das Haus interprets not the past but the present, not the distant but the front line.

It would be impossible to leave Das Haus without a feeling of admiration for those who have risked their lives to help others and the bravery of those who successfully or with tragic consequences try to escape; compassion for the families left behind; despair at the misery man can inflict on man; and anger at the brutality of a system that motivates people to jeopardize their own and others' lives for what we in the West consider to be basic and unquestionable freedoms.

Furthermore, it is impossible not to leave Das Haus and pass through Checkpoint Charlie into East Berlin without a highly charged mental agenda for what one is about to see.

The Message not the Media

The organization which set up Das Haus am Checkpoint Charlie was fired to tell the story of the Wall through a sense of outrage and a desire to publicize the contravention of human rights. Should not more – not all, but more – interpretation arise out of this same sense of outrage? This would be hot interpretation.

The stories and issues that interpreters address daily are no less worthy or capable of this type of treatment.

- the destruction of our towns and cities;
- the damage which is being done to the countryside, forests and wilderness;
- the killing of wildlife;
- the poisoning of our rivers, land, atmosphere and, ultimately, ourselves.

These stories are equally as powerful and important as the story of the Berlin Wall. They ought to inculcate and inspire the same sense of anger.

We have spent a great deal of energy and even more money devising new interpretive media and techniques in an attempt to get our message across more effectively. Has this effort been misplaced? Does not the power, persuasiveness and significance of the message lie in the story itself rather than the ever more complicated technology we use to communicate it? Should we not release the energy and feelings which initially motivated and inspired us to want to interpret our concerns about our heritage and environment to others? Why are interpreters unwilling or unable to interpret these issues with the same degree of intensity, passion and commitment?

Interpretation, however, is as much about changing behaviour as heightening awareness and understanding, and changing attitudes. Tilden (1957) and Aldridge (1972) have both forcefully argued that one end product of the interpretive process is the encouragement and development of a conservation ethic. Although crucial to the interpretive process, the link between changing attitudes and changing behaviour is far from straightforward. Psychologists have been wrestling with this issue for sixty years and have found it extraordinarily difficult to specify and predict the precise relationship between these two psychological constructs. Nevertheless, a question a psychologist might pose is can we turn hot cognitions into hot behaviour (Abelson, 1963)? Should not the interpreter ask whether we can turn hot interpretation into hot action?

The Re-Presentation of History

If the interpretation of contemporary conflicts and the need for hot interpretation raises important questions for interpreters, then the presentation, or rather the re-presentation, of history is no less problematic. The issues that emerge raise a number of challenging questions which interpreters need to address if the practice of interpretation is to have any integrity and self-respect over the next decade.

A view recently expressed by Wallace (1987) is that the interpretation of our past is typically deficient in three respects.

(1) We need to strive for a better connection of past, present and future to overcome the tendency of seeing the past as something that is finished with, and which now has simply nostalgic, academic or entertainment value.
(2) We need to stress that any moments considered are moments in larger processes – processes which are still in operation.
(3) Interpretation and presentation should take not only a larger temporal perspective, but a wider spatial and global perspective.

The consequence of this as Wallace puts it is, that 'an opportunity is being lost to inform visitors about great historical processes which have drastically affected their lives, and thus to empower them, by enhancing their capacity to understanding, to perhaps change, their world'.

Second World War

It has been estimated that perhaps as many as 13 million children were killed during the Second World War.

* Some died in bombings and battle.
* Many died through torture, slave labour or execution.
* They were killed separately or in groups – often in front of their parents and friends.
* They were killed in camps, at the side of roads, in their houses, in churches, in woods and fields.
* They were shot, burned, gassed, tortured, poisoned, beaten to death.

Does this make you feel uncomfortable? When did you last feel uncomfortable through interpretation?

Near Limoges in Central France there is a town called Oradour-sur-Glane. It has always been a quiet unassuming place, with little claim to fame. Even during the Second World War it was considered a safe area, with children from Lorraine being evacuated to the town. There is a great deal of

Figure 4.1 Oradour-sur-Glane: Before the Second World War.

Figure 4.2 Oradour-sur-Glane: The village was totally destroyed after the massacre.

uncertainty about why the events of Saturday, 10 June 1944 happened. There is no doubt though as to what happened (Pauchou and Masfrand, 1970; Hivernaud, 1988).

An SS unit belonging to the Das Reich Division surrounded Oradour-sur-Glane and assembled most of the inhabitants in what is called the market place. The 500 women and children were led away to the church where they assumed that they would be safe. The men were taken to three barns, two garages, one cellar and one shed. There they were shot. Straw was piled on their bodies and set alight. Five men escaped. Those who tried to avoid the initial rounding up were shot in their houses: again, a few men and one boy escaped.

The German troops then turned their attention to the church. Two soldiers left an explosive device in front of the altar, which exploded giving off a great deal of pungent smoke. Some were killed by the explosion, some by the subsequent fire and some by asphyxiation. As soon as some of the women and children tried to escape through windows and by forcing open a door, they were shot by the troops surrounding the church. The soldiers then entered the church and machine-gunned at random. They left, but returned again after a short time to pile up the chairs, pews and anything else that would burn, and then set the church on fire. The bell fell from the burning belfry and the intensity of the heat was so great that the bell melted. Only one women, Mme Rouffanche escaped and survived with five bullets in her thigh: she died only last year. The town – 123 houses, forty barns, twenty-two shops, four schools and the tram station – was burnt and destroyed.

Six hundred and forty-two people in Oradour-sur-Glane died on the 10th of June, of which 247 were children and 200 were women. The story as related here is the story as told by Jacques Hivernaud, a guide who with intensity and feeling interprets the events of 10 June 1944. He lost a number of relatives on that day. The survivors of the massacre chose to remember this atrocity by leaving the town as it was found – cars are still left abandoned at the side of the road, and buildings burnt out.

In addition to Jacques Hivernaud and his colleagues, interpretation is by means of a small collection of personal items such as spectacles, watches and identity cards collected from the ashes and rubble of the town. We must not forget that for the new town, built less than a kilometre away, the mere presence of the destroyed and abandoned town is interpretation. The environment itself is a book which can be read by those who choose to read, irrespective of the activities of a group of people called interpreters.

There is also a small shop for visitors, which sells booklets and leaflets that document what happened. The historical photographs on these pages are drawn from some of these publications. Oradour-sur-Glane is now a national memorial, managed by the government. The government and inhabitants of the new Oradour-sur-Glane have chosen to expose the public to the full horrors of the massacre by a sense of collective outrage, anger, despair and, one imagines, hope that lessons can be learnt.

Figure 4.3 Removing the remains of the women and children after the massacre in Oradour-sur-Glane.

Figure 4.4 One of the victims of the massacre.

Figure 4.5 Oradour-sur-Glane today: a place of remembrance and a tourist attraction.

The argument is not being advanced that the government and people of Oradour-sur-Glane are right to do this, or that it is always appropriate when it comes to the interpretation of war and conflict. It is, however, hot interpretation. Do we have the courage to interpret with this effect? Are we prepared to interpret war in this way at the risk of losing some of our market segments or market share? Are we prepared to interpret any of the major environmental issues of our time to awaken awareness in a similar fashion and shock the complacent into action?

Contrast the approach at Oradour-sur-Glane with the Tank Museum at Bovington Camp in Dorset. Amidst the tanks are amusement arcade games machines in which you drive a tank through a battlefield and see how many people you can kill. What is the motive behind this approach? What are the educational objectives of Britain's national museum devoted to the military – the Imperial War Museum – in selling cut-out Waffen SS helmets, other than, of course, capitalizing on an irresistible 'merchandising opportunity'? Indeed, where is the sensitivity of design which makes the museum shop look like the entrance to a promising discotheque?

First World War

So many museums devoted to war and conflict seem almost obsessively concerned with the display of uniforms. It is as if the most remarkable thing about so many thousands if not millions of people killed in battle is the clothes in which they died.

The new gallery devoted to the Second World War at the Imperial War Museum in London illustrates the point precisely. It should be stressed that criticism is not being directed at military museums. These are special cases. They almost seem to be private affairs between past and present members of the regiment – external representations of a collective consciousness, memory and rightful pride.

In so many museums and exhibitions that commemorate and present war and the military, one cannot help but agree with Horne's (1984) assertion that their main consideration in terms of theme and design is the best combination of colour and glitter. As Horne writes 'One room only has armour and another only has weapons – the gleaming metal could be placed in more effective patterns that way. It doesn't matter which particular event is celebrated: all fighting is fun and glory.' The Military Museum in Lisbon, housed in an eighteenth-century arsenal and palace suffers from its over-powering ornate environment: arguably the museum setting is more interesting than many of the exhibits.

The re-presentation of the First World War in the Imperial War Museum pays marginally less attention to the sartorial aspect of this conflict. It does at least try to capture the human dimension; it does convey how the efficiency, organizational skills and technology of the industrial state were successfully harnessed and transferred to the slaughtering of millions. Nowhere, however, does it really convey the scale of the carnage and the horrors of the war. If we just recall that in the Great War:

* 65 million people were mobilized;
* 18 million killed;
* 7 million disabled;
* millions became refugees or military prisoners.

Nowhere is the immensity of this human tragedy communicated. For me, at least, when I think of the Great War three images come to mind – gas, mud and trenches. The first of these – gas – because my grandfather was gassed with chlorine and coughed incessantly because of respiratory problems until the day he died in the 1960s. The following is the recollection of just one ex-soldier who contributed to the Imperial War Museum's oral history project. He is describing his experiences, and for him it left a permanent mental legacy.

The conditions in each year in the winters of '15, '16 and '17 were exactly the same. The trenches were generally up to your knees in liquid mud and there was only a period from May on to September that the trenches had a chance of drying out. We would start off, and it would probably be three miles to the Front, and if we did it in three hours we were lucky. It was dark, the duck-boards were icy and the men were weighed down like a Christmas tree: he was carrying extra barbed wire – a roll of that between two – or he was carrying two or three iron pickets – six feet long or four feet long. Men sometimes fell into a shell hole – it could be four feet deep. Firstly the men started to try and rescue the fellow, but you had to leave him – he'd gone, and there was nothing you could do about it. There was any amount drowned. (Imperial War Museum, 1986)

Unfortunately, in the exhibition the subject matter of gas and mud warranted just two small, dull pieces of text.

The visitor walks along a simulated trench, but one wonders how many visitors appreciate this gesture towards verisimilitude. As far as the exhibition designer is concerned the trench wall provides another opportunity to display medals and the prevailing technology. Large-scale mural photographs providing images of war serve merely as a backdrop to technological achievements.

Contrast this with Jacques Shier's museum at Sanctuary Wood in the Ypres Salient in Belgium. It is one of a number of museums devoted to the battles of the First World War (Holt and Holt, 1984; Glover, 1987; Neuburg, 1988). Here the visitor can view the original front-line trenches, which remain wet and muddy. The scale of devastation was so pervasive that even today, seventy years later, the fields continue to give up bullets, shells, and the other ironmongery of war, not to mention the bones of men and horses. These artefacts are on display in an unadorned fashion in the museum. The museum also has an extensive display of photographs and documents around the walls. However, it is its exceptional collection of contemporary stereoscope photographs that exposes the visitor to an experience of the full horror and misery of the trenches. No attempt is made to buffer the visitor from the affective experience of shock, sadness, if not nausea. Images of men and horses draped across the upper branches of trees as a consequence of shell blasts, and decaying bodies, cannot be construed as entertainment: it can be construed as powerful, effective, hot interpretation.

The Interpretation of Fascism in the Twelfth Century

In 1190, at a time of crusading enthusiasm under Henry II, many small Jewish communities in the East of England came under considerable pressure to be converted to Christianity (Roth, 1978). The choice was simple: they could be baptized Christians or be put to the sword. One such episode occurred in York. After weeks of rising tension and mounting anxiety for the small Jewish community, most of the Jewish population of York moved into Clifford's Tower. They were eventually besieged by the local people, incited by Richard Malebrisse. Anticipating their fate, many set fire to their possessions and themselves. In their own *masada*, they committed mass suicide.

This alone would have been horrifying enough. The next day, however, on Friday 16 March 1190 the besiegers gathered outside the gates of Clifford's Tower and persuaded those who had survived to open the gates, with a promise of clemency if they became Christians. As with the few women and children who survived the initial explosion in the church at Oradour-sur-Glane, it was a trick. The expectation of freedom was rapidly turned into the tragedy and horror of death. As the few survivors of the mass suicide left the tower, they too were all massacred. It is estimated that 150 died.

Clifford's Tower is now a popular tourist attraction managed by English Heritage. A three-sided interpretive panel has been erected within the walls of the castle, which describes its varying use over time as a fortress, a residence, a prison and its place in the politics of the region. Its architectural development, its ownership and its changing fortunes over nine centuries is also examined. Of the events of 1190, it simply remarks that 'In 1190 the wooden tower on the motte was burned down during anti-jewish riots. It was replaced by another, also of timber which survived until 1228 when it was destroyed in a great storm.' Although it is seen as relevant to note that its replacement was also made of timber, it makes no mention of the fact that people were killed, that scores of Jews committed suicide and the remainder of the Jewish population were massacred by the good burghers of York. It is left to the Jewish community to remember and to remind, with a simple plaque at the base of the tower.

Is this a case of being 'economical with the truth' to use Sir Robert Armstrong's elegant understatement? Is it because it was so long ago – too long ago to really concern us? Or is it a straightforward attempt to rewrite, or should it be re-interpret, history? Could it be suggested that while events in recent history are re-interpreted to become the acceptable face of heritage, embarrassing and distasteful events further back in time are forgotten altogether?

There is one issue in interpretation which rarely seems to be regarded as problematic by interpreters: whose interpretation? Whose view of the world are we presenting and re-presenting? Stories are told and relationships are revealed as if they are objectively true, as if there is only one way of understanding an issue, place or event (Uzzell, 1988). History is continually being re-presented, re-worked and re-interpreted.

Re-enacting the Past

Tony Fyson wrote a brief but provocative article on the interpretation of war, in *Heritage Interpretation* in 1982. He wrote:

Interpreters faced with the attraction which historic battlefields have for us all, should entertain the possibility that the need to know, see for oneself and understand what happened there, may be a powerful motive for a visit not immediately compatible with a fun day out.

The issue of the relative remoteness of our historic past and the acceptability of treating conflict and horror as entertainment is made all the more pertinent by the consideration of living history groups and historical re-enactment. Living history groups are flourishing, especially those whose main focus of interest is battle re-enactment. Giles (1986) lists some thirteen living history groups of which many stage mock battles from Roman times (the Ermine Street Guard), through the seventeenth century (The Sealed Knot; the English Civil War Society), the eighteenth and nineteenth centuries (The Napoleonic Association; the 68th Display Team) to the First World War (The Great War Society). Similar organizations can be found throughout Europe and the United States. These groups command large support. The Sealed Knot alone has 3,000 members, which is about eight times the membership of the Society for the Interpretation of Britain's Heritage. Some of the other groups attract members from all over Europe.

Re-enacting battles from the English Civil War or the Napoleonic Wars seems rather innocuous and good colourful fun. Its like men who graduate from playing with train sets to restoring Great Western engines or running steam preservation societies. In this case the graduation is from playing with soldiers to being them. This is not to criticize or devalue their activities. The contribution of these groups to our historical knowledge is probably considerable. The research they carry out on armour, uniform and clothing in order to enhance the authenticity of the displays is second to none. The correct stitching pattern of buttons and the faithful reproduction of colour through contemporary dyeing recipes is almost obsessional.

However, the idea that we can somehow re-create the past must be challenged. I start to feel a little uncomfortable when I read that the Great War Society 'has an excellent reputation for total authenticity. Members can join as either a "Tommy" of the recreated 4th Battalion, Middlesex Regiment, or as a German of the 63rd Line Regiment. Members not only re-fight skirmishes, but also give displays of period drill, weaponry and training' (Giles, 1986, p. 15). Of course, while every attempt is made at authenticity and accuracy, we know that the mud, the gas, the carnage, the horror is excluded for the sake of good taste and presenting 'an enjoyable day out for all the family'.

Freeze-framing our heritage ignores the psychological reality that neither those who provide interpretations of the past nor those who receive these interpretations can avoid loading them with their own twentieth-century perspectives. We cannot re-create the past or provide a 'truly authentic atmosphere', since visitors' perceptions of the past will always be influenced by their present-day attitudes and values. As Lowenthal points out, 'The press of numbers also inhibits a sense of the past: it is hard to suspend disbelief about the seventeenth century with hundreds of other twentieth-

Figure 4.6 Re-enacting the English Civil War at Kenilworth Castle.

century folk milling about' (Lowenthal, 1985, p. 298). If authenticity is of the essence and the suspension of disbelief vital to the spectacle, then there seems to me an element of voyeurism about rows of people sitting down to watch soldiers slaughtering each other. The presentation of 'slices of the past' permits the packaging of romantic and nostalgic vignettes of our heritage which is attractive to tourists and visitors. At best it reduces the educational value of history, and at worst it creates and reinforces myths and promotes sanitized versions of the past where guilt is removed and fantasy rules.

On returning to Oradour-sur-Glane recently after an absence of ten years, it seems to have become more 'popular' as a visitor attraction. One suspects that when the war generation first visited Oradour it was to pay homage – *souviens-toi* as the sign at the entrance to the town reminds us. As that generation ceases to be with us, so the motivations to visit change. It becomes less to do with remembrance and more to do with a day out. This was exemplified for me by a French mother who lined up her children for a photograph alongside the remains of a burnt-out car in the town square. But the nature of the place changes as well over time. It becomes less of a memorial and more of a tourist attraction. The detritus of the day visitor, such as empty film containers, lie scattered among the ruins.

The distancing of ourselves in time from the original event will influence not only our perceptions, understandings and appreciation. It will also affect our feelings and affective response. The edge gets blunted. We become more accepting of the role of voyeur. Are we as willing to watch a re-enactment of the Battle of Goose Green in the Falkland Islands, as we seem to be willing to witness a skirmish from the English Civil War?

Conclusion

Wilhelm Reich was a noted psychoanalyst and a contemporary of Freud. Like Freud, he became a victim of Nazi persecution and escaped from Europe and emigrated to the United States in 1939. Reich argued that fascism is not simply the product of socio-economic factors, as it has been commonly argued, to account for the rise of National Socialism in Weimar Germany (Reich, 1970). He also rejected the notion that fascism is an ideology or an act of political leaders, parties or nations. More profoundly, he asserted that fascist tendencies are not something out there, residing in extremist groups or political parties who have names like National Socialists or the National Front. Rather, fascism is something residing in here, latent in the minds of all men. Reich may not be right, but can we afford to assume that he was wrong?

Our museums and interpretive sites should be centres of excellence for telling the story of our cultural heritage in all its dimensions. Of course, we want them to be a celebration of the finest achievements of man, but if they are to be of educational value then they must also honestly re-present the more shameful events of our past.

To provoke an emotional response is not soft or weak. It is what it is to be human. We are deceiving ourselves if we think that when we stand in front of a case of medals, or guns or photographs of mutilated bodies we are looking at the past. We are looking also at the present and the future. If interpretation is to be a source of social good then it must recognize the continuity of history and alert us to the future through the past.

Interpretation should be interesting, engaging, enjoyable, informative and entertaining. But now and again it has to be shocking, moving and provide a cathartic experience. Tilden's fourth principle of interpretation was that 'the chief aim of interpretation is not instruction, but provocation'. He might equally have written that there is a need for hot interpretation.

References

Abelson, R.P. (1963) 'Computer simulation of "hot" cognition', in S.S. Tomkins and S. Messick (eds) *Computer Simulation of Personality*, Wiley, New York.

Aldridge, D. (1972) 'Upgrading park interpretation and communication with the public', *Second World Conference on National Parks*, US National Parks Service and

IUCN, Yellowstone, Wyoming.

Fyson, A. (1982) 'The interpretation of war', *Heritage Interpretation*, 25 (Summer), 3 – 4.

Giles, H. (1986) 'Living history groups', *Heritage Interpretation*, 33 (Summer), 14 – 15.

Glover, M. (1987) *A New Guide to the Battlefields of Northern France*, Michael Joseph, London.

Hildebrandt, R. (1983) *Es Geschau an der Mauer*, Verlag Haus am Checkpoint Charlie, Berlin.

Hivernaud, A. (1988) *Petite Histoire D'Oradour-sur-Glane*, A. Bontemps, Limoges.

Holt, T. and Holt, V. (1984) *Holt's Battlefield Guides*, T & V Holt Associates, Sandwich, Kent.

Horne, D. (1984) *The Great Museum*, Pluto Press, London.

Imperial War Museum (1986) *The First World War Remembered*, Extracts from interviews carried out by the Imperial War Museum, London.

Janis, I.L. and Mann, L. (1979) *Decision Making: A Psychological Analysis of Conflict, Choice and Commitment*, The Free Press, New York.

Lowenthal, D. (1985) *The Past is a Foreign Country*, Cambridge University Press, Cambridge.

Neuburg, V. (1988) *A Guide to the Western Front*, Penguin, Harmondsworth, Middlesex.

Pauchou, G. and Masfrand, P. (1970) *Oradour-sur-Glane: Vision D'Epouvante*, Charles-Lavauzelle, Paris.

Reich, W. (1970) *The Mass Psychology of Fascism*, Penguin, Harmondsworth, Middlesex.

Roth, C. (1978) *A History of the Jews in England*, Oxford University Press, Oxford.

Tilden, F. (1957) *Interpreting Our Heritage*, University of North Carolina Press, Chapel Hill.

Uzzell, D.L. (1988) 'The interpretive experience' in D. Canter, M. Krampen and D. Stea (eds) *Ethnoscapes*, Gower, Aldershot.

Wallace, M. (1987) 'Industrial museum and the history of deindustrialisation', *The Public Historian*, 9 (1), 9 – 19.

5

Opening Doors on the Past

Merlin Waterson

Recently I was fortunate enough to be in Florence, and revisited the Medici chapels. There could scarcely be a better place for observing how different nationalities respond to great architecture and, in this case, to masterpieces of sculpture by Michelangelo.

The many Japanese visitors seemed entirely preoccupied with taking photographs, choosing to see works of art through the viewfinder of a camera. Perhaps they regarded this as a way of ordering their response, rather as an eighteenth-century visitor on the Grand Tour would have been expected to note down inscriptions or draw rapidly in a sketchbook.

The American visitors behaved very differently. An Italian guide had been employed, and he lectured to them in a passionate, rather theatrical way on Michelangelo. To be rather more precise, he told them a good deal about Michelangelo's attitude to the female body and why his female subjects have such very large thighs. It is a fascinating subject – but not one which concerns us here. On other art-historical matters the guide's knowledge seemed distinctly shaky, and I don't suppose those American visitors left with any idea that Michelangelo was, for instance, also an architect.

Then there were the English visitors; and I found myself behaving in a way which is no doubt recognizably English. We have been conditioned, over centuries, to adopt a literary approach. The English visitor arrives with 673 pages of the 'Blue Guide', or something very like it. On entering, he or she can be observed refinding the place in the guide, which probably involves recourse to the index. Then, once on the right page, there is the agonizing business of trying to identify whether this is the Chapel of the Princes, or is in fact the New Sacristy. It's particularly difficult to decide, if the guide does not make it clear, whether the description of the works of art is going clockwise, or anti-clockwise, round the chapel. Having resolved these difficulties, the English visitor looks, very briefly, up at the ceiling, and leaves.

Perhaps we could explore some other peculiarly British responses to historic sites. There is a particularly revealing passage in the delightful and perceptive diary that the Reverend Francis Kilvert (1977) kept while he was living on the borders of England and Wales. He is writing of a walking holiday in 1870:

About a mile above Llanthony we descried the Abbey ruins, the dim grey pile of building in the vale below standing by the little river side, among its brilliant green meadow. What was our horror on entering the enclosure to see two tourists with staves and shoulder belts all complete postured among the ruins in an attitude of admiration, one of them discoursing learnedly to his gaping companion and pointing out objects of interest with his stick. If there is one thing more hateful than another it is being told what to admire and having objects pointed out to one with a stick. Of all noxious animals too the most noxious is a tourist. And of all tourists the most vulgar, illbred, offensive and loathsome is the British tourist.

What does that imply? Well, first that there is a long tradition of visiting historic sights in this country. Indeed, country house visiting was a popular pastime in the eighteenth century and before. Secondly, I think we had better admit that the British have a natural reticence which prejudices them against any too intrusive interpretation. Our embarrassment threshold is, I believe, reached a good deal more quickly than that of the average American or, say, Italian. And thirdly, there is a romantic streak in many of us, which sometimes means that we would rather savour the atmosphere of a place in solitude than have it explained to us; we like to be able to respond to the spirit of an historic site, even if we don't necessarily understand it.

One of the first qualifications for an interpretative planner, then, is to know when to leave well alone, when *not* to interpret. I remember being particularly grateful for a model example of restrained interpretation when I visited the Grand Canyon, where the US National Park Service deliberately keeps its reception building well away from the point where visitors confront that awe-inspiring phenomenon for the first time.

Similarly, any interpretation that intrudes on a visitor's first perception of, say, the west front of Chartres Cathedral, or the grand approach to Blickling, a National Trust property in Norfolk, is an impertinence. Both the Trust and English Heritage know that we are failing in this respect at Stonehenge; and we have plans for re-siting the car park there so that some of the dignity of the site is restored. What a contrast the present arrangements at Stonehenge are to the lonely, untrammelled beauty of Castlerigg in the Lake District, or Branodunum Roman Fort, in Norfolk.

All this may sound very negative – but is I believe a fundamental principle of sound interpretation. The siting of a car park, the building of a new road or the construction of an intrusive visitor centre can wreck the visitors' enjoyment and understanding of a property.

But getting those very basic things right does not usually happen by accident. Let me return briefly to Florence, to the Piazza della Santissima Annunziata, which I revisited this summer for the first time for twenty years. The piazza is no longer a public car park: you do not have to see Brunelleschi's Spedale degli Innocenti across a sea of shining metal. This masterpiece of Renaissance architecture has also been sensitively restored; yet it is still an orphanage. You can see babies being carried to and fro, below Andrea della Robbia's medallions of fifteenth-century children. Is that interpretation? I believe it is.

If it is necessary to acknowledge that very often it is unglamorous interpretation that is the most effective, then we should also admit that some of the most expensive and contrived presentation is sometimes wholly inappropriate.

One of the most romantic of all National Trust properties is Dunstanburgh Castle, on the Northumberland coast. It is approached on foot – and the walk is of such breathtaking beauty that this is one of those rare cases where there may be justification for not providing an easy access road and car park for less fit visitors.

Recently, the Trust has been agonizing over the rights and wrongs of building a new visitor reception building at Fountains Abbey. This World Heritage Site is our most visited property, and its extraordinary beauty can only be fully appreciated if visitors understand something of the Cistercian order, with its emphasis on austerity and the need for isolation in a remote, wild environment. Here, immediately, we had a conflict. It was only after lengthy heartsearching that the Trust was satisfied that we had found a site which would not intrude on the visitors' first views of the abbey, but would nevertheless work in a practical, useful way.

I have dwelt at some length on the need for reticence in planning for visitors. At the risk of appearing not only negative, but also reactionary, let me also admit allegiance to some of the most traditional methods of interpretation. In this country, for instance, the guidebook remains an indispensable tool – not the obscure, over-long, technical guide, written one sometimes thinks for the benefit of the author's scholar friends – but the guidebook as a way of opening the eyes of a visitor who may be curious, anxious to learn, but not particularly well informed.

The evolution of a house such as Ightham Mote is best explained in a series of simple, cut-away drawings. At a glance visitors can understand what would otherwise be a wordy and technical piece of architectural history. A new guide at Flatford Mill uses a bird's-eye view, which is so much easier to interpret than a map, to help visitors identify the exact spots where John Constable painted some of his most familiar works.

At Blickling we have introduced two new publications to help visitors. The first is *An Introduction to Blickling*: a folding leaflet with very little text, but with an axonometric drawing by James Dodds, showing the house before radical alteration in the eighteenth century. The numerous other drawings provide visual points of reference, hooks on which the visitor can hang key images. It is essentially a tool for helping visitors round the house – and has been very well received.

We have also produced a 'book of the house'. This is not a guide, but is for reading before or after a visit. The essays on architecture, the library, the

Figure 5.1 The Long Gallery, Blickling Hall, Norfolk.

Figure 5.2   Blickling at night.

park and estate draw together new research by leading authorities in the field.

A publication such as this can begin the process of interpreting not just the architectural history of the grand facades of our houses, or the art history of the state rooms, but their social and economic history. It can throw its net much wider. We are now far more conscious of the need to interpret the

Figure 5.3 Peter The Great Room, Blicking Hall, Norfolk.

social context of our buildings; to look below stairs as well as upstairs, to show the sometimes unattractive face of the industry or agriculture which supported them.

I hope we are getting better at acknowledging the human frailties of the families that created some of our grandest properties. The Paget family, for example, owed their title and their place in nineteenth-century court life to the role of the First Marquess at Waterloo, where he led the cavalry and lost a leg. Not surprisingly, the macabre survival of the blood- and mud-splattered trousers he was wearing at the battle are a relic which stirs the imagination of most visitors. But they are then told that the First Marquess was an enlightened and remarkable far-sighted Lord-Lieutenant of Ireland, who was recalled from that post after advocating Catholic Emancipation. At Plas Newydd there is not only an exhibition on the career of this complex cavalry commander, but also a display of photographs of his descendant, the 'Mad' Marquess, who devoted his life to amateur theatricals, in which he took leading female parts.

As it is almost exactly one hundred years since Henry Cyril, Fifth Marquess of Anglesey, embarked on his career in the theatre, it is opportune to give recognition to this long-neglected pioneer of the art of interpretation. As a young man he converted the chapel at Plas Newydd, now a National Trust property, into the Gaiety Theatre, to which he invited some of the most celebrated actors of the day. They were given very minor parts, while he played the leading roles.

Let a contemporary Dresden newspaper take up the story of his international contribution to the interpretation of German history. He appeared, we are told, under the pseudonym 'San Toi', in all sorts of fancy dress:

The splendour and the brightness of the colours, the tasteful combination, and the constant change of the beautiful electric light on the slender form of the artist, clothed in white, gladdened the eye. The likenesses of the German Emperors and the German heroes of the last decades were beautifully rendered. The production was received with great applause.

While we can never hope to tell a visitor the whole truth about the history of Plas Newydd during an hour or two, we do try to present a balanced picture, allowing space for the failures as well as the heroic successes.

Our concern to give visitors insight into the lives of both masters and servants at Erddig, in North Wales, persuaded the National Trust that reversing normal access arrangements would be justified. Visitors enter the house, not through the front door, but like a junior stable hand, through the estate yards. They see working blacksmiths and joiners, and a bakery which is still in operation. They see the portraits of staff, initiated in the eighteenth century and continued by successive generations of the Yorke family, who added descriptive verses. These are by no means all hollow eulogies, as witness the references to Mrs Penketh, a housekeeper whom the family took to court for stealing, but who, significantly, was acquitted:

Her coming we may here remark
Brought to a close a period dark,
For long on us did fortune frown
Until we welcomed good Miss Brown,
One whom this latter did replace
Did for five years our substance waste,
As foul a thief as e'er we saw,
Tho' white-washed by uncivil law.

At the beginning of this paper I suggested that in this country we, as visitors, tend to be literary and rather inhibited in our approach to places. We are, let's admit it, hypersensitive to fancy dress. But the special clothing, of no particular historic authenticity, that a blacksmith dons to do his job, conveys its own powerful message.

Those inhibitions apply much less to children. The Young National Trust Theatre involves annually thousands of schoolchildren in dramatized recreations of significant historical events, ranging from the terrors of the besieged garrison of Corfe Castle to the torments of the wounded from First World War trenches, recovering in hastily improved country house hospitals.

I have made little reference to exhibition panels and audio-visual displays. They have a place, but a limited one. Our aim should be to let visitors experience our historic buildings at first hand, whenever possible. Real life, real activity stays in the mind long after the display panel is forgotten. Which of these two images is the most memorable – the engraving of spinning in a nineteenth-century cotton mill, or the sight and deafening sound of the machines now operating again at Quarry Bank Mill, a museum to the cotton industry at Styal, in Cheshire?

In the quayside buildings at Cothele, in Cornwall, there are exhibitions about the relationship between the late medieval manor house and the history of the river traffic on the Tamar. They are well and competently done. But what my children remember is the sight of the *Shamrock*, one of the last of the Tamar barges and now restored to a seaworthy condition, thanks to the assistance of the National Maritime Museum. The *Shamrock* makes the point about interrelationships, about the wider economic base of a country house, better than any two-dimensional exhibition.

Similarly, at Wimpole the National Trust is preserving and presenting to the public a great estate. Its heart, historically, is an important house, with fine picture collections, books, drawings, furniture and textiles, calling for high standards of conservation and display, and which the Trust has enhanced through loans and acquisitions. The house, now and in the past, was supported by an agricultural estate of 3,000 acres, much of which is parkland landscaped by Capability Brown, Humphry Repton and others, but which retains evidence of medieval settlements in its field archaeology and earthworks. The Home Farm, now a rare breeds centre, provides a use for an outstanding collection of buildings, and gives visitors insight into the history of livestock and farming.

What distinguishes the Trust's work at Wimpole from most museums and from the hundreds of other country houses open to the public is that the visitor is encouraged to think of the estate as an entity. A conscious effort has been made to break down the barriers which so often limit visitors' perceptions and enjoyment. The appeal is to people of all ages, especially children, from all social and educational backgrounds. They can see works of architecture and art *in situ*, in their historical context, instead of being on a shelf in an intellectual display cabinet. It is an answer to those who want to divorce the Trust's work of preserving the countryside from the preservation of country houses, and who see these as separate, conflicting responsibilities.

Visitors are encouraged at Wimpole to understand how the pictures of people and animals in the house relate to the rare breeds, to the farm buildings preserved *in situ* and now more vigorously used than in the past, and to the historic parkland. The recently restored stable block and its exhibition on the evolution of the estate ties these themes together. Drawn by the Suffolk Punches, visitors can make the journey, physically and in their imagination, to medieval settlements, to the household of great patrons of the arts and of letters, and to a model farm.

In his novel *Howards End*, (1910) one of our great twentieth-century writers, E.M. Forster, used the phrase 'only connect'. To the seventeenth- or eighteenth-century creators of our great country houses, the connections between paintings, literature, architecture and landscape were usually very evident; the relationships were frequently fruitful and rewarding. In our own century, with its reverence for the specialist, the temptation to take a limited, blinkered view of history is considerable. However subtle or reticent we may be, it is the role of the interpreter to make these connections.

References

Forster, E.M. (1910) *Howards End*, Edward Arnold, London.
Kilvert, F. (1977) *Diary Selections 1870–79*, Penguin, Harmondsworth, Middlesex.

6

Heritage: A Post-Modernist Perspective

Peter Fowler

Introduction

Driving along the motorway recently, I passed a large white-on-brown sign. It exhorted me, in one and the same breath as it were, to visit the Derbyshire Dales, Gulliver's Kingdom and the Heights of Abraham. Such a sign has no space for explanation, let alone justification, of value judgements; but merely by carrying these three messages, this particular sign might be taken to imply that all three potential destinations were of similar validity. In that sense, it well serves my purpose here for it illustrates the 'anything goes', the 'it's all grist to the mill' attitude which seems to have infiltrated the working practices, even the rationale, of much that is made available as heritage for public consumption.

And that motorway sign is relevant to our considerations for it is one of the suite of tourist signs promulgated in a recent leaflet from the British government's Department of Transport (COI, 1987). The front of that leaflet, decorated with brown signs, also exemplifies my point: 'Camping Site' in one direction, 'Historic House' in another, 'Steam Railway' in another. Does it matter which we choose? Best of all, however, is 'Anywhere Castle'. Will any castle do, so long as it's a castle? Does it matter where it is, provided tourists can drive to it? An impression I am receiving from at least some of the heritage industry is that the answer to the first question is 'yes' and to the second 'no'. Worse, some of those involved seem unable to grasp that both answers are wrong, let alone appreciate that it is a matter of some moment for heritage presentation to be synonymous, not with expediency as a function of exploitation, but with integrity as a function of interest.

Post-Modern in Olde Tyme

In these cost conscious, entrepreneurial days, when balancing the books can so easily seem more important than integrity, we all make our individual decisions in the light of our local constraints and of what appear to each of us to be the best interests of our various heritage concerns. I know this, as head of a university Department of Archaeology, as Keeper of a regional museum, as a member of umpteen heritage committees, and as a private consultant. My thesis, following other analysts of the heritage scene such as Wright (1985) and Hewison (1987), is that the sum of these individual decisions contains, in some respects, certain characteristics which can be identified and commented upon critically; and that two of those characteristics can be helpfully discussed within a post-modernist perspective.

'Post-modernism' is of course a mode or fashion, applicable especially in literary and architectural matters, which has already generated its own library. For my purposes here, I turn to two short articles by the arch-apostle of current architectural post-modernism, Charles Jencks. Both are conveniently in the same book (Papadakis, 1987). One article is called 'Post-modernism and discontinuity', the other 'Post-modernism and eclectic continuity'; the titles neatly make his point in a 'smart alec' sort of way along the lines of 'take what you want, use it how you will, and make no connection'. Nevertheless, I do see a connection between that sort of approach and heritagism today; and in fact the two come together visually in Stirling's addition to the Tate Gallery in London in providing accommodation for a priceless part of our real heritage, the work of J.M.W. Turner, arguably England's one painter of world stature. Jencks' articles together highlight two of the salient strands, eclecticism and discontinuity, which seem to me to run through quite a lot of contemporary heritage presentation and interpretation. In so doing, they raise a number of questions, at least from an academic, and even ethical, point of view. Maybe such a point of view is, in the eyes of some involved, 'purist' and therefore anachronistic, unrealistic, marginal, even irrelevant. If so, the concern underlying my commentary is indeed justified.

Do we recognize where we are in this quotation? 'Many ... reacted by adopting meretricious ornament and cheap details, or robbed exotic styles and cultures for easy effects, or else produced designs that were meant to be no more than jokey . . . [It is] narcissistic nonsense, a minor pseudo-cultural event'. I hope we are honest enough to recognize elements of our own territory there, though in fact the words come from the definition of 'Post-modernism' in *The Conran Directory of Design* (Bayley, 1985, p. 209). We can all think of examples we have seen, perhaps even used ourselves, of 'meretricious ornament', of 'easy effects' and of jokey designs, in other words of eclecticism, to achieve particular aims. Together they amount to a trend, a characteristic of heritage presentation and interpretation.

Do not misunderstand: I am very definitely not thus characterizing, and by implication condemning, all our output. Like you, I can think of many individual showpieces that have not gone down that road; and since sooner or later I have to name names let me instance the Vasa in Stockholm, Greig's house in Bergen, Avebury (though under threat at the time of writing),

Kilhope, and Studely Royal, with Fountains Abbey in England, Birsay and Skara Brae in the Orkneys, the monuments of the New Zealand National Trust and, among many national and state park presentation in the USA, the Chaco National Park, the Roxborough State Park near Denver, and the Trapper Nelson Interpretive Site on the Loxahatchee River, Florida. Quite an eclectic list, with no historical continuity, so very much à la mode.

Forced to generalize, I would have to point to the sites of 'new' heritage, or of 'old' heritage now operating under new circumstances, as those where eclecticism and discontinuity are collectively manifest. Cley in Norfolk, Littlecote and the Weald and Downland Museum come to mind as English examples, though of course they pale into insignificance compared with Mr Disney's creations and those of his imitators in sundry parts of the civilized world. Nevertheless, by no means all of the new old is tarred with that brush. For example, the deliberately low-key open-air presentation by Hampshire County Council of Danebury hill fort in the light of long-term, still current excavations is entirely appropriate. Models too, in their different ways, are three indoor heritage attractions opened this summer in Northumberland: the Bagpipe Museum at Morpeth which, defying the apparent esotericism of its theme, launched itself on a high note by coming second in the 'Museum of the Year' competition; the tastefully modest presentation of Thomas Bewick, his work and his birthplace, at Cherryburn, which exudes an aura of homage and attempts no hype; and English Heritage's new site museum on Lindisfarne which successfully combines sound text, effective graphics and relevant objects.

Reflections on the Verb 'to Antique'

By chance, a particularly apposite publication (English Heritage, 1988) arrived on my desk while I gazed at a VDU, blank apart from my post-modernist title. It conveniently lends itself to comment for present purposes, rather as Jencks' papers do, for the generality of its contents, a point I stress since it is not my intention to appear to be picking on one particular organization: its problems as exemplified here are very much those central to our common concerns. The front cover of the magazine trails a medieval merchant's house restoration in Southampton, properties open to the public in Shropshire, and the restorative work on the gardens at Stowe and Painswick: at first glance perhaps eclectic but then this publication is a magazine and, more importantly, all three items fall within well-known, soundly based and long established policies of England's professional and statutory conservation body.

The back cover is a full-page, colour advertisement which has appeared widely. It is for a commercial company specializing in making, some would say faking, replica garden ornaments, and it beautifully illustrates the eclectic catholicism of our heritage world. It is coy, it is damning of human folly, it is quietly assertive of the quality of its up-market replicas with their 'authenticity' (surely a misuse of the word?) and 'noble patination of age' (one can but ponder the observation that, in a free market society, old age is 'noble' with things and anything but with people). Then, without blush or hesitation, it introduces us to 'Stoneage, our brush-on antiquing solution'. It introduces us to the verb 'to antique', meaning to give a spurious but authentic looking patina of age on the unstated premise that such a patina is desirable.

I fear that some of what now purports to be 'heritage' has been 'antiqued', not only in appearance but, rather more sinisterly, in being presented as if it was significant historically as well as merely ennobled by time. That thought of course takes us into a very grey area: what is historical significance? And is, or should, such significance be a significant part of the heritage business when its immediate priorities are more bums on seats and tourists through the turnstiles, to satisfy management requirements, committee directives or, quite simply, to survive?

The editorial in English Heritage's magazine (English Heritage, 1988) eloquently illustrates the dilemma and, not entirely unconsciously, demonstrates the characteristics of my thesis. Its own thrust is explicit in its headline: 'Making History Exciting', the implication being that, given excitement as a priority, the means are justified by that end. I wonder. In the first place, a lot of what happened in the past, just like much of day to day living now, simply was not exciting, neither to those involved at the time nor to our minds now. So to adopt as priority an excitement-making model for interpretation (*sensu* the title of the Second World Congress on Heritage Presentation and Interpretation), and the presentation that follows from it, is knowingly to bias interpretation (*sensu* an intellectual exercise in academic judgement). This is achieved either by omitting non-exciting history, or by making unexciting history into something that it was not, or by inventing history, perhaps even any history so long as it is exciting history, say in the form of non-attested events. Maybe that last is justified in the heritage ethic; it certainly is not in historical research or scholarship. The sobering fact here is that I should feel it necessary to have to state such a truism.

The past *per se*, but perhaps not that part of its product which we call heritage, is emotionally neutral. It is neither exciting nor dull, good nor bad, worthwhile nor worthless, without our intercession. These value-laden attributes come not from what has happened in or survived from the past; they come solely from our contemporary minds or, perhaps more precisely for we are not dealing the wholly rational, from that human ability to react which we identify in ourselves as an emotional response.

The editorial which has proved to be so stimulating anticipates criticism by admitting that English Heritage's summer programme of events includes various 're-enactments', or just fantasies such as 'Alice in Wonderland' at Belsay Hall, Northumberland, where the presentation does not actually accord with historical fact or legitimate association. 'Purists', it predicts, 'will almost certainly object, if only for geographical reasons, that these settings are inaccurate. Likewise, critics will protest with fervour at the manoeuvres of apparently French Napoleonic troops in indubitably English Palmerstonian forts. Never, they will declare, should English Heritage endorse such distortions of place, time and history.' Having smeared objectors as unreasonable pedants, we then get the patronizing put-down: 'These are serious points of view, which cannot be lightly dismissed.' In fact, they are then lightly dismissed in special pleading of an awe-inspiring poverty of thought and bikini-like ethics.

History can be manufactured and distorted apparently:

(a) because falsities over 'relatively superficial historical inaccuracies' such as who fought whom where and when do not do much harm;

(b) because – and here rumbles out the classic excuse of the miscreant on dodgy ground – 'such liberties are taken much more lavishly by other organizations';

(c) because we do not happen to have the right sites and 'education must *inevitably* be reconciled with the realities of enjoyable presentation' (author's italics).

This editorial is a particularly valuable passage. Of course one appreciates the difficulties of the organization: its brief is not just to look after a fair chunk of the perceived manmade heritage in the English landscape but also to promote enjoyment of it, increase the number of visitors to it and the cash crop from them, and to utilize as an educational resource more effectively than hitherto the splendid heritage it inherited from the Department of the Environment. On the other hand, the eclecticism, not to say opportunism, of the editorial tone is so blatant that one wonders if it was written tongue-in-cheek – or just cynically. There may indeed be acceptable reasons for twisting history but, at least for a prestigious and educational body, these are surely not they: eclectic empiricism simply is not enough, nor is the chronological discontinuity justifiable. Along this road lie 're-enactments' which have taken place of 'events' that never took place, such as the Napoleonic attack on Scarborough Castle (Historic Buildings, 1985, pp. 14–15) which occurred recently for the first time. And indeed, since one is only thinking of a difference of degree, one might well envisage a re-enactment, though it has not so far occurred, of the Battle of Waterloo between The Sealed Knot and the Ermine Street Guard at the Tower of London.

Of course, if such is done purely as theatre, rather as Shakespeare adapted history to dramatic requirements and his creative art, the objections of the 'purists' such as myself would dissolve; it is the presentation of false history as history that has to be criticized and indeed condemned. English Heritage, and other organizations, invite this criticism for, as the editorial states, its presentations, although 'lighthearted pageantry', have 'a serious purpose'. But perhaps I misunderstand. I at first took that to mean that the 'serious purpose' was to enhance the public's understanding of history; if it is the legitimate, but totally different, purpose of providing a bit of entertainment as an end in itself, then eclecticism rules, OK.

As a stuffy, pedantic professor, with a fogeyish and rather quaint predilection for old-fashioned concepts such as factual accuracy and a recognition of the limits of historical inference, I wonder about another facet of this re-enactment or living history scenario. Again, for convenience I can use our English Heritage editorial, but I could equally well have used examples from other prestigious national bodies or commercial enterprises. The purpose of generating *excitement* (its italics) is 'so that our members and other visitors may *feel* (my italics) as well as see'. I worry about these heritage feelies. Of course we can all react emotionally to our experience of heritage whether in its natural (if that is the word) state or presented for us in more assimilable, artificial form. We naturally wonder what it actually felt like to be a Stone Age farmer, medieval knight or nineteenth-century boy chimney sweep. The fact is, however, that we never can know what it was really like to be someone else in another age; and devices, however well-intentioned, claiming to give us that experience are fraudulent. In a sense they are worse than that, for they can send customers away believing that they *do* now actually know what it felt like to live someone else's life in the past. This is, of course, self-delusion and heritage events purporting to provide such genuine experiences are knowingly contributing to the delusion.

To say as much is not to decry all direct, imitative experience: to a large extent it depends on what the experience is being sold as. I am indirectly responsible for such experience provision as a trustee of the Butser Ancient Farm where, as part of our educational programme, my students can handle, in a wattle-fenced field of the same size and shape as prehistoric exemplars, an exact replica of a late prehistoric ard being pulled by two trained Dexter cattle: *not* the real thing but, on the basis of a great deal of interdisciplinary, academic research, as close to it in physical, tactile and visual terms as we can now simulate. And simulation is precisely what we are attempting. We are not offering 'real' history; we are not, through re-enactment, 'living history'; we are not attempting anything more than offering, as a participatory three-dimensional hardware model, a demonstration of just one way from several options of how an Iron Age farmer's life might have been conducted in certain environmental conditions. Involvement of the students in this situation gives them direct physical experience of method; with application, they can actually become reasonably proficient at ardmanship.

In no way, however, does it enable them to feel, or claim that they have felt, what it was like to be an Iron Age farmer, nor would we in any way encourage them so to think. It would be wrong for us to do so, if only because two thousand years of cultural accretion interpose between the perceptions and feelings of an Iron Age man and a 1980s student. And furthermore, of course our own interpretations change: our 1980s version is different from the 1970s model and will itself, I hope, be different again by the 1990s. For, as we all know, the past, or more strictly our perception of it, is both organic and dynamic. In contrast, so-called 'living history' re-enactments of it contain a built-in tendency, paradoxically but of their very nature, to perpetuate academically 'dead' and often pseudo-historical stereotypes. It seems to me therefore that those who lead people to believe they can experience a chunk of the past by dressing up as a medieval knight, or by dirtying their face and climbing up a chimney, are being both misleading and cruel. Whatever the external trappings and the physical experience, psychologically we are of the late twentieth century and we cannot recover in our outlook and sensitivities what our predecessors felt or even, I believe, how they thought (except by accident, and then how would we know?)

Of course, we can recover forgotten skills: we can reinvent by patient experimentation lost points on the course of technological development. We can do what our ancestors did and learn something of what they might have experienced physically. But even here we tend to be somewhat selective, going mainly for the fun things like jousts and fayres and banquets. I doubt if all this activity has contributed one iota to a deeper popular understanding of history. Indeed, the cynic could see evidence in the heritage product to argue that, far from being educative, it has had the effect of buttressing already deeply embedded perceptions. Nevertheless, it is easier, more fun, and more revenue earning than the perpetuities for so many, the cold and damp and hunger, the weariness and illness. Since the majority have not written down their thoughts for most of time, nor were there the appropriate organs of the media to reflect them, I would add to that list a sense of subjugation and a sense of either religious hope or individual hopelessness.

How do we put that over in our heritage interpretation, even if we wish to? And if we do, would the public let us display death, disease and dismay rather than the pap which panders to their expectations? I doubt it, but how often do we even try? No, rather do we encourage people to go via Gulliver's Kingdom, the Heights of Abraham and the Derbyshire Dales – not necessarily in that order – to Anywhere Castle.

References

Bayley, S. (1985) *The Conran Directory of Design*, Octopus Conran, London.

Central Office of Information (1987) *Get on Your Way with the New Tourist Signs*, London.

English Heritage (1988) *English Heritage Magazine*, July.

Hewison, R. (1987) *The Heritage Industry*, Methuen, London.

Historic Buildings and Monuments Commission for England (1985) *English Heritage Annual Report and Accounts, 1983–85*, London.

Papadakis, A. (1987) 'Post-modernism and discontinuity', *Architectural Design*, 57, pts 1–2.

Wright, P. (1985) *On Living in an Old Country: The National Past in Contemporary Britain*, Verso, London.

7

How the Ship of Interpretation was Blown Off Course in the Tempest: Some Philosophical Thoughts

Don Aldridge

The 'What' and the 'Why' of Interpretation

It must surely be obvious to any serious student of the subject of environmental interpretation that if we do not define our terms we shall not be able to communicate on this our chosen subject. I make no apology for this statement, even though it is quite incredible that it is necessary to make it, for of all people one would expect those professionally engaged in interpretation to have thought deeply about what they are doing. From the literature, however, this seems not to have been the case and some of the best recent contributions to the subject have come from critics of interpretation and of the so-called 'heritage industry'.

I must therefore begin with a definition of site interpretation as: 'the art of explaining the significance of a place to the people who visit it, with the object of pointing a conservation message'. (See Aldridge, 1972 and 1975 for a discussion of definitions.) I do not intend to parse this definition word by word; instead I attempt to provide in the following pages a do-it-yourself-kit which will enable the beginner to romp through philosophies which have informed interpretation in the last half century. The reader may come to realize that interpretation is not a science; that site significance is what makes the practice of interpretation worthwhile; that the interpretation is for whichever audience comes to the interpreter; and that to display a thing of significance to the public without attempting to communicate some of its values is irresponsible if not immoral (because it puts the thing at risk). Site interpretation is the core of interpretation, for it is where the subject began. The further one departs from it to off-site and global interpretation the more difficult it is to discuss. This is because interpretation is about place and the concept of place, about putting people and things into their environmental context, restoring provenance to artefacts that have lost their roots so that their significance can once more be seen.

The one thing that every contributor to this book seems to have in common is a stated interest in the conservation of the resources for which they are responsible. This responsibility does not prevent them from being entertaining people but neither does it mean that the primary aim of their job is entertainment. They all have two tasks: first and foremost to ensure that the resource is protected for the benefit of present and future generations; and second, that they should communicate with those who visit the site, and, although it is terribly unfashionable to do so, I shall refer to the end-product of this communication process as a message. One has to admit that the word 'message' raises difficult issues in interpretation because we have to communicate with the public about conservation ideas to stimulate them to think about values, without telling them what to think. This paper explores whether one person's interpretation is another person's propaganda, looking first at conservation philosophies and then at message philosophies. It might be useful at this stage and before leaving the subject of definitions if we boldly assert that it is not possible to interpret to children, following the definition we have just given!

In matters of environmental perception and understanding, children may become more skilled than their parents, but in appreciation, which involves a deep understanding of time scales, spatial ideas and the idea of place, they do not have enough experience to appreciate fully what is meant. We shall look more closely at the meaning of the terms perception, understanding and appreciation later, but for the present we draw attention to the fact that good interpreters working with family groups attempt to overcome these problems by encouraging interaction between parents and children to build appreciation of time and space relations. (For most of us the appreciation of historic time was, at least in part, initiated in the bosom of the family circle, by means of that process we now call oral history, rather than in the classroom.)

In Table 7.1 the major difference between site interpretation and environmental education for schools are summarized. This table compares these two distinct processes under seven headings to show that they have little in common, apart from their objectives. Anyone who attempts to provide for both functions simultaneously in a single centre is likely to face problems. It can be done by interpreters who are aware of these differences and, of course, it is important to introduce children at an early age to their environment. Improving the child's *perception* by such means as 'acclimatization' and other play techniques is fine, but environmental *appreciation* cannot be achieved by play.

What Messages? Philosophies of Nature Conservation

The literature of Western philosophy is vast, and many thinkers have applied themselves to questions which have a direct bearing on modern attitudes to nature conservation. In a paper of this nature we shall concentrate on the issues most relevant to interpretation. The key issue is that most of our ideas are inherited from a body of thinking which dates back over 3,000 years and

Table 7.1   Site Interpretation and Environmental Education for Schools

SITE INTERPRETATION	ENVIRONMENTAL EDUCATION FOR SCHOOLS
1. Objectives Always concerned to seek the significance of the site and put over a conservation message to visitors.	Rarely concerned with significance (since this requires adult judgement of a wide range of complex concepts). Teaching objectives seldom relate to site conservation.
2. Target Audiences Designed for the casual visitor. Anyone who comes to the site is a visitor. The norm is a family group. Visitors come for a recreational experience not for education or moral uplift.	Designed for a school class group of relatively uniform age and ability (compared to the variability of the interpreter's audience). School groups are paid for by the community or taxpayer to make visits on the assumption that they will be educational and that a teacher's presence is necessary.
3. Casual Audiences and Preparation Visitors are not prepared for the visit nor do they book for any services. Frequently the numbers involved are very large, more than a single ranger could manage. Hence interpretation employs media to reach visitors.	Educational groups should be prepared for a visit (as teacher's time is at a premium) and there should be follow-up after the field visit back in the classroom. A booking system ensures that a class gets help from the local expert or ranger.
4. Informal Play v. Formal Education Casual visitors are not likely to want to work or 'go back to school'. Interpreter makes use of the different experiences of child and parent	The best fieldwork often makes use of local identification keys, base maps and worksheets and is related to the school curriculum. Outdoor classes cannot utilize the differing child/adult experiences to anything like the same extent as the family recreation group.
5. Motivation To motivate family groups the interpreter establishes a good rapport, introduces elements of play and interactive techniques.	School groups least easy to motivate; often respond to play techniques. In this area teachers make use of the interpreter/animateur's techniques.
6. Reaching the Audience or Penetration of the Market No ranger service in the UK is large enough to meet all its visitors.	Ranger services in the UK have a strong belief that they are there to work with schools!

Table 7.1 contd.

SITE INTERPRETATION	ENVIRONMENTAL EDUCATION FOR SCHOOLS
7. Length of Stay and Educational Techniques	
The interpreter can expect to have an audience captive for 30 minutes or so. Good staff can extend this period. The use of heuristic methods is difficult because adults expect straight answers to straight questions! Visitor centres provide instant explanations.	School visits are usually for one day or half a day and they can therefore make use of heuristic or discovery teaching. Giving the answers to the child's questions prevents the child from having a first-hand experience, which was the whole point of coming out of the classroom. Visitor centres ought never to be visited by schools!

has been kept alive in modified forms precisely because it still serves a useful purpose.

Philosophy does not solve ecological problems but it can help to clarify issues, define terms, identify mysticism and expose mumbo-jumbo or 'ecotalk' for what it is. Nature conservation and the ecological sciences have one great drawback: they inevitably call for a global view of issues. It is but a short step from this to some kind of holistic mysticism in which everything is linked to everything else by cycles or chains. What follows is an examination of some of the ideas which feature in the philosophies of nature and scenic conservation today, summarized here as a mere two dozen concepts. Many of these ideas have been born in disputation and conflict, and most have been continuously modified to take account of new thinking and conditions. Before we interpreters start 'putting the message across' we might think about which of the twenty conservation messages we had in mind?

The most comprehensive account of this field is Clarence J. Glacken's *Traces on the Rhodian Shore* (1967) whose 763 pages are an eye-opener to those who think conservation ideas are post-1945 in origin!

Keith Thomas's *Man and the Natural World* (1983) covers the period 1500–1800 and complements Glacken's philosophical account with detailed explanations of changing attitudes to wildlife and a scholarly bibliography based on literary scholarship and biology. William L. Thomas's *Man's Role in Changing the Face of the Earth* (1956) presents an account of how changing beliefs affected land use, seen from a geographical viewpoint. Gordon Davies's *Earth in Decay* (1968), in stark contrast to all other accounts which are heavily weighted by the literature of biology, summarizes the ideological changes that stemmed from the evolution of earth sciences. I shall now list and briefly describe some twenty-six ideas which have played a role in formulating our attitudes to conservation. Those which cannot be regarded as ideas in support of conservation are included here because they continue to play essential roles in the debate and they also help to explain how some of our conservation philosophies were conceived.

Ideas Influencing the Concept of Conservation of Nature

First Group: Economic Reasons and the Argument from Design (A to F)

(A) *Creation* brought order out of chaos and waste. Hence land which is wild should be cultivated. It is a Greek view from Diogenes that God created order out of chaos for a purpose and Plato saw God as artisan – creator.

(B) Judaeo-Christian myth is different: God is the Lord-of-creation not artisan – designer and we are servants of the Lord, which is the origin of the idea of man's *stewardship* as a form of conservation.

(C) Man was given *dominion* over nature and commanded to go forth and multiply and subjugate the earth. *Homo sapiens* has this *uniqueness* and is not part of the animal kingdom but was granted privileges by the Creator, at the Creation (e.g. the apex of the food chain).

(D) Nature is a *machine*. God has ensured that the fertility of the earth is not eroded but is naturally replenished by the processes of denudation and decay.

(E) *Teleology* means that God designed everything for a purpose, which being translated today means a rational economic use. Animals can be domesticated, and even apparently useless animals have a purpose for mankind. Aristotle believed that plants and animals are for man's use, the rational end of the formative process or final causes.

(F) *Empiricism*: all knowledge is observed fact, there are no fundamental answers and no final causes. Spinoza's view that all values are human in origin is an important contribution here.

I have grouped together these ideas because they evolved together for thousands of years, from the time of Hesiod in the eighth century BC. In common with all other conservation ideas they did not then die away but are alive today in recognizable forms. We hear echoes of them in: 'Landscape is about land use, not scenery or wildlife habitats, what we need is good husbandry with a landowner keeping land in good heart.'

Second Group: Intellectual and Scientific Arguments (G to J)

(G) Ionian philosophers proposed that there was one *order*, which generates the whole in all its variety. According to Anaximander in 600 BC, order is achieved by a struggle between opposites. Empedocles in 490 BC introduced the four *elements*: fire, air, earth and water, which dominated scientific enquiry for centuries. The Ionians looked for fundamentals of the universe, introducing ideas of the *atomic unit, element, cycle, chain, balance or harmony, variety and interrelationship, unity.*

(H) The Judaeo-Christian view that God is not in nature led to belief that the study of nature and worship of nature was sinful. After the Fall the earth was in a state of decay or *senescence.*

(I) In the late seventeenth century the Cambridge Platonist religious movement resolved some theological difficulties and strongly influenced the geologists but left biologists unmoved. Whilst a new geology saw a *divinely created order*, biology continued with the older belief in a divine designer, recorded in Genesis as a vengeful judge bringing catastrophe and hazards which were punishments upon a sinful mankind.

(J) This schism divided book scientists from the scientific observers. John Ray, true to his biological colleagues, rejected the machine analogy of nature and accepted the divine design but was the first to reject the theory that the earth is in decay. *Deism*, or the belief that theological proof of these matters can never be found in the Bible and that God's works in nature provided abundant evidence, had a profound effect on science, fieldwork and field observation.

These ideas have helped to produce modern answers to the question: why conserve? Today we believe in: the principle of variety, the key to ecological diversity which ought not to be threatened; the concept of conserving typical sites; and the idea of a scientific record and conservation of rare species and plant and animal communities. Hence the philosophical basis of nature conservation is found in the modified deism: causes are sought by scientific field observation.

Third Group: Arguments from Sensory Enjoyment and Escapism (K to M)

(K) Ideas of *escape from the city* and return to nature date from the fourth century AD. Lecantius defined nature as that which a man sees outside city walls. The Greek Hellenistic period contributed many ideas that we think of as modern, such as Columella's 'the country was made by nature and the city made by man.'

(L) By 1850 *rural depopulation and the urbanization of the countryside* began to be a serious problem. The process continues apace today and poses social, economic and philosophical problems which cannot be solved simply by introducing urban thinking to the countryside (e.g. the view that rural areas are principally the playgrounds for urban populations). This has implications for nature conservation and interpretation.

(M) The park or *hunting* reserve had its origin in the Persian word 'paradise' which meant a royal hunting forest. The conservation of wild animals for field sports and the chase has long been cited as the origin of many conservation ideas, including the word conservation: the job description of a conservator in the Norman times, from whence it reached Britain. This use has probably caused more semantic confusion than any other. The urban park derives from play and escapism. Hellenic tree-lined walks, sacred groves and gardens were attempts to bring nature into the city. Virgil's *Eclogues* carried the ideas a stage forward: 'let Athene dwell in the cities that she has founded.' In sixteenth-century Britain the dissolution of the monasteries was the potent factor in focusing attention on the rural, as monastic sheeplands were sold to a new aristocracy and country seats became a feature of British life. In the seventeenth and eighteenth centuries time 'in retreat' could be spent making landscapes, gardens and groves, planting estates, improving the scene and, if possible, the pocket.

Fourth Group: Sensory Enjoyment and Aesthetic Arguments (N to P)

(N) Romanticism applied to landscape and nature (*Nature = Beauty*) is a form of particularization or idealism. It was a way of seeing through a special viewfinder. Environmental interpretation is a romantic pursuit, it cannot be otherwise. (This is discussed in a later section.)

(O) *Sublime* as the opposite of beautiful, invented by Edmund Burke (1756) in eighteenth-century England to develop his philosophical ideas of beauty in scenery. Beauty was smooth, rounded, sylvan, with green lawns and golden sunsets or silver skies and it induced feelings of peace and well-being. Sublime was rugged, aweful, with overhanging cliffs or avalanches, tempests or floods, with bandits lurking in the hills. Consequently it produced feelings of horror and fright.

(P) William Gilpin's (1792) wonderful compromise, *the picturesque*, was the type of scenery which was not too smooth or too rugged, not too dull or too exciting, with great variety of texture and with antique buildings, preferably in ruin, all inducing a desire for sketching or touring.

These eighteenth-century ideas motivate landscape and scenic conservation today and are seen in some of the elements of nature conservation found in heritage conservation, e.g. the special attention afforded to sublime or picturesque mountains, and to sublime or picturesque wildlife, such as birds of prey, especially eagles and ospreys, red deer, badgers and otters. (When we want to make bats and hedgehogs more popular we feature their more aesthetically pleasing and anthropomorphic features.)

We use the vocabulary of Burke and Gilpin when we propose to designate areas of natural beauty. Tourist literature still describes scenery in the language coined two centuries ago. Conservation is firmly rooted in eighteenth-century romanticism, which is essential to its survival: to attempt to rid conservation of its romanticism would probably prove fatal to both nature and wildlife conservation.

Fifth Group: Sensory Enjoyment and the Quasi-religious Arguments (Q to R)

(Q) *Wilderness: the challenge or escape paradox*: The religious idea of *wilderness* is complex, even paradoxical and has at least three main elements. Christ went into the wilderness because it was an abode of evil and the Devil and it therefore represented a challenge. He also went into the wilderness to be alone and commune with His Maker. These two reasons are, in part, the reasons why hermits chose to live in the wilderness but they also had a third motive, which was to escape the evil of the cities and fly from persecution by so doing. The modern ideas of wilderness are now even more complex.

(R) *Solitude and communion with nature* Nature is seen as a book of symbols which we should seek out. St Augustine put it clearly: 'some people, in order to discover God, read books, but there is a great book: the very appearance of created things. Look above you! Look below you! Note it, read it . . . He set before your eyes the things He had made. Can you ask for a louder voice than that?' In medieval times knowing the meaning of the animals as symbols produced a world of allegories and homilies. St Francis (1182 – 1226) urged a *solitary communion with nature*.

For those who seek wilderness today there is either a spiritual value in the experience or the challenge/escape paradox of an outdoor pursuit. If someone tells us that technically no English national park has wilderness because no place is more than five miles from a road, or that remote St Kilda is a hollow military base, the seekers after solitude will still continue to go there. There may be no more scared groves, no Eden, no paradise gardens left, but the experience of wild qualities is almost a symbolic fantasy as it becomes more difficult to find solitude in an overcrowded world. The reason why all conservation philosophies have something to say about wilderness is because it is a concept on which attitudes to nature can be clearly focused. It has become a metaphor for nature and scenic conservation.

Sixth Group: Arguments from Physical and Mental Health (S to V)

(S) Rejection of nature and the *irrelevance of nature*, was originally a religious idea: we are here on this earth in preparation for some other life, and earthly purgatory before entry to the City of God which is man's true habitat, and whilst we are here we should not be distracted from meditation by worldly things.

(T) St Bernard (1091 – 1153) thought that nature is *therapy* for weary minds and it may be that this is the source of our ideas of mental relaxation and outdoor activity contributing to mental and physical well-being. But there are more ancient and more important sources which have to do with the close links between war, war games, and sport which derived from classical Greece and the first Olympic games.

(U) The Greek idea of *sacrifice* and sport at funeral games was based on the belief that the blood and energy needed by the dead for the journey to the next world could be supplied by the athletes and gladiators. The links between war and sports, and what we now call outdoor pursuits, have not lessened over the centuries. Originally they had nothing to do with the conservation of scenery or wildlife.

(V) Nature is just *a backdrop to sporting activity*, part of the playground.

These sporting views of the environment as a playground or assault course where everyone has a right to walk, climb, sail, ski, dive, windsurf, hang-glide, fly, water-ski at any time, are especially dominant in our society. They were responsible for the establishment of the ten national parks of England and Wales: it was healthy exercise and sport (not beauty and nature conservation) that turned these ten areas into national recreation areas for outdoor pursuits. What is the place of interpretation in recreation areas? What are the best ways of communicating with sportsmen about environmental conservation? When is the right moment when they are hell-bent on their pursuit? All these are areas of considerably controversy and interest which reveal as much about the motives and approach of interpreters as of competitive sportsmen today.

Seventh Group: Current Attitudes to Nature Conservation (W to Z)

In the early years of this century there was a general acceptance that scientists were disinterested workers in pursuit of objective truth, but the Second World War and the second half of the twentieth century have demonstrated to many people that science is not value-free. Scientists are guided by research programmes which indicate which paths to pursue and which to avoid. The Baconian scientific method assumed two quite naive beliefs: that all observations are made through colourless spectacles, and that all testing of hypotheses is done with that *tabula rasa* mind that some researchers still believe in! Today science recognizes that observations can be 'theory loaded' and we have to admit that scientific studies in wildlife conservation can be affected by popular attitudes to nature conservation. We can now present four ideas which all have a relatively modern origin and come from scientific enquiries of the last hundred years.

(W) *Ecological balance of nature*: we have seen that balance has an ancient origin but we can invoke Buffon and Marsh as mid-nineteenth century exponents of the idea that man has profoundly disturbed the balance of nature. Conservation helps to restore an equilibrium, though scientists recognize nevertheless that this cannot be a stable state.

(X) *The population and resources equation* idea derives from Malthus and from Darwin. It is a paradigm at the very root of the question 'why conserve?' It is most frequently swept under the carpet.

(Y) The idea of the *gene reservoir* is a powerful argument for conservation today. It is derived from evolutionary theory and genetics but also has philosophical links with the way we now look at man and nature.

(Z) *Possibilism*, in conservation terms, is about keeping options open for the future and it relates closely to the previous idea. It is particularly germane to interpreters because it is sometimes stated as an objective of communication about nature and wildlife conservation. Scientists who produce data would resent being accused of presenting propaganda, i.e. telling people what to think.

Our Attitudes to Conservation Today

We can simplify and group these twenty-six examples of philosophies which have influenced our attitude to nature conservation into just four which are current today: the *economic* view; the *scientific* view; the *sensory enjoyment* view; and the viewpoint of *physical and mental health*, though there are many variations on each of these.

Telelogy and *economic* views of utility and land use now dominate our discussions about conservation. From roots in eighteenth-century *science* we have seen the growth of the Malthusian nightmare: its relevance today is obvious and largely ignored. Science has also taken us into the study of the natural world via modern evolutionary theory, ecology and genetics.

But not all of the philosophical developments related to environmental conservation in the last 200 years have been stimulated by economics or scientific enquiry. *Sensory enjoyment*, the key motivation for much conservation work, takes several forms. We have seen romantic and *aesthetic* ideas surviving intact from the eighteenth century and becoming the cult of worship of nature and scenery. An offshoot of these ideas was the worship of health-giving waters, sunshine and the designation of spas and resorts as sites for *relaxation*. We have seen the growth of another form of worship of nature, the *quasi-religious*, derived from Rousseau, from the mystical love of mountains, from an interest in oriental world views, from extra-sensory perception, from holistic 'hippies' and from the so-called Deep Ecology Movement of Arne Naess, which throws them together into a single cult.

The last major attitude we come across today is the argument from the standpoint of *physical and mental health*. Indeed, the strangest philosophical developments in our field in this century have arguably been related to the explosive interest in *competitive sport* which often affects the environment, particularly *outdoor pursuits* (which were originally simply techniques of surviving in wild country). These pursuits now challenge urban dwellers to seek out remote places.

Here then is a grouping of our attitudes to nature conservation (Table 7.2) which demonstrate how we regard the natural environment, landscape and wildlife, our feelings of responsibility in this connection, and our search for

Table 7.2 Nature Conservation Attitudes

Conservation Ideas	A Competitive? Social or Gregarious	B Fear/Risk or Curiosity Motives	C Attitudes to Landscape and Wildlife	D Moral View Rights & Responsibilities
1. Economic, teleology or utilitarian	Competitive work and economic competition or growth.	Untamed nature is a threat: introduces risks.	Dominion of man: scenic beauty was made by landowners.	Owner has right to use his land as he wishes and develop its resources.
2. Scientific	Some elements competitive.	Fear that man will destroy his own habitat. Curiosity is a motive.	Man has to manage the resources for present and future generations.	Rights limited by obligations to ensure survival of life forms. Responsibility to pass on knowledge.
3. Sensory, enjoyment: aesthetic	Competitive element in finding scenes, often gregarious.	Curiosity is the driving force.	Attractions should be accessible to sightseer.	Rights to enjoy travel and curiosity. Some responsibility to keep places looking nice.
4. Sensory enjoyment: aesthetic	Not competitive or gregarious.	Curiosity is a motive, beauty (romantic) and nostalgic (sentiment).	Those places which inspire should be preserved.	Man has a responsibility to respect wildlife and landscape value if it is not to be lost.
5. Sensory enjoyment: quasi-religious and deep ecology	Self-realization and contemplation of wild scenery, solitary.	Fear and curiosity are mixed. Fear of an impoverished planet.	Reverence for life and nature important for its own sake.	Man has a right to escape to experience the wild. Contemplation. All nature has rights.

Table 7.2 contd.

Conservation Ideas	A Competitive? Social or Gregarious	B Fear/Risk or Curiosity Motives	C Attitudes to Landscape and Wildlife	D Moral View Rights & Responsibilities
6. Physical and mental health: outdoor pursuits	Competitive. Not usually gregarious.	Risks are essential to character training and fear is also important in challenges.	Wild areas are a challenge. We have become soft and need to be toughened.	Man has a right to roam and use land for outdoor recreation at all times.
7. Physical and mental health: relaxation	Not competitive. Usually gregarious.	Neither fear nor curiosity. Health comes from sun and air, not from exercise.	Wildlife and landscape are just a backdrop to the relaxation.	Man has a right to get away from worries and responsibilities of everyday life for once!
8. Physical and mental health: competitive sport	Competitive. Gregarious.	Fear and risk. Health comes from the exercise in games and challenges.	Play no part in sport except as backdrop.	Man has right to use the country for sporting competition and games at any time.

solitary or gregarious experiences. Check out your own beliefs and you will see that you do not hold just one environmental ethic but a mixture of most of this oversimplified list. So, the interpreter seeking to communicate with an audience is really faced with a multitude of messages and a variety of audiences.

Changing Attitudes

Our list of attitudes shows why the call for better environmental behaviour, based on new environmental ethics, is not a realistic or even a helpful objective: we cannot change everyone's environmental ethic! If we can find the attitudes which lie behind patterns of behaviour we should be in a position to change environmental attitudes, if that is our role. Questionnaires cannot help us here because they cannot probe the value systems which have the greatest influence on our behaviour; they merely survey the peripheral areas. It has been shown that there is little correlation between surveys of value systems and behaviour patterns that are capable of being measured, and only the simplest questions can be answered by our evaluation techniques.

Suppose then that the interpreter wants to put across the message that everyone should help to 'ensure that the national heritage of wild fauna and flora and geological and physiographic features remains as large and diverse as possible'. This is a scientific concept but it has to be communicated in a language that will be understood by non-scientists.

The World Conservation Strategy, for example, employs the concept of *sustainable yield* and the concept of *using only the interest on the capital of our natural resources*, to get this message across to those to whom this is an acceptable conservation philosophy in a language which they can understand. Our efforts in seeking to change attitudes must therefore be targeted at those who are most likely to threaten the survival of wildlife populations.

It is always possible to argue that if we want to influence absolutely every citizen at the most formative period of his or her life when every fundamental attitude to the environment is being inculcated then we must take a leaf out of the Jesuit's book and get to work in the primary schools. This year is the centenary of the birth of Aldo Leopold (1888 – 1948) who was the first conservationist to use the term 'conservation education' and probably the first person fully to understand that it is not a subject but an attitude of mind. As we have seen in defining the subject, the site interpreter, whilst sharing many of the objectives of the schoolteacher, is involved in a different activity. Until interpreters fully understand that they will do little to upgrade our interpretation.

What Messages? Philosophies of Heritage Conservation

There is not sufficient space here to develop a list of conservation philosophies which have an equal bearing on heritage conservation, historic monuments, historic landscapes or the built environment. However, apart from the fact that many of the ideas in our framework of nature conservation philosophies have much greater antiquity than their equivalents in historic conservation, our framework works reasonably well for both approaches to the environment, at least as an attempt which may encourage others to go more deeply into the subject.

Stewardship and Preservation

The interest in preserving ancient monuments came partly from the stewardship concept which was prominent in the second half of the nineteenth century and which produced the first legislation on preservation in many countries. George Perkins Marsh identified the need to conserve both historic artefacts and nature in his seminal *Man and Nature* (1864).

Ideas of historic continuity have also played a part in the development of this philosophy and are particularly important in the rationale behind archaeological and folklife collecting policies.

Senescence and Decay

Nostalgia for an imagined golden age is a concept which goes back to antiquity. We live in an age in which this philosophy is again rife; as it is one which drives the tourist and souvenir industry it therefore has strong economic overtones. Interest in antiques, antique buildings and museums is high and some critics see this as a form of decadence.

Urbanization and the Superiority of the Past

Many artists and historians looked fondly at a particular past and grew acutely conscious of the effects of urbanization in Europe at the end of the nineteenth century. The arts and crafts movement identified the threat that machine workmanship posed to the quality of life. Today the interpreter may not fail to notice how the mindless pursuit of novelty has begun to produce a similar reaction or backlash in the arts.

Sensory Enjoyment, Escapism and Nostalgia

Escape from the city and urban values into the countryside is not only a matter of seeking healthy outdoor exercise, it is also an escape to rural values thought to survive there. Many of the traditional items sought by the urban escapees in their hunt for rural values are made available to them by other escapees who have got there first!

Sensory Enjoyment and Romanticism

National romanticism in the nineteenth century encouraged a growth in museums and the preservation of national sites and ancient monuments as the new nations recognized that their cultural heritage and treasures provided them with a national identity.

Ruin and Decay and the Wilder Shores of Experience

In Europe appreciation of ruins came before a love of the wild, partly because of the antiquarianism of aristocrats on the Grand Tour of Europe, particularly when such touring was made rational and intellectually respectable by scholars like Johann Winckelmann and then linked with touring in search of the picturesque.

Buildings in the landscape were only acceptable if they were ruinous and it became logical to create ruins where history had failed to do so. David Lowenthal (1985) suggests that as Americans were slower to recognize their own ruins and antiquities these same motives produced the quest for geological landforms and the creation of national parks. The curious (to European eyes) designation of American geological features as 'National Monuments' lends support to his interesting idea.

From Social Darwinism to Current Attitudes

In 1852, seven years before Darwin published his *Origin of Species*, Herbert Spencer drew attention to adaptations in human history in his *Theory of Population* and coined the phrase 'the survival of the fittest'. He opposed social provisions on the grounds that they would preserve the weak! This was a social ethic which had some appeal in Victorian England and it became the first cornerstone of social Darwinism.

Fortunately Darwin was influenced not by Spencer but by Malthus's *Essay on the Principle of Population* (1798) which suggested to him the dynamic which could drive the machinery of natural selection, and this he applied to the animal kingdom. Nevertheless the phrase 'survival of the fittest' is often attributed to Darwin rather than to that set of ideas called social Darwinism, which proved to have such an awful potency. Robert Owen contributed the second cornerstone of social Darwinism in his writings on education: he believed that if the environment could be improved, the child could be reformed. The third and last cornerstone of this unstable structure was the nineteenth-century belief in historical progress.

Interpreters will find relics of all three principles of social Darwinism alive today. Even as I write, the first principle of survival of the fittest applied to our social provision is being actively revived with the dismantling of many of those social achievements of postwar Britain which are fundamentally opposed to social Darwinism. The second principle is also alive and well in many schools, despite the fact that it remains unproven, and the third principle of belief in continuous progress still permeates the interpretation of history, not least in the recent explosive growth of heritage centres.

The creation of new historical myths has reached unprecedented proportions in America, Britain and Commonwealth countries with the growth of so-called 'living history' demonstrations by costumed guides, which is partly the result of widespread youth unemployment. Doubtless Herbert Spencer would have approved of the irony! Essential reading here is David Lowenthal's examination of the heritage phenomenon in *The Past is a Foreign Country* (1985), which touches on some of the philosophies of interpretation, but is itself strangely affected by this myth of continuous progress.

Because Darwin spoke of race and species in the same breath it was perhaps inevitable that social Darwinism should develop theories about racial superiority and conceive of an imperialism which claimed it had a duty to humanity to preserve standards of purity of race. The philosophy which could justify racism, fascism and global war had quite different effects when it was ameliorated by national romanticism and its many relatively less harmful variants.

Regional Ethnology

Yet the philosophy which inspired Artur Hazelius to begin the collection that became Stockholm's Nordiska Museum and the outdoor Open Air Museum at Skansen is now known as the highly respectable subject of regional ethnology: defined by Alexander Fenton as 'the study of the individual in the community which puts the emphasis on traditional ways of life'. Nationalism was never far beneath the surface and it was no coincidence that Hazelius's Danish disciple, Bernard Olsen, began his Frilandsmuseet folklife collections, near Copenhagen, with two buildings from Scania and Småland – parts of Sweden which were formerly Danish.

Both Hazelius and Olsen were inspired by the concepts of the Great Exhibitions seen in London in 1851 and Paris in 1878, which they had visited together. Neither could exhibit technology and machine crafts:

instead they were drawn towards traditional handicrafts and artistic skills. Their collections of farm buildings and folklife grew out of an appreciation of the skills that went into the construction of vernacular buildings and folk artefacts, rather than from any philosophy of environmental interpretation or museology.

Anders Sandvig in Norway was also influenced by philosophies of national romanticism and by an extension of ideas of evolutionary development which were much closer to Darwin than to the misconceptions of social Darwinism. He was aware of the dangers of diving head first into these murkiest of waters, as can be seen in his brilliant interpretation of Gudbrandsdalen. He avoided the worst pitfalls by concentrating on a region (instead of attempting to interpret the entire country). His interpretation selected four major themes which have stood the test of time: the agricultural way of life; the vernacular architecture; the development of crafts; the development of outfarms and transhumance. Furthermore, his insight demonstrated the many causal relationships between the four themes – through tools and techniques, lighting and heating and other similar aspects of living conditions which run through all four. His message was a far cry from either social Darwinism or the simplistic forms of determinism. He even gently debunked national romanticism in the *saeter* section of his open air museum. (Norwegian mountains were not discovered by Romantic poets and tourists that followed them: they were important because they were part of the transhumance system of summer grazing.) Sandvig advanced the subject of regional ethnology and upgraded the concept of the open air museum. He did this by a single-mindedness which won popular appeal without losing any of the scholarship required of a responsible curator.

From Determinism to Human Ecology

Larry Grossman in his paper 'Man–Environment Relationships in Anthropology and Geography' (1977) has charted the progress of environmental attitudes this century in these two complementary academic disciplines. He has shown that the development of Newton's ideas of space, time and causal relationships, Darwin's ideas of evolution and Spencer's ideas of social Darwinism contributed to environmental determinism. Then a reaction against racism in the 1930s led to a stress on the culture–environment relationship but a rejection of the simple cause/effect interpretation of the environment which is found in determinism. But as early as 1923 the American geographer H.H. Barrows had taken the first steps which led to the creation of the new discipline of human ecology. Then in the 1950s the American anthropologist J.H. Steward introduced the approach of cultural ecology, which returned to questions of human adaptation to the environment, causal relationships and evolution in ways which were once more acceptable.

Geographers focusing on landscape in their studies of human ecology came closest to the anthropologists' position when studying man's adaptation of the environment. They have very similar perceptions but look down different ends of the same telescope. Spatial questions and matters of scale are characteristic of one end of this telescope, and time relationships, change and the concept of homoeostasis (borrowed from biological ecology) are found at the other end; there is much to be gained by looking down both ends! Returning to the environmental interpreter, we can now look at this telescope! Environmental interpretation as we understand it today had two major points in origin: in the United States national parks where it was based on American ideas of nature conservation, and in the Scandinavian folklife parks where it was based on ideas of European regional ethnology. The philosophies common to the view of the human and cultural ecologist together with the biological ecologist include the general principle which affects all adaptations to the environment of all life forms: a universal need to maintain those properties essential to survival of the system. In addition there is a common interest and concern for the dynamics of change, the survival of communities, and the extent to which changes in the environment can be assimilated without destruction of the community or the species. Sadly, in practice the regional ethnologist rarely progresses analysis to the point where account is taken of all the biophysical relationships in the milieu which might explain the adaptations. Likewise the ecologist rarely progresses biological studies of living organisms to include all the implications for man.

Inescapable Romanticism

Romanticism is a key concept in environmental interpretation and conservation. It is often defined by reference to its opposites, as in the contrast with the 'ancient' or the 'classical', whose formal values we associate with mathematical theorems, Bach fugues, or scientific treatises, all characterized by their purity of form, abstract and strict rigidity of structure and precision. Hence romanticism is modern, free, boundless and universal, impressionistic or emotional, and inspired by organic and natural forms and landscapes. Clearly the art of interpretation demonstrates some aspects of romanticism!

In the eighteenth century two aspects of romanticism swept across Europe. They were national romanticism's 'vision of freedom' and the Romantic poet's 'ideal of beauty', and they became merged in the arts, in landscape appreciation and garden design. The link between freedom and environmental interpretation is less obvious than the link with beauty but it can be demonstrated. The eighteenth century was an age which rediscovered the glory that was Greece and Rome, and not least the Homeric legends of ancient national heroes. So it was not surprising to find that collections of German *Nibelungenlied* legends, and Gaelic and Welsh equivalents, could be pressed into the service of national romanticism.

Before regional ethnology could make its subject matter respectable in the late nineteenth century, that subject matter had to be refined; folklife and folklore were examined closely, and recently manufactured fakelife removed, though not without difficulty. For example, some of the ancient poems of Ossian were written by James Macpherson and some were not: what is significant about them is not the question of their authenticity but the incredible extent of their influence in every European country and the light which this sheds on the romantic movement (Jacobites, heroism, freedom, cultural identity). Such romantics as Macpherson were often more successful in identifying modern injustices than the politicians of their day. Here there is a direct analogy with the interpreter who does not seek to tell the public what to think and does not prescribe political actions. In encouraging his audiences to think for themselves Macpherson succeeded in being more 'effective' than the Prince! Likewise two romantic artists who could fairly claim to be the conscience of their age, Goya and Blake, made no such claims for themselves. As romantics they communicated effective messages without telling anyone what to think; they cannot be regarded as propagandists.

The Marriage of Taste and Nature

Turning from freedom to ideal beauty the links with the environment are more obvious and perhaps much more important aspects of romanticism. The ideas of the painter William Hogarth set out in his *Analysis of Beauty* in 1753 were borrowed by the philosopher Edmund Burke for his famous essay *A Philosophical Enquiry into the Sublime and the Beautiful* published in 1757 and were in turn merged with concepts of the sublime drawn from the theatre and written by Longinus in the first century! We have seen that this philosophy had a considerable effect on nature conservation and we should now explore its relevance to other areas of conservation.

It is interesting to note that at the birth of landscape appreciation there was this link with theatre. The adoption of the word 'scenery', which is derived from the stage, was built into the aesthetics of landscape at the very beginning and all attempts to replace it with such words as 'landscape' have met with no great success here because our attitude to beautiful countryside in Britain is a romantic notion. Were it not so we would not have the Countryside Commissions but Departments of Environmental, Social and Economic Rural Conservation and Development.

The recognition that there is a third type of scenery which is neither beautiful nor sublime, called the 'picturesque', was made by the Reverend William Gilpin in his *Essay on Picturesque Beauty* in 1792. He brought together many of his observations on the subject of scenery and history made in a lifetime of touring those areas of England which have since become national parks. It is no coincidence but a direct result of the influence of eighteenth-century taste that they have been so designated.

The importance of the picturesque for environmental interpreters is more profound still, for this aesthetic has so influenced us that we employ it in almost everything we do connected with scenery. As an important environmental philosophy it has come to mean particularizing. Every time you frame an object in the viewfinder of a camera you are doing what Gilpin taught us to do. Because the camera can only capture a segment of a view and because (with few exceptions) the decision to point it one way rather than another way is taken by a person, everyone has to compose a picture, nobody with a camera can escape the picturesque! The principle is one of selection and particularization, and whenever we do either of these with regard to landscape we are likely to finish up with a record of scenery, unless we are being deliberately perverse.

Even our excursions into the field of industrial archaeology, which may be thought to be far from romanticism, are particularizations. However hard we try we cannot but romanticize about such sites. We create the simple myth that one place was the birthplace of all industrial innovation (and the more complex myth that there was an event called the industrial revolution which happened one Wednesday afternoon in 1709 when Abraham Darby invented coke!). Even the act of designating industrial sites would have Gilpin's stamp of approval!

The same selection process affects the exhibition designer, the guide, the researcher and, of course, the interpreter: there is no escape from romanticism!

Philosophies of Hermeneutics

Transmitting a message to others requires a form of interpretation on the part of the transmitter and also on the part of the receiver. The former activity was much studied at the turn of the last century and continues to be studied today by the German school of philosophy. It has been called hermeneutics, the name derived from Hermes, messenger of the Greek Gods, to emphasize the fact that as a philosophy it was mostly applied to theological messages, in particular to the interpretation of the Bible. In the writer's view, environmental interpretation and museum interpretation have also taken on some quasi-religious characteristics which the study of hermeneutics helps to pinpoint. Just as Wordsworth's appreciation of nature amounted to worship, so Goethe compared his experience of a visit to a museum to 'the emotional experience of entering a house of God consecrated to the holy ends of art'. Readers will find it interesting and even instructive to seek out some of the other quasi-religious characteristics of environmental interpretation.

Two philosophers of the German school of hermeneutics: Wilhelm Dilthey (1833–1911) and Hans Georg Gadamer (b. 1900) have explored the nature of understanding and the meaning and significance of things. Their findings have relevance both for interpretation in the general usage of that word and also in its more specific environmental use, as we have defined it at the beginning of this paper. The meaning of a text can be understood in terms of the intentions of its author or in terms of an analysis of the structure and the implications of the text that the author may never have intended.

There may be a right or a wrong interpretation, or a real and an unreal interpretation, but Dilthey (see Bulhof, 1980) showed that science could shed no light on the matter; in his view the real world had to be interpreted like a text. For Dilthey this was the hermeneutical process of producing a message; he saw hermeneutics as a function of history and the arts and an essential part of what we mean by culture (and what our generation calls the 'cultural heritage' which we falsely profess to have such difficulty in defining!).

Western culture has only just begun to rid itself of its old imperialist attitudes and some credit for these changes in attitude may be attributed to hermeneutics. For example, Johann Gottfried Herder's contribution to hermeneutics was the view that everything is part of a continuous stream of human events and there are no external values. This has helped to engender tolerance but, paradoxically, Herder's view that nations have character was distorted by the social Darwinists to engender quite the reverse. Another related facet of this school of philosophy is the concept of continuity which is an important one in interpretation of the environment; without it many of the arguments for conservation of historic sites and landscapes are difficult to sustain.

I have attempted elsewhere to show how hermeneutics can be applied to the environment by drawing distinctions between environmental perception, understanding and appreciation. These three are of considerable importance in environmental interpretation and environmental education with regard to school fieldwork and streetwork. In the Council of Europe's 'Environmental Awareness' (Aldridge, et al., 1976) I suggested that the three elements differed in the following manner: environmental perception means recognizing a stimulus (as when an image or sound makes an impact on our senses before we pose any cognitive questions); environmental understanding means grasping in a cognitive sense the facts about that stimulus (such as identifying it); and environmental appreciation means going beyond mere perception and mere understanding to develop a concern for values (for example, by determining the significance, meaning and context of a place).

Returning to the philosophy of Dilthey, interpretation explored territory far beyond what he called 'mere understanding' to discover underlying patterns of interrelationships, in the real world or in the texts. The human observer isolates things (or percepts), putting them into the cardboard boxes of the mind, on to the shelves of a library classification or into some mental filing cabinets. But in reality they are not so isolated and it is the job of the interpreter to seek interrelationships and apply these to give coherence and relevance to the interpretation of the world. Without an appreciation of our cultural history we cannot understand the significance of human events, discover the meaning of the world stage, or any of its manmade phenomena.

In order to act responsibly we need roots, a sense of belonging and shared values. Interpreters make discoveries and communicate them to others: interpreters are messengers who, according to Dilthey, aim to produce changes in human behaviour which they do by communicating a message relevant to their audiences.

Social and cultural elements of our world can only be understood through interpretation of the human condition. The scientist studying the natural world claims to understand its phenomena without the need to examine the meaning of texts or the significance of causal relationships.

In Gadamer's (1960) hermeneutics the interpreters' insights are essential to the appreciation of the reality and to how interpreters communicate their messages. He would claim that one cannot understand and appreciate a text, an historical event, or a place without having some (preconceived) idea of its time context. Thus our appreciation of the cultural landscape arises out of our position in an historical tradition and Gadamer sets out to fuse the historical outlook with his own. Thus interpreters do not merely make the appreciation of a place relevant to their audiences (as Freeman Tilden's [1957] first principle implies), they incorporate the appreciation of a place into the lives of their audiences.

The Ship of Interpretation

I have focused attention on the several different ways in which the term 'environmental awareness' is being used today – sometimes to mean perception and at other times to mean appreciation. This ambiguity is at the root of the current confusion of objectives in environmental education for schools.

This has gone so far in the UK that the statutory bodies engaged in the work seldom recognize that there is a significant difference between environmental studies, which are designed to use a place simply as a reservoir for teaching perception, and environmental education, which is designed to recognize values, clarify concepts, develop skills and attitudes ranging widely over all three of the educational elements we have attempted to define.

The application of hermeneutical philosophy to environmental interpretation illuminates two other important and topical areas: the question of provocation and the problems of evaluation. The fourth principle of interpretation in Freeman Tilden's *Interpreting Our Heritage* had been much misunderstood: 'the chief aim of interpretation in not instruction but provocation'. Later chapters in his book make it clear that Tilden was not intending to impose his solutions to political and social problems on his audience, or suggesting that interpreters should do the same. Dilthey said that the world should be encouraged to run its course and that hermeneutics was not about prescribing political actions.

So interpretation is about encouraging people to think for themselves, not about telling them what to think, or setting society's objectives. It is hard for the young revolutionary manning the barricades to understand this philosophy but it would be unwise for him or her to write off all artistic communicators as ineffectual, simply as a consequence of their role as messengers! The clue to understanding the problem of what interpreters mean by a message is to be found in art, and our example of Goya and Blake could be matched in other media. Because interpretation is an art, it is naive to think that it can be done scientifically and objectively. Artists and historicans select what they think is significant and however much they may strive to be authentic or true to the reality in their interpretation, their work cannot be evaluated objectively. University departments applying their minds to the question of evaluation of interpretation find themselves trapped by the practitioners' definition of the subject. For example, *Interpretive Views* (1986), edited by Machlis, escapes from the trap by the simple device of not defining environmental interpretation, but in omitting to do so he removes all credibility from the debate.

Researchers tell us that much environmental interpretation is too complex to evaluate and they monitor only that which can be measured, such as factual recall. This is a far cry from the world of interpretation mapped out by hermeneutics philosophers and by the first environmental interpreters in America and Scandinavia. The real tragedy is that evaluators are now designing evaluation around what is easy to evaluate when the whole point of evaluation for the interpreter is to encourage more creative interpretation. Some evaluators have shown that they want to reduce creativity, spontaneity, and flexibility to nil in order to produce standardized interpretation which will be easier to evaluate. In the same way, award schemes for interpretation and heritage provisions can actually lower standards as developers strive to build into their schemes the kind of novel components which, although not relevant to interpretation, are nevertheless good for winning awards. We are forced back to definitions and to consider the hermeneutic philosophers (whether we accept them or not) and to sanity.

Acknowledgement

The writer is grateful for permission to use previously unpublished material which first appeared in an assignment written for the Nature Conservancy Council.

References

Aldridge, D. (1972) *Upgrading Park Interpretation and Communication with the Public*, (paper presented at the Second World Conference of National Parks, Yellowstone.)

US National Parks Service and International Union for Conservation of Nature and Natural Resources.

Aldridge, D. and Fenton, A. (1973) *Environmental Awareness in Scotland: Regional Ethnography and Environmental Awareness: Regional and National Interpretive Plans*, Museums Journal 73(3).

Aldridge, D. (1975) *Principles of Countryside Interpretation and Interpretive Planning*, HMSO for Countryside Commission for Scotland and Countryside Commission.

Aldridge, D., Epler, G. and Wals, H. (1976) *Environmental Awareness*, Council of Europe, Strasbourg.

Aldridge, D. (1984) *A Sense of Place: An Exercise in Interpretation and Communication* in Fenton, A. and Palsson H., The Northern and Western Isles in the Viking World, John Donald, Edinburgh.

Bulhof, I.N. (1980) *Wilhelm Dilthey: a Hermeneutic Approach to the Study of History and Culture*, Martinus Nijhoff, The Hague, Netherlands.

Burke, E. (1756) *A Philosophical Enquiry into Our Ideas of the Sublime and Beautiful*, London.

Davies, G.L. (1968) *Earth in Decay, a History of British Geomorphology*, Macdonald, London.

Gadamer, H.G. (1960) *Truth and Method*, (English trans., 1975), Sheed and Ward, London.

Gilpin, W. (1792) *Essay on Picturesque Beauty*, London.

Glacken, C.J. (1967) *Traces on the Rhodian Shore*, University of California Press, Berkeley, Calif.

Grossman, L. (1977) 'Man–environment relationships in anthropology and geography', *Annals of the Association of American Geographers*, 67 (1).

Hogarth, W. (1753; 1955) Burke, J. (ed.) *The Analysis of Beauty*, Oxford University Press, Oxford.

Lowenthal, D. (1985) *The Past is a Foreign Country*, Cambridge University Press, Cambridge.

Machlis G. (1986) *Interpretive Views: Opinions on Evaluating Interpretation*, National Parks and Conservation Association, Washington DC.

Marsh, G.P. (1864; 1965) Lowenthal, D. (ed.) *Man and Nature*, Harvard University Press, Cambridge, Mass.

Thomas, K. (1983) *Man and the Natural World*, Allen Lane, London.

Thomas, W.L. (1956) *Man's Role in Changing the Face of the Earth*, University of Chicago Press, Chicago, Ill.

Tilden, F. (1957) *Interpreting our Heritage*, University of North Carolina Press, Chapel Hill.

8

Looking for the Future Through the Past

Marc Laenen

Imagine you're travelling as a tourist in a coach through Belgium from Brussels to Waterloo and suddenly see Napoleon, accompanied by his field marshal, hitch-hiking along the road. He will accompany you to his tent then escort you to a part of the battlefield of Waterloo. What would you feel like? This extraordinary experience might indeed happen to you in Belgium these days.

This story is not a *captatio bene volentiae* as you might expect, but an amazing reality when visiting Brussels in the 1980s if you order this programme and pay for it.

Flanders has such a rich heritage that every historical city or village has its own cortège, its own giants, its own folklore or crafts market, its own harvest or dance festival. Calendars burst with them. And if one village happens to have lost or never has had an historical tradition, a new one is easily and quickly invented, in order to attract tourists to increase the cash flow.

The past and the cultural heritage have become a lucrative business. This is made possible by the 'retro' climate that has occurred during the last decades.

In general I would not interpret the attention to the past and its heritage as negative. I still feel positive about this increasing interest in the past even when it is not due to genuine motives. However, we do need to distinguish between the historian and museum director who studies or collects heritage on one hand and the TV historical series scriptwriter on the other; between the farmer who reuses old farming methods because they appear to be more efficient and the ecologist breeding Brabantian horses as pets; between members of a bowls club continuing an old tradition, and the production of cultural heritage by the tourist boards who ignore historical authenticity and integrity. The bigger the competition, the more far-fetched, grotesque and fantastic the performance becomes.

Economic exploitation of heritage is not often very compatible with historical veracity, authenticity and integrity. One of the most fundamental problems is the subjective and often inaccurate interpretation and presentation of the past, originating in our inevitable links with our own time and culture and in our own prejudices and projections.

One part of the problem is having an accurate understanding and interpretation of the past. The other, however, consists of transmitting the historical image to the public in the correct manner. This is a communication problem which museums in particular are facing.

Re-presenting the Past

It is obvious that there are different approaches to re-presenting the past. I can introduce Napoleon as a man who developed a progressive and more just jurisdiction in Western Europe ignoring the fact that he deprived our farms of young and vital workers, thus undermining the economic foundation of our families and of society. Enthusiastic industrial archaeologists consider the eighteenth and nineteenth centuries as a major thrust forward for the human race. Sociologists, however, see it as a low point of the human condition. This is, of course, a matter of emphasis and selectivity. A rose-tinted interpretation of a past that never existed is another matter. The rose-tinted selection and presentation of the past responding to unfulfillable needs of dreams of power, comfort and prestige appears to be a matter of consumption rather than a cultural issue for making people aware of their identity. History is interpreted to stimulate nostalgia, idealize the past, and leads to a selective understanding of the past that has more to do with fantasy and fairy tales than veracity. In Belgium, and perhaps elsewhere on the continent, you can see newly built farmers' cottages called *fermettes* in city agglomerations. Rural interiors furnish modern flats. Romantic dresses for women and *borsalino* outfits for gents following Alain Delon suggest feminine and masculine roles no longer so clearly defined. Our feeling for romanticism makes us appreciate historical farmsteads but without the smells and the flies. We enjoy a flock of sheep and caress the lambs but we'd rather not get up in the middle of the night to assist with the lambing. We like to identify with the landowners but surely not with the servants, and we are satisfied with lace of Bruges, albeit made in Hong Kong.

However, one cannot in principle reject all commercialization of history and cultural heritage. Commercial use of historic facts and images like Shakespeare quotations on anniversary calendars, valuable historic buildings and landscapes on plates, postcards and calendars, crafts and games on beermats, only help to introduce and to spread cultural items to the general public. Only when economic interests prevail over cultural identity or when businesses use the past for mere profit regardless of excesses, should it not be encouraged, especially by the government. In these cases the same objections should be made as will the extreme commercialization of theme parks, sensation projects, eroscentra etc.

Cultural Decline

The substitution of present-day culture by artefacts of the past should be seen as cultural decline: a definite part of modern architecture consists indeed of renovating old buildings instead of encouraging a new architecture.

As far as I am concerned, the main reason for the boom of the past and heritage is to be sought in the moral, social and identity crisis that we have experienced increasingly during the last decades. Notwithstanding 1968, the welfare society has failed in its purpose. Out of the ruins of the Second World War Western Europe became prosperous. In our welfare states most basic human needs have been fulfilled: life is sustained by sufficient food, housing, clothing and hospital care, employment and communication. The basic conditions for the development of the more fundamental and non-material aspects of the human condition – the intellectual, emotional, aesthetic and social needs – are all faculties of well-being. Although the latter is dependent on the first, they do not necessarily coincide. The cultivation of material welfare has led to large-scale mass production, uniformity and above all a levelling down, which appears to be a reversal of goals and means.

We have known other instances of uniformity in history. But the achievements of the Roman Empire, the Ottoman culture and others prove that uniformity need not necessarily be identified with loss of quality. The difference this time is that production is not defined by human and social needs and has not grown organically out of society, but has been imposed on it through production methods and the absolute priority of economic profit. This has obviously led to a lower quality of life. Perhaps for the first time in history, Europe has a welfare orientation (or least had, a few years ago) but has witnessed a decrease in the quality of life.

One of the most relevant examples of this situation is the modern super-urbanism with its cool, unfriendly skyscrapers, its segmentation into so-called specialized town quarters (trade centre, cultural centre, shopping centre, dormitories, working areas, recreational areas) and its large-scale traffic system. In this new development towns and villages break brutally through the varied and vernacular response to local dwelling and living needs. This development hardly corresponds to a socially conceived urbanism. The old neighbourhood activities in cities and villages, the welcoming of new members, the activities linked to birth, marriage and death, the shop on the corner, have disappeared. Strict individualism and shopping centres have come in its place. Instead of traditional food and table culture, we eat from dispensers in the street. Everything is focused on immediate pleasure. More of the same, *tout et tout de suite* as the French say. The problem is so deeply rooted in society that the youth that have grown up in this situation don't even realize it any more and are thus not able to evaluate an alternative. In this brave new world they try to satisfy their individual and social needs. How far are we away from Aldous Huxley's vision of the future?

The question, however, is whether nostalgia, apparently stimulated by commercial groups, and the commercial selling of past are the right answer. If not, I am afraid that 'selling the heritage' only stimulates consumption, aggravates the need, and leads to more hunger for the past, so worsening the problem.

Heritage, History and Cultural Identity

Perhaps our interest in the past should be examined more clearly. Is it a demand or a product, such as a need for clothing, eating, transport, etc.? Can it be met by commercial production until satisfaction? Is it an attempt at compensation for the present-day culture crisis, a kind of alternative because present-day society cannot satisfy our fundamental needs? Is it to be compared with the interest in religion? Is it an essential human need to place oneself in time and to develop a cultural identity? Or is it one of the means of improving the quality of our lives? Cultural levelling threatens to make uniform different cultures and to lead to their disappearance. Different organizations and institutions have pointed out the importance of their own traditions, their own roots, their own past and heritage for the recognition and development of cultural identities. 'To know who we are we should know how we were' is the eloquent slogan they produce. The history of native cultures such as those of Australia, Greenland, Africa and North America show the vital role of history and heritage in the cultural awareness and identity of communities and individuals in the mere process of survival. At a negative level it appears that the loss of traditions, social patterns, cultural expressions, roots, and the abrupt substitution of external and imposed cultural patterns leads to loss of identity and a gradual breakdown in society. The testimony of Chief Dan George of the Capilano Indians in British Colombia, Canada, is very significant. He wrote an open letter with the title 'I was born 1000 years ago'. Confronted suddenly with Western culture swamping his society, he wrote:

We did not have time to adjust to the upheaval around us; we seem to have lost what we had without replacement; we did not have time to take our twentieth century progress and eat it little by little and digest it. Do you know what it is like to be without moorings? Do you know what it is to live in surroundings that are ugly? It depresses man, for man must be surrounded by the beautiful if his soul is to grow.

The idea that our knowledge of the past and experience of heritage are necessary for asserting and further developing a cultural identity can be confirmed by several examples in history. This is not only so for native cultures which are confronted with Western culture. It is also valuable to smaller cultural entities in Western Europe, as the case of Flanders demonstrates. The geographical position of Flanders in Western Europe has always been of vital importance. In the fifteenth and sixteenth centuries

Flanders acquired a strong economical and independent position and developed a rich and high-level culture inspiring the whole of Europe north of the Alps. Nowhere else is so much heritage to be found in such a small area.

Flanders was a highly desired prize and was ruled in the seventeenth and eighteenth centuries by foreign powers. After independence in 1830 the entire social, economic, cultural and political life was in the hands of the French-speaking bourgeoisie. This supremacy oppressed the Flemish population, and Flemish cultural identity was strangled. The Flemish emancipation movement of the nineteenth and twentieth centuries was a long and difficult process that is still leading to social, economic, cultural and political independence in a federal state. The protagonists of this emancipation movement made sure that it was reinforced by a knowledge of Flemish history and heritage. In a constructive way a consciousness of the past helped to develop a cultural identity.

One could ask if it would not have been better for Flanders – and you might extend this to other smaller cultures – to be integrated into the important French culture which was present in the French-speaking bourgeoisie in Belgium. It is difficult to tell how a completely French-speaking and thinking Belgium would have looked after several generations. The question of large- or small-scale, uniformity and diversification is related to the question 'what kind of world do we want?': a uniform, easier to organize society or a multifaceted one. I don't think anybody will dispute the richness of variety: most people acknowledge this for animals and flora by supporting the world wide Fund for Nature. What is true for animals and plants is more true for the complex human species. I wouldn't feel comfortable living in a world or part of a world with only one kind of landscape, one kind of dwelling, one kind of culture. The human species is so complex that it needs many mirrors to define itself. Therefore, variety in cultures is an idea worth supporting and stimulating.

The diversity of cultures is particularly important for the 1990s. The almost magic milestone should bring Europeans together economically, culturally and politically. I cannot imagine yet a pan-European culture. On the contrary, one of the most fundamental characteristics of Europe is its variety of cultures. The vitality, dynamism and force of Europe lies in its polyculture. Eventually a European feeling, consciousness and culture can grow out of this multiplicity of cultures when Europe's identity has developed in a new economic, social, cultural and political climate.

The conclusion to draw from this is that history and its expression in heritage must be recognized as a basic resource for asserting and further developing cultural identity.

However, the function of the past and of heritage is not only to maintain and support a cultural identity. Elements of the past can possess qualities that our present societies have lost. If the past and the heritage contain qualities that we don't find any more in present-day life, can we continue these values and reintegrate them? If so, how is this to be done? If this is seen as desirable, the past and the heritage can contain a social constructive function or a function in cultural identity development. It can have a substantial part to play in the development of the quality of our life. This aspect is stressed in the philosophy behind the conservation of architectural heritage. These ideas have grown through several meetings organized since 1965 by the Council of Europe and Europa Nostra, culminating in the year of Architectural Heritage in 1975. In this campaign it was made clear that the environment value of architectural heritage was situated in the relationships which exist between streets, squares, light, space, green, water, colours, volumes and forms, and the regional response in cities and villages to local needs. Research has pointed out that this morphology has grown spontaneously out of the evolution of functions and relations that permanently integrate and adapt the heritage.

Here, historical research goes far beyond the study of the concrete cultural heritage. It concerns the basic ideas, concepts and values that our predecessors cherished. The facts are less important than the values out of which they are derived.

In Alden Biesen, near the German and Dutch border, the gate of the castle leading to the main entrance of the buildings was placed on top of a specific hill much higher than the castle. The gate is not important; the particular hill is not important. The point is that standing at the gate one looks over Germany, Holland and Flanders, thereby symbolizing European power. The figures and steps we dance and the rules of the games we play are less important than the relations we express while performing them. The sense of neighbourhood, scale, proportions, beauty, the relation to green space, sun, light, water etc., is more important than the concrete expression of it in the architectural heritage.

The integration and continuation of cultural heritage, and the attainments and cultural values of the past are based on their inherent qualities and their validity to present-day society.

The Validity of the Cultural Values of the Past

The most essential question remaining is whether former cultural values still have a meaning and validity in today's society. Some of the values of the past are irrelevant today: I do not feel any need to live in a small historic cottage without enough space for my twelve children, and my wife does not feel any necessity to do the laundry near the river with the village women singing a working song. Women prefer their social position in today's society to that of their ancestors in previous centuries: I suppose nearly everyone will reject the social class system of earlier times. Only the values and ideas that still have a meaningful function today are desirable.

It would, however, be a mistake just to copy the past. New developments in the social and technological field have their merits and contribute to the quality of present-day life. Soulless copies of the past exclude any social vitality and are in fact neither past nor present and often represent a step backwards.

The past is not important in itself. It is the presence of the past and our attitude to it that matters. The restoration of old buildings and settlements, or making replicas of the fifteenth or sixteenth century, might be a hobby or can be done for museological reasons, but makes no sense, since I don't want to live in the straight-jacket of a fifteenth-century environment, but in a house of the fifteenth or sixteenth century *now*. The values expressed in historical architectural heritage should be continued in a present-day context. The old principles of situation and orientation of buildings, materials, techniques, proportions and volumes could inspire our architects. Lately, folk games have been revived in our country, with important social benefits: bowls, popinjay and closh used to be played locally with the neighbours in the local inn. You always could play these games with only one hand; in the other you were supposed to hold your drink. Social contacts are no longer determined by the place in which we live but, thanks to modern communication, are now chosen more freely on the basis of common interest. These new social groups are happy to receive these old folk games as a means to live and to express their relationships in a playful way. The fun of it all is not to be authentically historical and to reconstruct these games in the most authentic way, but to enjoy together an activity that needs some dexterity but not training or anabolic steroids! These games of local origin are now enjoyed everywhere in Flanders. Our museum, in co-operation with the Physical Education Department of the University of Leuven, carried out the research on these almost forgotten folk games. The results were presented in an exhibition where the social value of these games was experienced by actually playing them. This was such a success that it was possible to start a folk games institution which now provides kits of folk games which can be hired or bought for private, school, club or neighbourhood use. Regional consultants are available to introduce the system everywhere in Flanders.

In this way an organization has been conceived to study the past, to evaluate the cultural values of the past for present-day use and to integrate them into society. Here different institutions are involved: the Research Centre of the Physical Education Department of the University of Leuven, the Museum by conserving objects and presenting them in an exhibition, and the social organizations which organize the games. From these examples we can conclude that:

1. Not everything from our past is worth reintegrating into present-day society, and only the cultural values that are significant and have a constructive function for society should be considered;

2. Reintegration is not to be interpreted as a reconstruction of the past. Cultural heritage should be fostered in a creative way.

One could easily think of new concepts and new cultural phenomena or introduce cultural items from elsewhere. Why not? If our own cultural heritage fits into this process it is because it has adapted itself over the centuries to local geographical, historic, physical and societal conditions. Because James Joyce couldn't have written what he wrote without Chaucer and Shakespeare, and the Baroque is impossible without the Renaissance, it is obvious that the achievements of the past are a necessity for present-day creativity. We can only feel sorry that now we have to speak of reintegration instead of enhancement.

This is not to stress that only the past and the cultural heritage are capable of improving the quality of present-day life. New developments are not to be rejected, especially if they have originated in a confrontation with the past. Evolution urges a dialectic relationship with the past and forces us to assemble and harmonize the old with the new. This is the tremendous challenge of every generation.

It has been my intention to argue that a commercial approach to cultural heritage and a false nostalgia are not the right answer to the fundamental human need to care for the past. Attention to the past is much more than a compensation for a present-day crisis situation. Apart from its constructive function in terms of cultural identity, the past can contribute to the quality of our present-day life.

9

Is an Archaeological Site Important to Science or to the Public, and is there a Difference?

Hester Davis

One of the most perplexing things which has entertained American archaeologists over the past fifteen years is on what basis to establish the significance of archaeological sites which may be destroyed by public monies and which therefore may also be preserved and/or investigated with public monies. In this same time frame, the concept of 'public archaeology' has gained acceptance, that is, the understanding that if public money is being spent on archaeological research the public should in some way benefit. Over this time, a very large amount of government money has gone into investigations of prehistoric archaeological sites which would in one way or another be affected by federal projects. The question quickly arose as to how and why the archaeologists chose the sites upon which this money was to be spent. Was benefit to 'science' appropriate and adequate justification? And if, indeed, it was agreed that this was an appropriate *basic* justification, was there not some obligation to interpret the information recovered in a way that the 'Great Unwashed Public' could understand, either through 'popular' publications, through exhibitions, or through preservation and interpretation of the sites themselves.

To Europeans it may seem unnaturally naive that American archaeologists have only recently considered this as a consequence or as a responsibility of their research. Except for the obvious and spectacular archaeological sites, such as Mesa Verde or Serpent Mound which have been preserved and interpreted for over fifty years, most archaeologists in the USA, prior to about 1974, were accustomed to choose sites to excavate which interested them, and almost without exception told only their colleagues about what they found. In addition, they normally spoke and wrote in a language known only to themselves.

Guidelines came from the federal government about how to judge the significance of archaeological sites, the one most quoted being that the site must 'contribute to the history or prehistory of an area'. Well, that didn't narrow things down much; any archaeologist worth his or her salt could explain how any site could so contribute. The arguments raged. A particular federal agency, not used to paying for 'pure science' would read the proposal for archaeological investigations from an archaeologist, not understand a word of it, not see the significance of the expected results, and question the expenditure of several thousands, perhaps hundreds of thousands of dollars on yet another 'lithic scatter'. They might accept that the scientists felt science would benefit, but would the public benefit? If not, why not?; and if the public should benefit, in what ways?

This brings me next to answer the questions in the title: Is an archaeological site important to science? Yes, almost always. Is an archaeological site important to the public? Not always, but it does depend upon the site and which portion of the public one is talking about. Is there a difference between sites which might be important to one but not the other? Yes, I think there probably is and I will pursue this in a moment. There is, of course, the unasked question as to whether there are sites which are not important to either science or the public? And yes, I believe there are sites of this ilk also. In fact, US law requires archaeologists to make this decision, i.e., if a site is not significant according to the definition in federal regulation, then it should have no importance or significance to anyone.

I have cheated, in a way, in asking my questions, because actually I do believe there are *sites* which are significant scientifically, in which the general public would not be interested, but I also believe that if there is significant scientific information in a site, then the public should be told about it. One can certainly think of archaeological sites which have no real features to see – no foundations, no trash pits, no mounds or barrows. The significance lies in the associational context of the material culture (archaeological jargon: significance lies in where things are found and what they are found with). This is recorded by the archaeologist as the site is excavated, but cannot always be 'seen' at any one time in the ground. So in point of fact, the information from all significant archaeological sites should be of interest to the public, but not necessarily the sites themselves.

When this concept is assumed then decisions can be made about those sites which can best represent certain cultures or time periods or patterns of activity in the past which have both important information and features which can be seen and therefore more easily interpreted to the visiting public. We can, in fact, justify public acquisition of these sites, in addition to expenditure of public money for investigation. These are the sites which have become or should become county, state, provincial, and/or national parks or preserves; or in some similar way should be preserved and interpreted for future generations.

The final part of the equation, which reads 'archaeological sites + science = public interest and interpretation,' is the public. As we all know, the public comes in all guises, from schoolchildren to elected members of the government, from people with no knowledge of research, science or archaeology to those who, while amateur in one sense, have fully professional knowledge of the subject. In the US and Canada, we also have the native

Americans as an often interested and sometimes very vocal group with an interest in archaeological sites which may differ considerably from all other groups. In point of fact, interest by varied groups of people often requires different means of interpretation, from on-site tours for sites which have visible features, to publications about information which is important.

In almost all countries there are laws, in the name of the public, which indicate that there is, indeed, intrinsic value for the nation in what has gone on in the past. In the US, archaeologists have for so long talked only to each other that we are now faced with two very real and pressing problems in explaining why a particular archaeological site is important. The first is a problem in communication, and the second is that sites are important to native Americans, to archaeologists, and to the American public for very different reasons.

To understand the communication problem one needs only to read a 'popular' article or book about archaeology in the US written by an archaeologist. Most archaeologists simply cannot communicate about their expertise without using jargon: many – I might even say most – in my country do not have and are not trained to have skills in writing (this I find to be in great contrast to British archaeologists, for example). As a consequence, journalists or interpreters who may not be well acquainted with the science of archaeology or with how information is analysed, are doing the interpretation, often perpetuating stereotypes (archaeologists are old and bearded, or like Indiana Jones). They, quite naturally, write and/or talk about the things they *can* understand or about things in which *they* think the audience will be interested. People are interested in mounds, or in ruined buildings – things they can actually see. They are also interested in human burials. And therein lies our second problem.

In the case of US media of all sorts, if there are human burials being uncovered, that is what fascinates the press. Native Americans, an important part of the American archaeologists' public, have recently expressed offence at published photographs of prehistoric human burials and at the display of bones, and in many cases they have objected to the excavation of prehistoric human remains at all. Archaeologists and museums have in the past fifteen years recognized the nature of this sensitiveness, but information from human remains, from the prehistoric people themselves, is vital to understanding many aspects of prehistory, so while museums no long display human remains, and archaeologists usually don't include photographs of excavated burials in their reports, the excavation, study and appropriate final treatment of these remains is still an area of controversy. Archaeologists feel that science and the public should have information on diet, disease, health, environment, and similar kinds of information which can be gained from the study of human remains. Many, although not all, native Americans do not want prehistoric burials excavated, much less studied. Because archaeologists in the now somewhat distant past often ignored both the public and the native American, the difficulty of communication is sometimes doubled.

Some native American groups, whose aboriginal culture is extinct, recognize that the only way that information about their own past can be acquired is through archaeology, but this particular part of the archaeologists' public has different interests and different concerns to most of the other publics. The general public, those who have enough interest about the past to read about it or to visit sites, should have good science interpreted in ways that provide relevant information about ways of life, and not just about itemized curiosities. Plundering and vandalism comes not only from a sense of greed, but from a lack of identity with the people who left those remnants of their life. Sites with intrinsic importance to both science and the public are ravaged by individuals with whom archaeologists have failed to communicate. People dig for artefacts in graves, throwing out the bones as if they were not aware that these were once people. This particular group of the archaeologists' public is, if anything, even more antagonistic to archaeologists than are native Americans because of sheer competition for the artefacts. Communication in any form is often non-existent with this group.

We in the US are learning, often the hard way, that it is the public interest in archaeological sites to which we must pay more attention. We have learned that the public is varied and often wondrous to behold. It is not educated in the niceties of stratigraphic data, or to the sheer wonder of lithic technology. It loves metal detectors and three-wheelers. In Europe it is interested in things of its own past, a long and often documented past. Documenting for native Americans their own past is one thing; documenting this long history for non-natives is another. Scientists can justify to themselves the importance of most sites in this endeavour, and the legal mechanisms in the form of federal and some state laws are in place to allow recovery of significant scientific information. But the scientists have yet to convince several of their various publics that expenditure of large amount of public monies is always justified. In America, efforts must be more strenuous, to communicate appropriately and effectively the scientific information which is contained in most archaeological sites whether there is actually something to see at the site or not. This is indeed the story of our human heritage. The information is of importance to us all.

10

The Eternal Triangle: Archaeologist, Builder and Public

Marion Meek

The changing ethics and fashions in presentation can often create major disagreements in the treatment of monuments. The *archaeologist* wants to display everything he has found, even it if means exposing originally buried foundations, displaying underground water pipes, or stripping plaster off churches and houses in a way that earlier builders would never have agreed to. The archaeologist also wants to preserve original material only, without any additions whatsoever. The *builder*, on the other hand, likes to see a perfect structure and is particularly unhappy if the original construction was at fault. Following his arguments can lead to reconstructing more than the purist likes, but the exercise can also lead to more thorough understanding of structures. Putting a roof on a tower house (Narrow Water) makes the building easier to maintain, and having to deal with the drains, angle towers and other irregularities sharpens our wits too. The *public* is not a cohesive force in its wishes. Some people would like to see all monuments completed, castles roofed and glazed, prehistoric tombs enclosed in their cairns and mill wheels turning. But few people wish to see stonework correctly rendered with harling, or crisp new stonework replacing the weathered remains that survive. In fact many people are horrified if ivy is removed from a ruin, because they like how it looks and believe it holds the fabric together.

A number of case studies illustrate what decisions have to be made.

Londonderry Walls are a vital part of the city centre, comparable to York or Caernarvon. Londonderry was besieged many times, and re-enactments of the shutting of the gates to shut out King James in 1688 have been performed for 300 years. The city has expanded beyond the walls, and many alterations have been made. None of the original four seventeenth-century gates survive, and four new ones have been added. Two of the corner bastions were demolished in the nineteenth century, and there are often calls for them to be rebuilt. On the other hand, business properties outside the walls want to make use of their walkways. Many applications have been made to allow the parapet to be breached. Some pubs would like access to spread outdoor trade on to the walls. Most properties are looking for fire escapes on to the walls.

Figure 10.1 Londonderry Walls with attached houses removed, presented as
'perfect'.

We have in fact resisted requests for both rebuilding bastions and breaching the parapets, but realize that our judgement differs markedly from that of previous generations. In this case, almost nobody is happy. The archaeologist cannot stick to his 'leave as found' philosophy, the builder and visitor is not allowed a total reconstruction, and the public in the form of local business cannot understand why he cannot cut into the walls for access as he could have forty years ago.

In **Carrickfergus**, walls of the same date, but without earth ramparts and without the same growth of town, have recently been rediscovered by the citizens. They want the town to thrive like Chester or York, and would like us to expand its wall walk (only one metre wide) and build in a few more features. The fact that this would be expensive, historically meaningless and still not very exciting is brushed aside as mere detail. In this case the archaeologist is determining the display for the time being, but under a lot of pressure.

Castles in Northern Ireland are seen by many people as the property of invaders. The Anglo-Normans often succeeded in integrating with the Irish, but war amongst neighbours meant that castles, large and small, had a turbulent history in medieval times and often into the seventeenth century. **Greencastle**'s thirteenth-century keep was besieged by Edward Bruce in 1316, sacked twice more in the fourteenth century by the Irish and refortified but modernized by Bagnell in the 1590s. With very little effort its outer curtain wall could be restored to full height, making a much stronger impact, but to do so would be to deny its history of being slighted. The seventeenth-century fortified house and bawn of **Tully Castle**, Co. Fermanagh was built for the Scotsman Sir John Hume in 1612. A ruthless attack on the castle on Christmas Eve, 1641, left it burned and abandoned. When the ruin was taken into care in 1975, it was overgrown with ivy and cracked in several places. The ivy was removed and the cracks were knitted together. All it needed for completion was a thatched roof – but that would be a denial of its fate. We have however started a formal garden in the bawn. Are we confusing history? Or playing to the crowds? So far everyone seems to accept the situation.

Abbeys provide a classic example of historic destruction. The dissolution of the monasteries in the sixteenth century included not just disbandment, but the sale of their property, and often the buildings were sold as scrap. In Northern Ireland the cloisters survive very poorly, and it can be quite hard to explain how they looked to the many schoolchildren who visit. The practice of grassing ruins, making no distinction between inside and out, adds to the confusion, and although reconstruction drawings are always on show, not everyone can make the jump from ruin to reconstruction drawing.

Roofing a building can allow for improved preservation and presentation. At **Knockmany**, a denuded passage grave with fine megalithic art was a joy

Figure 10.2   Clough Castle with stone tower near collapse in 1980.

Figure 10.3 Clough Castle interior in 1980.

to see. But its position – on top of an easy-to-climb hill in a forest park – led to a tendency for people to carve their names on the stones, and so an antiseptic concrete dome was set over it in 1956 and this was grassed over to simulate a cairn. It fools no one and it does its job. However, most people would prefer to do without it.

Some thirty tower houses survive in Co. Down. They date from the fifteenth to the seventeenth centuries. Often their quoins, windows and doors have been robbed, their roofs have gone and their harling is missing. In the 1950s and 1960s we replaced roofs and windows in several cases but found that the interiors remain very damp. Part of the solution is to harl or render again, but that is not popular with the public. Another is to heat the buildings, an attractive but expensive alternative. In one case recently a privately owned tower house, **Quoile Castle**, was put in state care after one corner had collapsed. We could have restored 'as new' but chose instead to leave the corner exposed like an architectural section.

Multi-period sites can cause conflicts of interpretation, and even problems with analysing causes of collapse. A bulging church wall may be caused by the loss or spread of the roof. Or it could have been alterations to the fabric,

Figure 10.4   Clough Castle – over-restored or not enough?

elongation, the introduction of a crossing tower, the insertion of bigger windows. Or it may be that the medieval church overlies earlier archaeological remains, an early cemetery perhaps, leaving soft spots underground. Unless you diagnose correctly, collapse may happen despite remedial works. There may be two or three causes. At **Grey Abbey**, for example, the nave wall is severely bowed, arising partly from previous roof pressures and partly from adjustments in the seventeenth century, when the nave was used as a parish church. In 1908 the solution decided on by the Board of Works was what Ruskin would have called 'a visible crutch', large flying buttresses which were highly criticized for changing the appearance of the church. Nevertheless they saved the church from collapse, and we now have to think again about how to deal with the severe deformation of the walls.

At **Newtownards Priory**, bad construction and a fire in the fourteenth century caused the westernmost arch of the arcade to push out. In the late nineteenth century the wall tops were planted with flowers and creepers. No serious collapse was created until a tree that had replaced the core of the arcade buttress died and shrank. The arcade began to shift again. We were able to slip a steel beam into the cavity, and tie it into a Z formation along

Figure 10.5 Grey Abbey drawn by J.J. Phillips in 1874.

the top of the arcade and along the ground, making the structure stable again. Nothing shows, but we can continue to display the medieval fire damage and collapse. At other churches the ever popular ring-beam holds the structure together. However when foundations are the problem, removal of late burials can create local distress and the public would prefer to see the building fall rather than disturb burials. In an attempt to minimize our interference with burials, we cut narrow slots beside the walls, creating an ugly appearance and unsatisfactory working conditions for all, as at **Banagher**. Once again judgement cannot be easy. In the last fifty years, enthusiastic archaeologists have removed and destroyed many tombstones that the present generation of genealogists would value.

Where carved stonework has deteriorated badly or had been removed, the builder is anxious to restore as new. The practice of replacing quoin stones to prevent collapse is rarely challenged. But decorative features are a matter of dispute. Nineteenth-century owners replaced detail without compunction and modern conservation experts have reacted against their predecessors' often insensitive alterations. We have recently undertaken two replacement tasks that may well be challenged. The first was a set of three niches high on the east wall of **Down Cathedral**. The medieval Benedictine Abbey church was burned down in the sixteenth century and reconstructed in the eighteenth century. The three niches survived all this, but during repairs in 1984 we found that the stone was pulverizing. We recorded the original in detail and then replaced it. We knew that it would be fifty years before anyone would climb that height again, and by that time the fourteenth-century detail would have disappeared.

Figure 10.6   Grey Abbey as restored in early 20th Century with honest, but obtrusive, flying buttresses.

At **Dunluce Castle** very little of the originally fine sixteenth and seventeenth-century detail of stone doorways and windows survives. Three-storey bay windows of the stylish Great Hall were collapsing because they were robbed of detail. We could pull them down, support them with steel, or reconstruct. So far we have inserted one reconstruction, but have we done the right thing? If not, we can reverse the process, an expensive experiment. So far the public is divided between those who want total reconstruction (supported by the builders) and those who prefer the undisturbed, crumbling ruin.

Methods of marking new work with a line, or by recessing additions are worthy and effective. They can also be visually obtrusive, spoiling the appearance of a wall, especially indoors. My own belief is that periods can be distinguished by conservation staff through the character of the mortar. Our building staff actually dyed the mortar for some years to aid this distinction until I pointed out that twentieth-century mortar is easy enough to recognize without dye.

Finally I return to the eternal triangle of archaeologist, builder and public. The archaeologist is continually trying to learn and hold out for authenticity. The builder looks for strength and perfection. The public is willing to accept whatever we present, and will stimulate us by their criticism and questions. Together the result can be dynamic.

11

Interpreting the Historic Scene: The Power of Imagination in Creating a Sense of Historic Place

Bruce Craig

Recently I stood on the Gettysburg battlefield gazing over the broad field where a little over 125 years ago, Robert E. Lee's army of Northern Virginia boldly advanced on General Mead's army of the Potomac. In the distance, perhaps a mile away, I squinted to see the statue of the great southern general mounted proudly on his horse Traveler. To my left, stood a National Park Service interpreter, enchanting a group of visitors with the dramatic tale of Pickett's Charge.

He seemed to do everything right. He wove historical facts into a vivid portrayal of the battle. His talk had a central theme, a strong story line and was peppered with fascinating anecdotes which gave life to the presentation. He referred to the historic scene; he pointed out cannon positions on distant hills as well as the famous clump of trees where a few Confederates broke the Union line before retreating. Indeed, the interpreter had the audience in the palm of his hand and by nearly all measures of interpretive evaluation, he did a superb job. Yet, something was still missing from the presentation.

Freeman Tilden in his now classic text, *Interpreting Our Heritage* tells us in his often quoted line that 'The chief aim of Interpretation is not instruction but provocation' (Tilden, 1957, p. 9). Colonial Williamsburg's Cary Carson develops Tilden's concept and says that 'interpretation should engage visitors' feelings. Feelings are the pass-key to history' (Carson, 1987).

If feelings are the pass-key to history, then imagination is the latch that must be unhooked to open the door to the past. Calling upon the visitor's imagination is an often neglected tool of 'provocation'. If we can unlock the visitor's imagination, we can promote revelation, education and perhaps help an individual gain a greater appreciation for and sense of historic place.

Thinking back now on my Gettysburg experience, I believe that interpreter had painted a vivid portrait of the event; he had supplied not just a sketch of the battle but had included all the colour as well. Nothing was left to the imagination. I was merely the passive spectator. To be truly effective, the interpreter needed to unlock his listeners' imagination and, if at all possible, let them experience a moment of time passed.

Breaking the Left Brain Barrier

In recent years, considerable attention has focused on the concept of 'left brain, right brain' processing of information. Brain and mind system studies over the last decade have demonstrated the difference between the functions of the left and right cerebral hemispheres and their influence on behaviour and learning (Levy, 1985). Betty Edwards, in her book *Drawing on the Right Side of the Brain* (1979), suggests that one should try to break away from verbal analytic processing of information, so-called left brain processing, in order to develop the creative hemisphere of the brain, 'right brain' processing. One only needs to listen to a few interpretive presentations to realize that historical interpreters rely nearly exclusively on left brain processing techniques (the use of analytic verbal techniques) to present history to the public. In general, this limits the effectiveness of their interpretive programmes. It is rare indeed to find an interpreter who effectively draws on the right side of the brain and is able to unlock not only their imagination but the creative powers of visitors as well.

Through the use of imagination, it is possible to draw on the right side of the brain and consequently stimulate in the visitor's mind a 'sense of historical place'. With this in mind, perhaps the goal of an interpretive presentation should not be merely to describe historical events and personalities, but rather to seek to instil in visitors a feeling for a moment of 'time passed'. The interpreter is, in essence, the catalytic agent who enables visitors to feel virtually transported in time through the power of imagination to 'experience' a moment of history.

But before visitors can 'experience' a moment of history, three important elements of the interpretation process must be considered. First, the issue of historical accuracy; second, the concept of 'time passed'; and third, the inter-relationship of historical description, objects and artefacts, historic scene and imagination which, when properly combined, enable the mind to create an impression of 'time passed'.

Historical Accuracy

Historians and historical interpreters are generally over-concerned with 'historical accuracy'. Interpreters engaged in 'living history' often go to great lengths to try to create exact replicas of historic clothing. Curators of historic house museums strive to re-create historic interiors so that they appear 'as it actually was'; and historians pore over primary sources and archival material to discover 'what really happened in history'.

David Lowenthal, in his recent book *The Past is a Foreign Country* (1985), questions traditional standards of exactitude. According to Lowenthal, 'no historical account can recover the totality of any past events, because their content is virtually infinite. The most detailed historical narrative incorporates only a minute fraction of even the relevant past; the sheer pastness of the past precludes its total reconstruction.' Lowenthal advances the notion that, 'no account can recover the past as it was, because the past was not an account, it was a set of events and situations. Historical narrative is not a portrait of what happened but a story about what happened.' And he asserts, 'Unlike memory or relics, history usually depends on someone else's eyes and voice: we see it through an interpreter who stands between past events and our apprehension of them ... The past we know or experience is always contingent on our own views, our own perspective, and above all our own present' (Lowenthal, 1985, pp. 214–17).

According to Lowenthal, interpreters assert their views of the past, colour their stories to fit a specific vision of the historical 'reality', and seek to impose this view on listeners. But if these views of history are fragmentary at best, why should interpreters feel that it is so important to convey a fragmentary view of historical reality to visitors? Why not give visitors broad latitude to discover history for themselves? Why not let them create their own sense of time past and fill in the huge gaps that exist in our understanding of the past?

Theodore Sande, in his article 'Presenting the truth about the past' (1984) suggests that historical integrity should be measured in terms of historical plausibility rather than fact. He writes: 'Plausibility reaches beyond the factual basis and intellectual understanding, and attempts to meld them with an emotional certitude that raises the visitors' experiential level to a heightened realization of the past.' Furthermore, Sande suggests that 'meaning', for the visitor is not a series of facts but 'the sum total of the experience' (Sande, 1984, p. 2).

Thus, historical sites, museums, objects and artefacts may be viewed not only as cultural resources but also as stage sets and props which, when combined with the visitor's imagination and willingness to fantasize, can raise the visitor's experiential level to a heightened realization of the past. To a certain extent several outdoor museums seek to deliver to visitors this type of interpretive experience. What becomes of paramount importance in such museum settings is the sum total of the historical experience. Unfortunately, I doubt whether interpreters will ever raise the visitor's experiential level to a heightened realization of time past until they transcend the limitations they place on themselves when striving so intently for 'accuracy'. Perhaps what Sande suggests is an obtainable objective: interpreters should be concerned more with historical plausibility than with accuracy.

Time Passed

The second concern relates to the notion of 'time passed'. We are all products, perhaps victims, of our culture. To the Western mind, time is measured in minutes, hours and years. History flows linearly and our perception of history exists only in this context. But in many other cultures time, and hence history, is perceived differently.

John Hanson Mitchell, in his recent book *Ceremonial Time: 15,000 Years On One Square Mile* (1984), advances a notion of 'time passed' held by native American groups. He writes that land possesses a 'vague almost indefinable quality of time, or space or history' and that this quality tends to linger in an area. We rarely recognize these qualities, but Mitchell was able to gain a vision of the past – that 'secret world that lurks beyond the night windows and at the fringes of cultivated backyards', as he describes it, when introduced to a concept called 'ceremonial time' (Mitchell, 1984, pp. 9, 12 – 13).

As explained to Mitchell, the native American concept of 'ceremonial time' as held by several eastern woodland tribes may be defined as 'a heightened awareness or perception of the way things must have been' rather than 'the way things necessarily were'. Mitchell's guide into this previously unperceived world of time passed stated,

If you see things in your mind, you must believe that it is what happened. That is the only thing you can know . . . You can see people and animals who have been dead for thousands of years; you can walk in their place, see and touch the plants of their world. (Mitchell, 1984, pp. 12 – 13)

Ceremonial time, as explained to Mitchell, does not flow linearly from past to present as it does according to Western tradition. It is not measured by minutes, hours or years, it is not exacting, rather it stretches itself out or contracts or even reverses on occasion. The past and present are one.

Experiencing a feeling of time passed using the techniques of 'ceremonial time' is not dependent on eating magic mushrooms or relying on drug-induced trances. Each of us has probably experienced the feeling of 'time passed' using the ceremonial time concept without realizing it at one time or another. There are moments in everybody's past when the remembrance of a past event seems especially real. At these times we feel more in touch with our own sense of place. For example it was this intimate familiarity with the landscape, the remembrance of events and people that enabled Civil War veterans to vividly recall moments of their past when they visited the battlefields where they had fought years before. For today's Vietnam war veterans, the emotional response may come when they visit their memorial in Washington DC. For others, the feeling of time passed may come by reading a particularly vividly written book, perhaps by smelling a fragrance, or hearing a song that triggers a childhood memory. In each of these cases, the imagination plays a central role in bringing their past to life.

I suspect that nearly all historians who pride themselves on high standards of scholarship would laugh at the notion that the use of the ceremonial time concept could possibly be a valid tool for historical research. Indeed, accepting one's own 'vision of history' may more appropriately be termed an historical delusion, if not illusion. But interpreters must ask themselves, what is the perception of historical reality to historic site visitors? If one recognizes, as does Lowenthal, that even the best historian cannot possibly uncover the 'whole story', then the use of the ceremonial time concept in interpretive programmes need not constitute an abuse of history. Though the concept probably is not a valid technique for the writing of scholarly history, it can be a useful tool for 'provocation' and can help visitors explore the past for themselves, thereby making history more meaningful to their lives and personal experience.

It is the application of the concept of ceremonial time that enables people to uncover the mystery of the past by unlocking their imagination. But, more importantly, it enables visitors to gain a heightened sense of historical place and their relationship to that place. Whether marching across the Gettysburg battlefield picturing in the mind's eye some 10,000 grey-clad soldiers with scarlet banners flapping in the breeze, or standing alone in awed silence in the assembly room at Independence Hall (where the American Declaration of Independence and Constitution were signed) allowing the mind to absorb the atmosphere of that historic chamber, when one invokes the concept of ceremonial time the mind can be freed, if only for a moment, from the confines of time.

Historical Description, Objects and Imagination

Outdoor museums are often remarkably successful in conveying to the public a sense of time passed. This is due at least in part to the participatory nature of their exhibitions as well as their evocative environmental setting. For example, at Old Economy in Pennsylvania, sensory awareness – where visitors feel cobblestones under their feet when they walk or smell wood burning from hearths – helps create an environment conducive to unlocking the imagination.

Although some may suggest that outdoor museums are essentially 'anti-museum museums' (i.e., they are not places of hushed reverence, not places where objects are protected behind display cases), outdoor museums do help bring visitors nearer to the past because of interpretive techniques of display and presentation that emphasize activity, participation and process.

At such museums, interpreters engage in role playing, often creating fictional historical characters. Here again, it is historical plausibility that is one of the goals of the interpretive experience. While the use of reproductions is widespread in most such museums, I think there is no substitute for contact with original objects in order to stimulate one's imagination; objects indeed are the link between past and present, person and concept. Although prolonged and repeated contact with original objects creates wear and tear on artefacts and indeed may eventually destroy such objects, the fact remains that there is no experiential substitute for the direct link for visitors who are able to have immediate contact with original objects.

Creating Our Own Past

Theodore Sande summarizes the frustrations of many historical interpreters when he writes:

the placement of objects from a historical period in rooms of that time or the setting aside of a parcel of land . . . no matter how well preserved, does not guarantee the re-creation of a true feeling of an earlier time. Something more is needed to breathe vitality into these settings; yet, I am unable to say what that something is, or whether it can ever be found. (Sande, 1984, p. 2 – 3)

That 'something' Sande was unable to define yet which was needed to 'breathe vitality' into historical settings is, I believe, the imagination. While professional historians skim the surface of the past, interpreters can delve deeper into the realm (however murky it may be) of 'time passed'. And if interpreters are willing to expand their imagination and teach visitors to explore their own visions of historical reality, then (perhaps for the first time in their lives), visitors will gain a sense of historic place.

References

Carson, C. (1987) Presentation to 'Workshop for Historians', National Park Service, Steven T. Mather Training Center, Harpers Ferry, West Virginia.

Edwards B. (1979) *Drawing on the Right Side of the Brain*, J.P. Tarcher, Los Angeles, California.

Levy, J. (1985) 'Right brain, left brain: fact and fiction', *Psychology Today*, (May) 38 – 44.

Lowenthal, D. (1985) *The Past is a Foreign Country*, Cambridge University Press, Cambridge.

Mitchell, J.H. (1984) *Ceremonial Time: 15,000 Years On One Square Mile*, Anchor Press/Doubleday, New York.

Sande, T. (1984) 'Presenting the truth about the past', *CRM Bulletin*, 7 (4) (December) 1 – 3.

Tilden, F. (1957) *Interpreting Our Heritage*, University of North Carolina Press, Chapel Hill.

12

Is There an 'Excluded Past' in Education?

Peter Stone and Robert Mackenzie

A Contextual Framework

This paper reflects some initial thoughts stimulated by our working together as joint editors of a volume in the One World Archaeology series entitled *The Excluded Past: Archaeology in Education* (Stone and MacKenzie, 1989). The series results from the First World Archaeological Congress held in Southampton, England in September 1986 (see Ucko, 1987).

From its outset the Southampton World Archaeological Congress intended to challenge the common understanding of archaeology as an introspective academic discipline solely concerned with excavation and the minutiae of a chronologically interpreted past. It set out to be a truly 'world' gathering that not only attracted, and listened to, students of the past, but also attracted those whose lives are actively affected by the study of the past, for example, North American Indians and Australian Aborigines (Ucko, 1987). This commitment to a broad understanding and interpretation of archaeological study has been fundamental in the development of the new World Archaeological Congress organization (see, for example, Day, 1988). It was within this environment that the concept of the 'excluded past' came to light.

This paper chronicles the development of an awareness of the importance and power of education about the past through archaeology – a discipline that, hitherto, has shied clear of its responsibilities in this field. The realization of these responsibilities towards education around the world, a realization stimulated by the First World Archaeological Congress, is only one aspect of a general acceptance of responsibility that is of equal relevance to interpreters and presenters of the past (Cleere, 1989; Layton, 1988; Gathercole and Lowenthal, 1989). What we choose to teach, interpret and present, and equally what we do *not* choose to teach, interpret and present, is a fundamental dilemma common to all of those empowered to communicate about the past.

The Past in Education at the Southampton Congress

Initially the educational content of the congress was limited to a few papers subsumed within a part of one of the major themes. By the time the congress took place there were not only two full sub-themes (with contributions from ten countries) discussing education, but also an exhibition and a series of 'open events' that linked the academic discussion of the congress to more informal evening presentations of educational resources, including films and drama.

We have come to use the term 'excluded past' in relation to both formal education from the primary school to university and informal and non-formal education. This paper concentrates particularly on formal school education.

What is the 'Excluded Past'?

There is a dual sense in which the term 'excluded past' is used that encompasses both the virtual exclusion of the prehistoric past from school curricula around the world and the suppression of the versions of the past held to be true by many indigenous and/or minority groups.

In the case of Mozambique, for example, both aspects were evident during colonial rule. Sinclair explains how the present Mozambican government has attempted to increase public awareness of the, previously untaught, indigenous cultural heritage – a heritage that, because of its non-literacy, equates with Mozambican prehistory. The new government initiative attempts to counter this exclusion:

For many years Mozambique has been considered one of the blanks in African archaeology. Notwithstanding the early reports of rock paintings to the Portuguese Royal Academy in 1721 very little notice has been taken of Mozambican prehistory before the beginning of the twentieth century . . . colonial archaeology can fairly be said to have almost completely neglected the recent past apart from Portuguese colonial relics. (Sinclair, 1989)

Blancke and Peters, writing about how the past of the native peoples of North America is taught to native Americans, add a new slant to the problem when they quote the Cherokee, Gerald Wilkinson:

The history of the Indian people is not taught as Indian history, but as the history of Indian/White relations. This approach gives the impression that Indians would have no past at all if it had not been for the European invasion . . . It is difficult to see how an Indian young person could get any perspective on himself when his past is presented to him as a mere side-show in the panorama of human existence. (Blancke and Peters, 1989)

From these and other examples it is quite clear that there are vast areas of the study of the past that are almost totally ignored in school curricula.

Wilkinson claims that the North American Indian past is only taught within a particular context. In Europe the prehistoric past is relegated to providing a starting point for what is regarded as 'proper' history. The past is only worth studying once 'civilization' arrives. This approach assumes that society takes on a recognizable form once civilization arrives, leading to a sympathetic environment for 'progress' only once there is literacy and history. As one English textbook puts it:

When we talk of the history of man, we can only mean real history from the point in time when man began to use a means of writing which would be understood by those who came after him. Before that there is no true history . . .

and again:

To us the life of prehistoric man would seem very, very dull. Lower Palaeolithic Man did not live in an organized group, and for a long time made no contact with his fellow men. He wandered haphazardly about the land or dozed sluggishly beneath a tree in the noonday heat. He didn't meet another man very often, and when he did he probably ran away – not really in fear, but because there was nothing to say to him . . . Early man was therefore shut up in himself, he could not tell the others the things he felt, he could not laugh or smile, he could yell in pain but that was probably the only sound he ever made . . . (Boddington, 1965)

These statements can be derided and attacked for being sexist, sweeping and downright silly; the fact that many such textbooks are in use today is almost unbelievable. However, the real danger in these and similar passages is that children are being encouraged to feel contempt for the prehistoric past; it is our contention that it is an easy step from feeling contempt for the prehistoric past to feeling a similar contempt for any pre- or non-industrialized society.

Why Is There an 'Excluded Past'?

First, there is a universal cry of 'overcrowded curricula!' The argument goes that time cannot be given over to a 'new' subject when many that have been long accepted are now fighting for their lives in curricula that are increasingly being dominated by the need for job-related training.

Second, teachers have allowed the 'excluded past' to be excluded through their own ignorance. The little of the excluded past that is included in syllabi is taught under great difficulties because of a lack of suitable materials. As indicated by the above quotations from Boddington, endless examples could be given of history textbooks used in English schools today that ignore contemporary understanding of the prehistoric past. If the little that can be inferred about the prehistoric past is ignored in this way, and unsustainable interpretation put in its place, then a situation where the past is falsely interpreted on purpose can be envisaged. Individuals who take on the responsibility of teaching must be in the vanguard of those ensuring that such a situation never becomes a reality.

Mammini describes the situation in Italy where, after the rise of urban 'rescue' excavations,

The interest in archaeology, fed by municipal enterprises and press coverage, reached, above all, the primary schools. The Roman schools, urged by the requests of parents and teachers' Associations, were obliged to satisfy the desire for archaeological information, even though they were not provided with suitable programmes, equipment or teachers with the necessary training. (Mammini, 1989)

Mammini's response, as a practising archaeologist, was to try to help the teachers with information from his excavations. Similar assistance is being provided, in England for example, by the Council for British Archaeology, the English Heritage education branch, and a number of archaeological projects based in university departments of archaeology (for example, the 'Archaeology and Education Project' based at the University of Southampton between 1985 and 1988) and archaeological field units (for example, the Education Unit of the Manchester Archaeology Unit). Unfortunately, funding for the latter projects is usually of limited duration. In Canada, once teachers have been introduced to the methods of archaeology they quickly see its value as a tool for exploring the relationship between evidence and interpretation. Teachers begin to see the opportunities archaeology provides for children to test (and if necessary reject) hypotheses, and for them actually to put into practice cross-curricula activity and experimentation.

Third, the study of the prehistoric past is seen as an indulgent luxury that has no direct bearing upon today's society. In England the Historical Association has produced guidelines for a core national curriculum in school history that effectively cuts out all but the most cursory glance at prehistory (Historical Association, 1986). English historians seem to have bowed without resistance to the dogma that the real value of teaching about the past is to set the modern world into a narrow chronological framework that relates solely to the recent past.

We do not argue with the premise that children should be taught the recent national and world political history that has directly and most immediately shaped the world in which they live; we do argue, however, that only to do so is to ignore and exclude the wider view of humanity and the longer time dimension of human development which alone can give a complete context to national and world political history.

Chakrabarti chronicles a similar situation in India where, until recently, even at university, archaeology 'meant only a set of techniques' and that it 'was plainly unheard of in the schools'. He goes on to explain that:

The study of prehistory was in a kind of academic limbo because this had no general nationalistic appeal in a country singularly rich in historical relics. Even the discovery of the Indus civilization . . . did not lead to a change in this except in the fact that history textbooks started printing photographs of the brick-built drains of Mohenjodaro with an almost religious regularity. (Chakrabarti, 1989)

What use is prehistory in schools when national identity can be satisfied by recent history?

Finally, the 'excluded past' may be excluded for political reasons. In the case of South Africa this is overt, resulting in a concentration of archaeological work on the extremely remote fossil hominids and the virtual absence of studies of later prehistory. When it became impossible to ignore the evidence of later Stone Age and Iron Age cultures, the only acceptable interpretations were those that focused on the existence of disparate tribal groupings – interpretations that stimulated the production of schoolbooks using derogatory stereotyping of the presumed groupings. Meli argues that: 'the struggle surrounding the interpretation and explanation of South African history is an aspect of the struggle for human dignity' (Meli, 1986).

Less extreme forms of political exclusion are equally damaging to the people concerned, for example where, in Bolivia the past of the indigenous peoples is classified as prehistory. It is therefore made to equate with the 'primitive' and 'uncivilized' thereby denying any pride in the people's own heritage and even leading to the extraordinary situation whereby Bolivian Indians are made to pay for entrance to their own sacred sites (Condori, 1989).

Such exclusion allows the promulgation of the accepted values of the dominant group in society. This does not have to imply an overtly conscious politicization of the past implemented by a repressive dominant group, although this certainly can, and does, happen. The degree of overtly political involvement does not need to concern us here as the end result is effectively the same. Kehoe makes the point eloquently with regard to the United States of America:

'American history' begins, according to American schools, when Christopher Colombus landed on San Salvador, October 12, 1492. The twelve millennia or more of human habitation of North America are dismissed in a few brief pages in the textbooks used in American schools. This allocation of textbook space, fewer than a dozen pages on pre-Columbian America versus several hundred pages on the history of the United States, makes a powerful statement: America did not exist before European colonization. That assertion is the framework moulding discussion of the American past . . . Archaeology as the study of human occupation of the American continent is incompatible with the mission of the schools in the United States. (Kehoe, 1989)

Heritage Interpretation and the 'Excluded Past'

The extent of the power, and its associated responsibility, held by educators, interpreters and presenters in their transmission of the past is almost without rival. Together they transmit almost the sum total of knowledge about the past, and its relevance to the present and future, that the majority of the population will ever receive. Such responsibility is awesome to those who are

Figure 12.1 Stonehenge: a world heritage site.

aware of it. It is unperceived and therefore inappropriately discharged by those who are not.

Those carrying out original research about the past need to work closely with educators and interpreters, not to give a formalized view of a definitive past, finalized in all its details, but rather to do the opposite: to impart and distinguish between what is known, what can legitimately be inferred, and what is complete fabrication.

Most of the examples used in this paper have been of clearly definable groups denied, through lack of formal education, their traditional views of the past. We now turn to look briefly at prehistory, and a monument for which one of us bears educational responsibility – Stonehenge (Figure 12.1).

The educational (and associated presentational) responsibility at this monument is to ensure that all of the different legitimate views of the past are easily accessible to both visitors and students. Certainly, within any educational material prepared for that monument, the views of antiquarian, hippie, modern-day 'druid', archaeologist, ley liner, tourist and astronomer must be allowed space. To do less, to simply display Stonehenge in 'romantic isolation' or only to disseminate the contemporary scientific archaeological understanding of the monument is to remove much of the relevance to today's society of arguably Britain's most famous landmark.

In the educational material being prepared for Stonehenge at the moment all of these different attitudes to the monument will be discussed as actively held interpretations of how the monument should be regarded and used. Children must be given the opportunity to discuss and sift such views in order for them to come to a reasoned, contemporary understanding of the monument.

Conclusion

Until we, as interpreters, educationalists and indeed as a society, decide what it is we think is worthy of forming part of curricula about the past, suitable for different political and social situations, it must remain in some ways premature to decide on what aspects of the past heritage management and interpreters should concentrate. This chapter attempts to illustrate that what is chosen to be highlighted and revealed to visitors and students is extremely complicated and riddled with all sorts of potential and actual implications. It is only by recognizing why some aspects of the past have been excluded and others included in different contexts that we can hope to improve the situation for the future by having a clearer rationale for deciding what is taught and, by implication, what is excluded.

At a specially organized extra meeting at the Southampton congress a number of suggestions were put forward (MacKenzie, 1987). Two of these required specific action. First, that in as many countries as possible there should be meetings to discuss the nature of the relationship between the excluded past and education. In this way it was hoped to widen the database for discussion at any future international gatherings. This suggestion was followed up in Britain by the 'Archaeology Meets Education' conference (Richardson, 1988). The topic was also a considerable focus of debate at the 1987 Third New World Conference on Rescue Archaeology, Venezuela. Second, archaeologists are requested to recognize the importance of their subject in formal and informal education.

The new World Archaeological Congress lists seven areas 'on which it hopes to focus attention': one of these is 'education about the past' (Day, 1988, p. 7). As a result, education is mentioned first in the list of topics for discussion at the Second World Archaeological Congress to be held in Venezuela in 1990.

This is an exciting indication that what we have called the 'excluded past' may eventually find its rightful place in curricula around the world. It is only when this happens that as educators, interpreters and presenters we will be able to confront the implications of Podgorny's discussion of what she has termed 'the excluded present' with Argentina, when she states:

I agree with the view that the past is part of our identity, that the American and Argentinean prehispanic past is unknown, that the multiculturality of Argentinean society is ignored, and that the vision that we have is based on stereotypes that have been put forward by others. I also agree with the view that all this is part of a reality that can be modified, little by little, from the bottom up, and in its totality. (Podgorny, 1989)

References

Blancke, S. and Peters, J. (1989) 'The teaching of the past to the native people of

North America in United States' schools', in Stone and MacKenzie (1989).

Boddington, J. (1965) *The First People on Earth*, Hamlyn, London.

Chakrabarti, G. (1989) 'Archaeology in Indian education', in Stone and MacKenzie (1989).

Cleere, H. (1989) *Archaeological Heritage Management in the Modern World*, Unwin Hyman, London.

Condori, C.M. (1989) 'History and prehistory in Bolivia: what about the Indians?' in Layton, R. (ed.) *Conflicts in the Archaeology of Living Traditions*, Unwin Hyman, London.

Day. M. (1989) 'Final report to the World Archaeological Congress Steering Committee', *World Archaeological Bulletin*, 2, 4–12 (available from the Department of Archaeology, University of Southampton, UK).

Gathercole, P. and Lowenthal, D. (1989) *The Politics of the Past*, Unwin Hyman, London.

Historical Association (1986) *History in the Compulsory Years of Schooling*, London.

Kehoe, A. (1989) '"In fourteen hundred and ninety two, Columbus sailed . . .": the primacy of the national myth in American schools', in Stone and MacKenzie (1989).

Layton, R. (1989) *Who Needs the Past?*, Unwin Hyman, London.

Mammini, S. (1989) 'Rediscovering Rome's hidden past', in Stone and MacKenzie (1989).

MacKenzie, R. (1987) 'The future of the past in education', *World Archaeological Bulletin*, 1, 37–8 (available from the Department of Archaeology, University of Southampton, UK).

Meli, F. (1986) 'The past in South African education'. Paper presented at the 1986 World Archaeological Congress, University of Southampton (September).

Podgorny, I. (1989) 'The excluded present', in Stone and MacKenzie (1989).

Richardson, W. (1988) 'Papers for the AME! Conference', *Education Bulletin*, 6 (Council for British Archaeology).

Sinclair, P. (1989) 'The Earth is our history book', in Stone and MacKenzie (1989).

Stone, P. and MacKenzie, R. (eds) (1989) *The Excluded Past: Archaeology in Education*, Unwin Hyman, London.

Ucko, P.J. (1987) *Academic Freedom and Apartheid*, Duckworth, London.

13

Interpreting the Countryside and the Natural Environment

Adrian Phillips

Firstly, I wish to comment briefly on the title of this paper: 'Interpreting the Countryside and the Natural Environment'. The two subjects embraced in the one title are, of course, very different. The natural environment we take to mean the natural world around: the fauna and flora, the ecological systems which sustain them and of which they are part. When we create a national park, in the internationally recognized sense, we do so in order to safeguard part of the natural environment, and we use interpretation to serve that end. But 'countryside' is a more subtle concept. It implies a harmony between man and nature, it embraces the built environment in rural areas and the cultural and social dimensions of rural life, as well as the natural world which humankind will have adapted and altered. Interpretation of the countryside, therefore, has a lot to say about people and about how they interact with nature – and there is inevitably a strong cultural and historic component to the countryside story. The United Kingdom is, along with other parts of Europe in particular, a place where the concept of 'countryside' is deeply rooted – so much so that our own national parks reflect a very different concept from those found in most countries (and are, incidentally, internationally recognized as protected landscapes, not national parks *sensu stricto*). I stress this difference because those from other parts of the world may wonder why I use so many examples of interpretation which are not concerned exclusively with the natural environment, but more with man's place in it. And because the two strands in the title of this paper run through the history of the evolution of interpretation.

Historic Resumé

Many of you will first have encountered interpretation, in the sense in which it is to be used in this paper, in North America. Certainly my first full exposure to what interpretation could mean – a very exciting experience – came when I had the privilege of visiting a number of Canadian and United

States national parks in 1971 in the now disbanded international seminar on national parks and equivalent reserves. It is right to pay special tribute here, at the outset, to the leadership role which the United States National Park Service has played in interpretation. Not only has its interpretation work within the national parks of the US been an inspiration to those who have seen it, but through its generously funded programmes of advice and assistance, it has spread the message worldwide. Through involvement in the work of the International Union for Conservation of Nature and Natural Resources (IUCN) I have seen the influence of the park service in many countries in the developed and the developing world, and interpretation of the natural environment has been one of the outstanding features of this impact. Although, of course, each country has adapted the approaches pioneered in the US to its own circumstances, there is a common strand to much of the US-inspired work on interpretation: its reliance on sound ecological fieldwork and its concern with promoting an understanding among visitors and local residents of the importance of conserving the natural environment.

But if you come from Scandinavia or Central Europe you may, with some justification, be reluctant to accept the primacy of American interpretation and point to what, at first sight, seems to be an entirely different approach to interpreting the environment, one which is less ecologically orientated and more people-based. You might then claim that continental ethnologists discovered much of what we now label as environmental interpretation of country life, and all this well before the United States National Parks Service was established in 1916.

In fact this strand of interpretation concerned with country life and agricultural museums began with Artur Hazelius and the collections of those whom he inspired. He created both the Nordiska Museum in Stockholm and the world's first open-air country life museum based upon scholarship, known as the Skansen Open Air museum, also in Stockholm. These two museums, the indoor and outdoor, were designed to be places where complementary interpretive experiences could be gained. The idea of the Nordiska collection was conceived in 1872 (it was opened in 1886) and that of the Open Air Museum was conceived in 1878 (and opened in 1891).

Although 1872 was, of course, the year in which the Yellowstone National Park was established, there is no link between that event and the simultaneous development of Hazelius's thinking in Scandinavia. His inspiration came from the English and French efforts to show off their wares in the Great Exhibitions of London (1851) and Paris (1878). Bernard Olsen of Denmark, who was the creator of Copenhagen's famous open-air museum, met Hazelius at the Paris Exhibition; and King Oscar II of Norway is usually credited with establishing the first folk museum in 1881 in Oslo.

Fifty years later, returning home to the USA from a trip to Europe, John D. Rockefeller Jnr waxed enthusiastic about the Scandinavian folk museums. A direct result of this was the creation of Colonial Williamsburg; indirectly it led to all those other replicated American historic villages. Thus, the ethnological strand of interpretation, brought to the New World from the Old, was able to merge with that related to the natural environment which was already well established in the USA. It is this blend of the ethnological with the ecological which gives the best of modern day countryside interpretation its strength. It does not deal with people apart *from* nature, but with people as a part *of* nature. The more we understand the many and complex interrelationships between human beings and the rest of the natural world, the more we see the need to look at the two perspectives together – the more, indeed, we come to realize that they are two parts of one and the same story.

Having very briefly traced the historic evolution of interpretation, let me now look more closely at experience in Britain. The pioneers of countryside interpretation were our own national parks, especially the Peak District National Park, which had the good fortune to be served by both John Foster and Don Aldridge in the 1950s and 1960s. The establishment of the Countryside Commission for Scotland in 1967 and the Countryside Commission (for England and Wales) a year later created a national focus for work in this field. The Commissions had the mandate and the resources to bring US experience to our shores and to encourage a large number of bodies in the public, private and voluntary sectors to introduce interpretation as part of their countryside schemes. They were greatly helped by the Countryside Acts of 1967 and 1968 which empowered local authorities and others to create country parks as places in the countryside to which large numbers of day visitors could be attracted (there are now nearly 230 of these in England and Wales); and by the strengthening of the administration of our ten national parks in 1974 which gave them all access to the professionalism and resources previously enjoyed only by the Peak District and the Lake District.

The two Commissions came together to produce a guide to interpretive planning in the early 1970s. This was the first United Kingdom text on that subject, and it gave us definitions, a philosophy, principles and practical examples relevant to, and designed for, the UK. The guide has served us well without stifling innovation or debate.

The guide defined the subject: in Don Aldridge's very helpful words, interpretation is 'the art of explaining the significance of a site to those who visit it, in order to communicate a conservation message'. Let us take that definition apart.

First, the 'art'. Interpretation is not a science, although it draws on scientific analysis and materials and often uses technology to convey its message. But when we say it is an 'art', we mean that it calls for flair, imagination, creation: it follows, as Freeman Tilden recognized, 'that since interpretation is an art, it is therefore only partly teachable'. In assessing your professionalism and the need for training, do not overlook the limits to what can be taught.

Second, 'explaining the significance of a site'. Interpretation is about revelation, discovery, illumination. It is about revealing the essence of a place, be it Gettysburg, Ngorongoro or the Lake District. Therefore, the prime measure of success is whether the significance of the site has been conveyed to the visitor.

Third, 'to those who visit it'. And here I admit to a little difficulty. It is not that I question the definition, but rather that I see in the definition the limitations to interpretation. Because, of course, our understanding of the significance of a site depends not only on what we learn about it when we get there, but also upon our formal education, what we read, what we see on television, what values and attitudes guide us – and so on. I want to return to this point later.

And finally, 'in order to communicate a conservation message'. To me, this overrides all else. If you believe that the conservation of our natural environment and of our countryside is of the greatest possible importance, then the true value of interpretation is to be found in the contribution which it can make in this respect. If visitors' understanding of conservation needs is increased, above all if their values and behaviour are affected, through the interpretation experience, then the whole exercise becomes worthwhile – if, on the other hand, interpretation of the natural environment and the countryside makes no contribution, however direct, to conservation, it seems to me that it is in danger of being no more than entertainment. Which is not to dismiss the value of entertainment as a means of capturing the visitors' attention; nor is it to devalue the desire to increase the recreational enjoyment of visitors. Both of these are very worthwhile aims, but in my view they should be means to an end: the communication of the conservation message.

Countryside Interpretation in the UK Today

Against that historical background and the definition of interpretation, how does interpretation of the natural environment and the countryside stand in the UK today – twenty years after the setting up of the two countryside commissions which were specifically charged to promote conservation of the British countryside and its enjoyment by the public?

First, the concept is widely accepted. Interpretation as a process is well embedded in the minds and work of countryside planners, rangers and countryside managers. Virtually every countryside management plan has an interpretation element. Virtually all ranger services offer some interpretation to visitors. Though, of course, the quality of interpretation varies considerably, its integration into site planning and management in the countryside is perhaps the greatest single achievement of the past twenty years. You will now find interpretation provided at literally thousands of countryside localities, many of them grant aided by one of the Countryside Commissions.

Second, interpretation has spread into new areas of countryside experience. Take the extraordinary growth of interest in interpretation of industrial and social history. This has largely happened from scratch over the past twenty years. Indeed, in 1968, local authorities and others were happily demolishing industrial structures which would now be carefully preserved, restored and interpreted. You will find such interpretation not only in places which compete with each other to be called 'the birthplace of the industrial revolution' – which, when you think of it, means a certain licence with the truth – but also in our national parks and elsewhere in the countryside.

Another new area for interpretive provision is the urban countryside and city parks. If we recall that part of the definition of interpretation is concerned with explaining the significance of a site, then its significance can be a function of location as well as intrinsic value. A small woodland on the edge of a large city may have greater interpretive potential than a fine forest 100 miles away, precisely because of its accessibility, especially to children. Some of the most exciting developments in interpretation have been in such areas, particularly where they are linked to community participation in the care of such sites.

Thirdly, there is a growing professionalism and expertise in an area where there is no clearly defined profession, and this applies to interpretation of all kinds, not only that concerned with the natural environment and the countryside. Those involved in interpretation often have other duties, other professional allegiances. That is healthy – far better to integrate the conservation ethic into a large group than to concentrate it amongst a few. Such a dispersal of interpretation expertise does, however, need external support in terms of training, advice and contacts with fellow interpreters. This is especially so in the light of the results of a survey undertaken some ten years ago which showed that over 50 per cent of self-styled interpreters in England had not attended any training course in the topic (hopefully the position today is a little better).

Professionalism among interpreters in the UK is reinforced by the work of the Society for the Interpretation of Britain's Heritage (SIBH) set up in 1975. SIBH is especially valuable as a focus for practitioners because, by the very nature of the work undertaken by interpreters, they are often geographically isolated and therefore have a special need for access to professional networks. The Centre for Environmental Interpretation, founded in 1980 at Manchester Polytechnic is of particular value to the Countryside Commission as a source of professional consultancy advice. And there is a growing number of highly impressive private consultants in the field. None of this existed twenty years ago.

Fourth, there are many more actors on the scene. Twenty years ago, countryside interpretation – such as it was – was largely a public sector business, with local authorities (including the national parks) the most active providers. They still play an important role, of course but a host of other bodies have become involved in countryside interpretation of various kinds. There are national agencies, like the Nature Conservancy Council, the Forestry Commission, and English Heritage. There are many trusts with environmental purposes, ranging from the nationally important, such as the National Trust, the Royal Society for the Protection of Birds, the Wildfowl Trust and the network of Groundwork Trusts, to local trusts with more localized aims. There are community groups: parish councils – our lowest level of local authority, equivalent to the commune – in particular are taking a lively interest in interpreting the local countryside. Commercial and tourist operators are, of course, far more involved than in the past. And some landowners and farmers are becoming increasingly engaged in aspects of countryside interpretation.

Funding now comes from a range of government bodies, not only the Countryside Commission but also the tourist boards and the Rural Development Commission; from local authorities, from business and commercial sponsorship, and from charitable foundations. And a massive free labour resource has been available through government job creation schemes. On the other hand, the relative ease with which funds could be obtained from public sector sources is a thing of the past. More stringent commercial tests are increasingly applied to requests for funding for interpretation projects.

Fifth, interpretation has become more overtly associated with tourism. I sense that some people fear that relationship can be corrupting to the ideals of interpretation, just as tourism is a two-edged sword in relation to conservation generally. For my own part, I feel the tourist interest in many kinds of interpretation is broadly to be welcomed. It injects resources, creates exciting new possibilities and provides 'political acceptability' by associating interpretation closely with a much favoured industry. But interpretation of the natural environment in the countryside must not be hijacked by those solely interested in conveying a commercial message – tourist investment is welcome as long as it helps put across the conservation message.

Sixth, interpretation is playing an exciting part in the social and economic renaissance of formerly depressed industrial areas, such as the fascinating work undertaken by the Ironbridge Gorge Museum at a world heritage site. Local trusts in places such as Hebdon Bridge in Yorkshire, Rossendale in Lancashire or Allenheads in Northumberland have harnessed the pride of *local* people in their own surroundings, attracted new investment into old buildings and improved the green environment adjacent to built-up areas – bringing the countryside back into towns. Interpretation has played a key role in stimulating an awareness and concern about their environment amongst local people, as well as visitors. Increasingly visitors are drawn to experience the revived atmosphere of such places, thus generating income, creating jobs and supporting services which are helping to rebuild the local economy: a virtuous economic spiral in which interpretation has been an essential element.

Lastly, interpretation looks set to be an accidental beneficiary of the success of the Common Agricultural Policy. Because of the need to cut agricultural output and the costs of support for farmers, landowners are being encouraged to consider supplementary ways of earning a living from the land. In some cases, the most profitable 'crop' may be people – people who seek peace and quiet, attractive scenery and a place to relax. Farm-based interpretation, for which government funding may be available, will play a useful, if low-key, role in welcoming people to the farmed countryside and putting across a simple conservation message. I have seen some particularly attractive farm trails in England, which contain that very special ingredient which often guarantees a successful interpretive project: the hospitality and personal pride of the owner in what he is showing to the visitor. With farming facing similar difficulties elsewhere in Europe, I wonder whether those from other European Community countries foresee the same opportunities for on-site farm inter-pretation?

Some Signposts to the Future

Let me now try to erect a few signposts for the future, which – I trust – will have a wider relevance than in the UK alone.

I suggest that interpreters of the countryside and the natural environment should be guided by four messages:

- know your customer;
- plan and evaluate systematically;
- avoid the professional traps;
- keep your eye on the conservation ball.

Our customers are many and varied. But if the trends in Britain are anything to go by, there are some important developments which should condition our thinking. We know that a sizeable part of the countryside visiting public is now relatively well informed about conservation, perhaps seven or eight million in all. They have gained their knowledge from the huge expansion in formal and informal education on every aspect of our environment. There is a whole generation of young adults who have been exposed to programmes of environmental studies in school (which did not exist twenty years ago). And having left school, or university, they have access to the many hundreds of local guides to the British countryside which are published each year; to many column inches on the countryside in the newspapers; and to many hours of TV time devoted to this subject. Moreover, with higher car owner-ship and an increasingly dispersed settlement pattern, many more people live in the countryside, or have very easy access to it. Proximity may not always lead to understanding, but it helps.

So whereas twenty years ago we felt we were in general planning for visitors who would understand little of what they saw, that is no longer so much the case. Of course, there is still a great deal of ignorance about the natural environment, but millions have now acquired the self-confidence to explore the countryside themselves. The Countryside Commission wholeheartedly welcomes this development: acting with our partners throughout England

and Wales, we are launching a number of initiatives to help more people acquire higher levels of confidence and ability about the countryside.

Now I am not, of course, arguing that there is therefore no longer a need for on-site interpretation. The first-hand experience of visiting a site and having its significance explained remains of unique value. But clearly this trend amongst the visitors to the countryside has implications for how you pitch your message. I suspect it also means that interpreters have to make a more conscious effort to see themselves as partners with many others – schoolteachers, media people, conservation leaders in the business of environmental enlightenment, rather than the lone standard bearers of the true message (though I doubt that many interpreters are still attracted by that single-minded view of the place of interpretation in the world).

My second message is about planning, evaluation being systematic and the need to get good value for money. In other words, a group of organizational considerations. First amongst these, I would emphasize the need for area-wide or regional planning – something we do not always do particularly well here in the United Kingdom. Without it, there is a real risk that interpretive provision will be duplicated and as a result some schemes may fail. I think this will be a growing problem, particularly as the development of tourism based upon rural life and rural landscapes becomes more widespread. Local authorities in particular who are seeking to develop attractive tourism identities in their own areas need to look to their neighbours to avoid duplication. Regional planning may be too formal a process but at the very least we need greater co-operation between different local authorities, agencies and interests. Let me give you a couple of examples.

In Scotland, there are nearly fifty whisky centres explaining how whisky is made and inviting visitors to imbibe their product. One of the commercial distilleries – United Distillers Group – has actually employed a regional interpretive planner to ensure that their seven centres do not duplicate each other and has commissioned local interpretive plans for each to ensure that the narrative is closely related to the locality. And in the north Pennines area of northern England, once a world centre for lead mining, a group of local authorities and others has come together to ensure that the interpretation of the various mining centres complement each other: some concentrate on telling the story of mining and the related technology; others on the social and community aspects of life in lead-mining villages.

There needs, too, to be more work done on evaluation. Given that interpretation is indeed an art, has evaluation any place at all? I think it has. It seems to me important to seek to assess whether the significance of a particular site has indeed been revealed to the visitors, whether the visitors have received the conservation message and so on. Of course it is a 'soft' form of evaluation, dealing with words and ideas rather more than facts and figures. Often, too, it will be done by observation of visitors' behaviour rather than the direct use of questionnaires. But unless we can demonstrate the impact of interpretive provision, I cannot see that it will be possible to persuade public and private sector sponsors to invest in it, particularly in the interpretation of the countryside and the natural environment on which the straight commercial returns will clearly be very limited.

My third message is about avoiding the professional traps. Let us not have too much of a good thing. Much of what is special about any place can be left unsaid. Interpreters need to conserve some of the mystery of the environment, leave room for people to form their own impressions, leave space for people to discover for themselves. Interpreters need to know when *not* to interpret. Perhaps there is a need for 'interpretation free zones'.

Let me give you an example of when interpretation can be counter-productive. I recently heard an account of an archaeological site, a chambered tomb. It looks unimpressive as you approach it through the grassy meadow, but crawling inside, bent double to reach the inner chamber, you cannot fail to be excited by the experience. But now it has been interpreted. Before reaching the entrance you are arrested by two very large intrusive signs which seek to depict the magic of the interior and insist on informing you that the tomb was broken into 3,600 years after it was built. That seems to be a case not so much of interpretation as of vandalism (and I am not sure whether it is the looters of the tomb or the earnest interpreters who are the bigger vandals). I am sure that you will feel that such insensitivity harms the cause of interpretation and discourages visitors and interpreters alike. To destroy the special quality of a place through interpretation is indeed an unforgivable thing.

On the other hand, there are many, many places which still cry out for interpretive provision. This is especially so in developing countries where, understandably, interpretation comes far down the list of items which command support from a modest conservation budget. Faced with a choice of saving the rhino, or interpreting it, surely the priority has to be measures to enhance its protection. But when many national parks and other conservation areas in developing countries attract international tourists, I do feel the importance of interpretation should not be overlooked; perhaps interpretive projects could be sponsored by the international hotels and airlines who make money from tourists, thus enabling them to put the conservation message across to visitors – and to local people too. After all, it is in their own long-term interests that that message should be widely understood and the conservation resource which draws visitors be conserved.

Technology is of course another trap for interpreters, although my impression is that interpreters are more wary of it now – they have generally learnt that 'presentation' is not the same as interpretation. Again, let me give you an example, also relating to archaeology. In the Vercors region of France there is one of the principal prehistoric 'factories' for flint arrowheads and axes. A splendid multi-media presentation takes place in a large, airless building – looking like a supermarket. The sonorous commentary is interspersed with blasts of Beethoven and each statement is emphasized with spotlights to illuminate particular artefacts. After a few minutes I struggled out from this with great relief and found a few yards down the road a man making flint arrowheads from a pile of stones using exactly the implements of our prehistoric ancestors. This was pure magic and I can remember to this day exactly how the arrowheads were fashioned. So do let us avoid the obsession with techniques. When enthusiasm for the means of communication takes precedence over the message, then the activity becomes mindless.

The last of the technical dangers for interpreters, it seems to me, is that they can get carried away with nostalgia. In talking about the past especially, the interpreter's job is to tell the truth. In portraying rural life as it was, the interpreter should reflect the sheer hard work, the dependence upon nature and the harvest, the simple living conditions, the health or lack of it – as well as the rosy-cheeked happiness of the besmocked, clay-piped yokels leaning over gates. The countryside was never a museum and we should avoid portraying it as such.

Which leads to a more general point. There is a reaction, in Britain at any rate, to what is seen as an obsession with conserving and portraying the heritage. Some critics consider that interpretation has already gone too far, and is encouraging people to look backwards not forwards – an unhealthy preoccupation with the past and not with the future. Personally that is not a view I share but the danger is certainly there, and the surest way in which to bring it about is to encourage a sentimental, nostalgic view of the past. I sense that some of the large, tourist-based interpretive facilities do run that risk; as professional interpreters, you should challenge your clients if you feel you are being asked to convey a cloying, even dishonest, story.

My last message is about keeping your eye on the conservation ball. I put this last not because it is least important, but because it is most important: if you forget all else, please remember this. It is, I believe, the aspect which makes interpretive work most relevant to the needs of society around. Conservation problems now have an urgency and a universality which few could foresee only twenty years ago. Threats of a global nature, ranging from damage to the ozone layer and climatic change, to the terrifying rate of genetic loss now taking place with the destruction of tropical habitats especially – literally millions of species being destroyed – call for a response by each of our countries, individually and collectively. The effectiveness of that response will in turn largely depend upon the level of public understanding and here, of course, interpretation can make its contribution. My particular appeal to interpreters would be to help people see *the connections*, between their behaviour and the problems which beset the planet, between the problems of a particular site and those facing other parts of the world. Our desperate need is for a citizenry which has a global view and is environmentally literate: interpretation can, and must, contribute to that end.

Acknowledgment

I wish to thank Don Aldridge for his help in summarizing the history of interpretation, and my colleague Peter Ashcroft for assisting with the drafting of this paper.

14

Nature Interpretation:
A Threat to the Countryside

Kenneth R. Olwig

Introduction

What is perceived as 'natural environment' by one person may be another person's native countryside – a cultural landscape reverberating with social meaning. By labelling an area 'nature', interpreters can, unknowingly, pave the way for those for whom the local countryside heritage is an impediment. This, in the end, can result in the destruction of the very landscape which the interpreter seeks to present. Heritage and nature interpretation can only work for the maintenance of a living countryside if they are perceived as interpreting two sides of a physical unity which reflects both the nature of society and its ecological state. This will be discussed on the basis of a Danish example, but references will also be made to examples from the Third and Fourth World.

Is Nature Countryside?

At the Second World Congress on Heritage Presentation and Interpretation one theme was 'Interpreting the Countryside and Natural Environment'. Note the 'and'. Does it mean that the countryside is not the same as the natural environment? It is common in modern discourse to oppose nature to culture. Heritage is often explicitly linked in the conference programme to culture, and it is indeed difficult to conceive of heritage in other than cultural terms. The environment, on the other hand, has connotations which lead one to think more about 'nature' than about heritage when one comes across it today. This difference points out the underlying assumptions which can be hidden in the agenda of such a conference. Such agenda, I will argue, are related to issues which are of more than semantic interest to those concerned with the state of our countryside.

If we examine the titles of the papers presented in the countryside and natural environment theme of the conference, they appear to deal more with 'nature', as defined above, than with (cultural) heritage. We find that their subject matter tends to be, for example, birds, the sea, the forest, ants, monkeys and biological data banks. Heritage, on the other hand, appears to be something which involves, for example, Shakespeare, archaeology, Indians, gold rushes, buildings and religion. What nature and heritage appear to have in common, judging from the conference programme, is that both can be presented and interpreted, and that both can be marketed and/or funded. From this perspective, the content of what is presented, interpreted, marketed and funded may be less important – it's the technique for doing it which counts. Nevertheless, I would suggest that the similarities and distinctions between, say, Shakespeare, archaeology, and Indians on the one hand, and birds, ants and monkeys, on the other, are worth exploring because the way one interprets the meaning of nature and heritage not only has a marketing impact. It also has an impact on the life of the thing which is being marketed; it is this creature, after all, which lays the golden eggs that others market. The following Danish interpretation tale, in which it is a bird called the lapwing that lays the golden eggs, illustrates this point.

Nature v. Countryside – Is a Cow Nature?

An advertisement for a 'nature co-worker' to man a new nature presentation and interpretation centre recently appeared in the Danish press. The intention of the centre was 'to present activities in and about nature in the widest sense'. The applicant was to have qualifications, the notice continued, 'as a biologist, a teacher with a major in biology or some similar relevant degree' (*Magisterbladet*, 1986). I later visited the centre and saw the new interpreter in action. He was a biology teacher and an amateur ornithologist. The centre itself was located at an abandoned farm adjacent to an area of meadows lining a lake, on the outskirts of one of Denmark's major urban areas. One guest asked what the interpreter clearly viewed to be 'stupid' questions. The guest wanted to be shown some nature, and the interpreter showed him the many birds, such as the lapwing, which nested in the meadow. The guest, however, kept asking questions about the cow grazing in the meadow. The cow, the interpreter explained in an irritated tone, was not nature. The message was that if the guest wanted someone to present and interpret cows, the guest had come to the wrong place.

The question of whether cows belong within the domain of nature to be presented by the interpreter raises issues which are of vital importance not only to the lapwing, but to the life of the countryside itself. To put it bluntly, no cows, no lapwing, no countryside heritage! It is because of the cow that Danish farmers have for centuries mowed and grazed various wetlands and thereby created meadows of a particular height and species composition. The lapwing is dependent on the cow because it primarily breeds and nests in such meadows. By ignoring the cow, the nature interpreter was ignoring, in effect, a whole heritage of human interaction with the environment which created the countryside that formed the basis for the 'nature' that the interpreter interpreted.

One can well understand, however, why the interpreter may not have wished to dwell on this particular example of Danish countryside heritage. The meadowlands surrounding this lake had long been abandoned by farmers, and it was the city fathers who saw to it that this characteristic Danish countryside was preserved. The meadows were thus mowed as part of a job scheme for unemployed youth, and they were grazed under contract. This particular countryside, therefore, was in effect a sort of natural stage scenery created to solve both a social problem and an environmental one (the loss of characteristic flora and fauna). It also sought to preserve an image of a particular form of countryside which the city fathers believed their constituency expected to find on a weekend picnic. One might thus extend the argument: no welfare state, no cow; no cow, no lapwing; no lapwing, no nature interpreter! It would be understandable if an interpreter had little desire to present and interpret such a chain of being. It somehow lacks the ring of authenticity one expects from both heritage and nature.

The issue, however, involves more than authenticity, it touches upon forces shaping the countryside on a much larger scale. The fodder produced in the meadows was not only important because of the meat and dairy products which it generated, but also because of the fertilizer produced. The meadows, until recently, were the farmer's most valuable resource, and they were known as 'the mother of the grain fields'. Today, agricultural intensification and specialization has created a situation in which dairy production is concentrated in the economic periphery of the country, where the cows are often kept indoors and fed on high protein speciality fodder. The consequent concentration of manure production in one area has had the result that this product no longer has the status of fertilizer, but has become a pollutant. At the same time, the concentration of grain farming on the better soils of eastern Denmark where the major urban centres are also located, has led to a dependency on artificial fertilizers, which has also created a pollution problem. The meadows, on the other hand, have become largely superfluous, and they are in the process of being either abandoned or drained and ploughed. To add insult to injury, the reward for this process of specialization and intensification is an overproduction of agricultural products, which creates economic problems as well as a tendency to rural depopulation, and this, in turn, creates social problems. We are thus dealing with a situation where not only a vital visual element in Denmark's countryside heritage is being threatened, but the very social, economic and ecological life of that countryside is in danger.

Whereas the problems which underlie the state of the countryside are diffuse and by their nature invisible to the individual observer, the abandoned meadowlands are highly visible because they become covered by impenetrable scrub and weeds, so that they lose the characteristic flora and fauna which the population expects to find. This visible change has led to various Danish nature lobbies to make a call for what they term, literally translated, 'nature nursing' or 'nature care'. The primary motive for 'nature nursing' is to preserve the habitats that support the flora and fauna which are of interest to the nature lobbyist. The flora and fauna mentioned by them are usually various rare, and hence threatened, species of flowers or animals, but there is also some concern for common flora or fauna, such as the lapwing. Because the countryside is seen as merely providing a habitat or setting for the *nature* which interests the nature lobbyist, it does not matter particularly how this setting comes into being. Nature nursing can thus be accomplished by labour-extensive mechanical mowing machines or labour-intensive 'make-work' projects. It can also be accomplished by state-owned cattle (Olwig, 1986, pp. 113–31).

There are a number of problems with nature nursing. One of them is the so-called 'Humpty-Dumpty' syndrome. There is an obvious limit to how much welfare state nature the economy can support. All the queen's horses and all the queen's men cannot restore a countryside that has been functionally broken apart. If the countryside is not under the yoke of an economically, socially and ecologically viable agriculture it will not, in the long run, retain the physical appearance which is the golden egg that interpreters present. By focusing, however, on the lapwing rather than the cow, the nature interpreter, in effect, draws attention away from the basic dynamic factors forming the environment which he presents, and instead gives the impression that the key to environmental understanding can be found in unspoiled nature. Public debate thus tends to be deflected from the real issues, towards what could be termed environmental and social cosmetics.

An alternative to such 'nature'-focused interpretation would be to interpret, for example, our lakeside meadows as an ensemble of physical elements reflecting the Danish agricultural heritage. The same pitfalls, however, await such an approach if this countryside is treated as a static museum for the preservation of the remnants of an irretrievable past in the form of 'Heritage'. Such a reified heritage is just as capable (or incapable) of being preserved by machines, labour-intensive job creation schemes and state cattle as is the countryside perceived primarily as a habitat setting for nature (Lowenthal, 1985; Olwig, 1986). Heritage and nature interpretation, I would argue, can only work for the maintenance of a living countryside if interpretation is perceived as dealing with a physical unity which reflects both the nature of society and its ecological state. The problem, however, is that in attempting to institute such a form of interpretation, we are confronted by what has been termed 'the great divide', that is, a conceptual and institutional division in our perception of what is nature and countryside heritage which makes it difficult for an interpreter to deal with both lapwings and cows (*Landscape Research*, 1988, pp. 1–10). We cannot do much about the institutional situation here, but we can address the conceptual issues.

Can the Natural be Cultural?

The word nature is notoriously tricky to define. This is one reason, I believe, why a number of alternatives for the word 'nature', such as 'environment' and 'milieu', have been promoted. Such words have the appeal of apparently straightforwardly denoting our surroundings. Nevertheless they have, along with words like landscape, countryside and ecology, become cult words which have attracted many or all of the connotations of 'nature'. These words thus become even more surreptitious than 'nature' because these hidden connotations are unofficial lexical baggage, whereas the definition of 'nature' is available to anyone who opens an etymological dictionary.

If one examines the definition of 'nature', it can be seen to encompass the meanings of both environment and countryside heritage which have been discussed here. Such an examination could thus help explain how it is that such seemingly diverse subjects can be treated under one theme, or in one conference. What is equally important, however, is to understand how the etymology of 'nature' can explain the way we differentiate between these subjects. That is, help us understand why it is that both cows and lapwings can be seen to belong under the heading of countryside heritage and natural environment, and why it is that we may nevertheless experience difficulty in presenting and interpreting them under the same heading.

The definition of nature in *Webster's* (1963, p. 563) dictionary reads as follows:

Nature:
(L. *natura*, fr. *natus*, pp. of *nasci* to be born – more at NATION)
1a: the inherent character or basic constitution of a person or a thing: ESSENCE b. DISPOSITION, TEMPERAMENT.
2a: a creative and controlling force in the universe. b: an inner force or the sum of such forces in an individual.
3: general character: KIND.
4: the physical constitution or drives of an organism.
5: a spontaneous attitude.
6: the external world in its entirety.
7a: a man's original or natural condition.
7b: a simplified mode of life resembling this condition.
8: natural scenery.

If we start with the beginning of the word's evolution, we see that its primary meaning is derived from a Latin word meaning to be born. It is therefore also related to the word 'nation' in the sense that word refers to a people or folk – as when we refer to the Sioux nation. The nation is, in this sense, 'the native born'. When the word 'nature' is used to mean inherent character (def. 1) it essentially refers to characteristics which might be termed 'inborn'. The word 'born' as used here should not be used too literally, however. As the philosopher John Passmore has written:

The word 'nature' derives, it should be remembered, from the Latin *nascere*, with such meanings as 'to be born,' 'to come into being.' Its etymology suggests, that is, the embryonic, the potential rather than the actual. (Passmore, 1974, p. 32)

The nature of the nation is thus an inherent character which is 'inborn' in the sense that it is a kind of embryonic potentiality (def. 2) which comes into being naturally (def. 5) through activities of the native born which are in harmony with the heritage (def. 7b) of those who gave birth to the nation (def. 7a). We are apparently using 'nature' here in a different sense than is the case when, for example, the US park service preserves 'nature' (def. 8) in a national park. The difference, however, is more apparent than real. When one visits Mount Rushmore, for example, it becomes clear that Americans do identify the nation's physical nature with the nature (def. 1), or character, of the nation. The identification is made obvious by the fact that the visages of the nation's founding fathers who figuratively gave birth to the nation are carved into the side of a mountain in order to inspire the people to emulate their behaviour. Physical nature (def. 8) is thus, in this sense, the material manifestation of the character or nature (def. 1) of the nation. Natural scenery is the embodiment of the nation's heritage and, in this sense, an expression of the nation's values. This connection is less concrete in national parks, such as Yellowstone, where visages have not been carved into stone, but the literature written by and about the national parks makes clear that they are perceived as preserving the landscape which provided the setting for the American pioneer heritage (def. 7a) where Americans can relive that heritage (def. 7b). One writer thus describes the parks as preserving the memory of an era in American history when the 'exemplary virtues of rugged individualism and free enterprise were the foremost commandments of Manifest Destiny' (def. 2a; Everhart, 1972, p. 6). The nature we preserve, in this sense, is clearly an expression of cultural values. Physical nature hereby becomes an expression of the kind of character which we perceive to be natural for a native of the nation.

How Natural is Nature?

The word 'nature', as we see here, readily comes to be used in ways which implicate cultural values. This happens, however, in such a subtle way that we are not necessarily aware of the fact that when we are concerned with physical scenery (def. 8), for example, we may also be dealing with values concerning the inherent character (def. 1) of, for example, the nation. It is easy to forget, when absorbed by the beauties of Yellowstone, that nature is, to use A.O. Lovejoy's words: 'the chief and most pregnant word in the terminology of normative provinces of thought in the West' (Lovejoy, 1927, p. 32).

The word nature is closely tied to our conception of the natural, the natural being that which is in agreement with the nature (def. 1) or character of something. Words such as 'natural' (or character – 'he has a bad character') are enormously value laden. Witness the way the advertising industry uses nature to identify certain values with a product. The problem is that the use of the word 'nature' can, to quote Lovejoy again, 'slip more or less insensibly from one ethical or aesthetic standard to its very antithesis, while nominally professing the same principles' (Lovejoy, 1927, p. 444). This problem can be illustrated by returning to our last example, the US national parks.

When the United States preserves nature in Yellowstone or Yosemite in order to 'preserve the memory of the pioneers who founded the country' by colonizing the virgin land in the name of manifest destiny, it is preserving an embodiment of the national character which by nature (def. 1) must be represented as wilderness (Smith, 1970; Nash, 1973). It would not have been possible, for example, to preserve the same landscapes both as the virgin wild nature of the Anglo-American pioneers and as an American Indian cultural landscape. The first tourists to Yellowstone's nature, in fact, had to be protected by army troops from Indians who viewed the area as their native land (Graham, 1973, p. 195). The combined preservation may be possible today, however, when there seems to be an increasing willingness to define the United States as a fundamentally multi-ethnic society. A number of the papers in this book, in fact, are concerned with the interpretation of 'Indian' heritage. One essay brings the matter to a head, however, by substituting the appellation 'native American' for 'Indian', thus suggesting that there is only one natural native of the nation.

Yellowstone is not the only example of a colonial (or neo-colonial) power redefining the cultural landscape of a colonized people as wild nature after which it is transformed into a natural park. This issue has been treated, for example, in relation to the US national park on St John in the American Virgin Islands. Here, park policy is to preserve the landscape in its pre-Columbian state, despite the fact that the island's flora and fauna stem virtually entirely from the plantation era which lasted for several centuries (Olwig, 1980, pp. 22–31; 1985). Similar examples can be taken from African natural parks (Graham, 1973). The irony of most such attempts to preserve fundamentally cultural landscapes as wild nature is that such preservation inevitably has the effect of destroying the very landscape which it is intended to preserve. This is because the removal of the traditional human use of the land alters the ecological balance leading to often dramatic shifts in the composition of flora and fauna. The landscape thereby becomes quite different from that which inspired preservation (Olwig, 1986, pp. 132–40).

The question of whether the cow or the lapwing is nature reflects a number of issues, one of which is related to the way in which the redefinition of one social group's cultural landscape as nature can facilitate the process by which another social group takes possession of the landscape. The present-day Danish nature preservation lobby tends to be dominated by biologists and nature lobbyists (ornithologists) of urban origin who belong to an educated elite. They have spearheaded an attempt to take over control of the management of the rural landscape from the farmer in the name of nature and the environment. This may well be a good thing for the health of the environment, but it is nonetheless an ideologically and politically loaded issue, which is fundamentally concerned with the control of power. For this elite it is naturally (def. 1) vital to define nature as a lapwing rather than a cow. It is also vital for a technocracy, whose legitimacy is rooted in the ideology of the physical sciences, to define nature in terms of our most primeval nature (def. 7a) as a pre-cultural, biological being (defs. 3 and 4) (Söderqvist, 1986). Our heritage is thus stripped of its cultural trappings to become co-equal with our biological environs (Penning-Rowsell and Lowenthal, 1986).

When the issue of power over the landscape becomes a matter of historic, or even prehistoric interest, so that it is no longer a contemporary issue, it becomes easier to win general acceptance for the notion that an environment can be both a cultural landscape and nature. In Europe it is thus common for cultural landscapes reflecting a sufficiently pre-modern stage in the development of the nation (def. 7a) to be preserved as nature. In Denmark, the archaeological remains of the nation's forebears are explicitly protected under the Nature Protection Act. Indian ruins, which are ancient, and thereby distant from contemporary Indians, have long held a privileged place in US national parks. Shakespeare, archaeology, Indians, gold rushes, buildings and religion when seen in this light can all be perceived as phenomena which, when manifested in the countryside, express the 'natural' heritage of the nation. The naturalness of what is designated as nature clearly depends, however, upon who is doing the designating, and for whom.

Can Both a Cow and a Lapwing be Nature?

While it is possible, with a little goodwill, to see how Shakespeare, archaeology, Indians, gold rushes, buildings, religion and cows can be presented and interpreted in the context of nature, it may seem more difficult to encompass the sea, the forest, ants, monkeys, biological data banks and lapwings under the heading of heritage. It is possible, however, to view wild species both as nature and as cultural heritage. It should be realized that the local society 'cultivates' wild nature and takes possession of wild nature by absorbing it into the local culture as an expression of natural (def. 1) values. Flora and fauna are thereby transformed into an expression of local culture when they become embodied in folklore or artistic expression. The lapwing is thus not only of 'scientific' importance to the ornithologist, but also of cultural importance to the farming population as part of the rural heritage of the countryside in which the cycle of fertility manifested by the changing of the seasons is vital. The lapwing has been given a significant role in the culture through which the rural population relates to this natural (def. 2a) cycle both in the form of folklore and in the use of this folklore by creative artists. The popular Danish rural poet, Jeppe Aakjær, thus begins a poem about the return of love and fertility to the land, which has become the text to an immensely popular song (with music by Carl Nielsen), with the lines:

Now the day is full of song,
Now the *vibe* [lapwing] has come.
The snipe, the whole night through,
works the love drum.

Pluck, pluck bedewed straw,
Pluck, pluck reeds by the stream,
Pluck, pluck flowers. (Aakjær, 1918, p. 70)

The bird is thus directly identified with the natural values of growth and rebirth which return us to the most fundamental meaning of nature: 'to be born,' 'to come into being.' Its etymology suggests, that is, the embryonic, the potential rather than the actual.

If this notion of nature was made the focus of nature presentation and interpretation, it could conceivably have the effect of strengthening national awareness of issues involving rural agricultural heritage and its implications for present-day farm policy, and environmental issues involving both ecology and our values concerning the desirable 'natural' state of the nation's flora and fauna (Clifford and King, 1984). Such a form of nature interpretation need not be a will-o'-the-wisp. Not every Danish nature interpreter has trouble dealing with both cows and lapwings. But when presentation and interpretation make rigid distinctions between the natural environment on the one hand, and the countryside heritage on the other, then it implies a threat to the countryside.

References

Aakjær, J. (1918) *Samlede Værker*, vol. 2, Gyldendal, Copenhagen.
Clifford, S. and King, A. (eds) (1984) *Second Nature*, Jonathan Cape, London.
Everhart, W.C. (1972) *The National Park Service*, Praeger, New York.
Graham, A.D. (1973) *The Gardeners of Eden*, Allen and Unwin, London.
Landscape Research (1988) 13 (1), 1–10.
Lovejoy, A.O. (1927) '"Nature" as aesthetic norm', *Modern Language Notes*, 42 (7), 444–50.
Lowenthal, D. (1985) *The Past Is a Foreign Country*, Cambridge University Press, Cambridge.
Magisterbladet, 4, 1986.
Nash, R. (1973) *Wilderness and the American Mind*, Yale University Press, New Haven, Conn.
Olwig, K.F. (1980) 'National Parks, tourism and local development: A West Indian case', *Human Organization*, 39 (1), 22–31.
Olwig, K.F. (1985) *Cultural Adaptation and Resistance on St. John: Three Centuries of Afro-Caribbean Life*, University of Florida Press, Gainsville.

Olwig, K.R. (1986) *Hedens Natur*, Teknisk Forlag, Copenhagen. English version: *Nature's Ideological Landscape* (The London research series in geography 5), Allen and Unwin, London, 1984.

Passmore, J. (1974) *Man's Responsibility for Nature*, Scribner's, New York.

Penning-Rowsell, E.C. and Lowenthal, D. (eds) (1986) *Landscape Meanings and Values*, Allen and Unwin, London.

Second World Congress (1988) *Heritage Presentation 1988: Preparing for the 90s*, University of Warwick, Coventry, England (30 August–4 September 1988). Provincial programme.

Smith, H.N. (1970) *Virgin Land: The American West as Symbol and Myth*, Harvard University Press, Cambridge, Mass.

Söderqvist, T. (1986) *The Ecologists: From Merry Naturalists to Saviours of the Nation. A Sociologically Informed Narrative Survey of the Ecologization of Sweden, 1895–1975*, Almqvist and Wiksell International, Stockholm.

Webster's Seventh New Collegiate Dictionary (1963), Merriam, Springfield, Mass.

15

Interpretation in Australian National Parks and Reserves: Status, Evaluation and Prospects

Elizabeth A. Beckmann

Introduction

Interpretation in Australian national parks and similar reserves is considered part of the continuum from promotion to environmental education, and aims to provide recreational, educational and management benefits.

North American interpretation philosophy and practice quickly crossed the Pacific and became part of the national park ethic in Australia. This was especially true in the 1970s and early 1980s, partly because of a deliberate modelling of Australian park management approaches on their North American counterparts (O'Brien, 1985), including specific interpretation-orientated visits to North America by a succession of Churchill Fellows (e.g., Carter, 1979; King, 1985), and partly because of the concurrent growth of public interest in national parks, conservation and heritage issues.

In Australia, responsibilities for land and natural resource management, and hence national parks, lie with state, rather than federal governments. National parks are thus managed by a number of state, territory and federal agencies. Although their approaches to interpretation vary considerably, most view interpretation not only as 'an educational activity . . . to reveal meaning and relationships' (Tilden, 1957) but also as a means of creating 'a desire to contribute to environmental conservation' (Aldridge, 1974).

Interpretation is also seen as a potentially valuable tool in managing increasing visitor pressure. As early as 1972, the then Director of the New South Wales National Parks and Wildlife Service stated that 'the most important method of managing our National Park resource is to implement a well-designed interpretation program, which seeks to inform the visitor of the values of the park and of nature conservation, not by direct teaching but by experience' (McMichael, 1972).

Australia's first national park (and the world's second) was the Royal, near Sydney, which was established in 1879 as 'a splendid piece of natural landscape suitable for public recreation' (Turner, 1980). Although recreation remained the most common reason for declaring national parks, fauna preservation soon became another reason. For example, Wyperfeld National Park in Victoria was proclaimed as early as 1909 primarily for conservation of Mallee fowl habitat (Turner, 1980).

Thus the concept of Australian national parks as both recreation and conservation reserves has long influenced management, and hence interpretation strategies. The funds available for park interpretation have tended to be minimal, as funding priorities have lain with the acquisition of new areas for conservation and with the management of existing reserves. Staff, too, have almost always been rangers involved primarily in management, with various degrees of interpretive responsibilities, rather than full-time interpreters.

The unique characteristics of the Australian environment – the range of habitats from arid plain to tropical rain forest; the Aboriginal people and their desire to participate in management of their cultural sites; the range of unique and wonderful natural features; the wealth of wildlife, from brightly coloured parrots to hopping kangaroos and nocturnal possums, from 'cuddly' koalas to not so cuddly crocodiles – have also contributed to 'the development of a distinctly Australian approach to interpretation' (O'Brien, 1985). For example, Aboriginal traditional owners interpret their art and customs; spotlighting walks allow interpretation of the nocturnal animals; interpretation of zoning helps management in the Great Barrier Reef Marine Park; boardwalks give access to the many wetlands; and interpreters improve the salt-water crocodiles' public image (and hence its conservation status) while preventing misadventures.

Current Status of Interpretation

Detailed information on the current policies and status of Australian interpretation in a national context has not been readily available, in contrast to the overviews available from other countries, for example: USA (United States Department of the Interior, 1970; Paskowsky, 1982), Great Britain (Aldridge, 1975; Pennyfather, 1975), and New Zealand (New Zealand National Parks, 1983). The author therefore carried out a survey in 1987 to examine interpretation/education (including approaches to policy development, funding, staff training and development, programme evaluation, and future directions) in the major Australian agencies involved in the management of national parks, state forests and similar reserves (Beckmann, 1987a). Some of the main findings are summarized in Table 15.1 and below.

Policies

National parks are seen as important educational resources (Fox, 1980). Although the interpretation/education function is incorporated into the legislative base of Australian national park management agencies (O'Brien,

Table 15.1 Australian National Park management organisations, and specific staffing/funding levels for interpretive services

Organization	Acronym	No. of specialist Interpretive Services Staff	Other staff Involvement	Specific Interpretive Funding*	% of Total Funding
Australian National Parks & Wildlife Service	ANPWS	6 full-time (FT) admin/ planning	7 seasonals + % ranger time	$223,000 (85/6)	2.5
Australian Capital Territory Parks & Conservation Service	ACTPACS	7 FT admin/planning/ production	% ranger time	$85,000 (86/7)	φ
New South Wales National Parks & Wildlife Service	NSWNPWS	2 FT admin/planning	% ranger time	$20,000 (85/6)	0.05
New South Wales Crown Lands Office	NSWCLO	No FT specialists	% 20 staff	$90,000 (85/6)	16.1
Victoria, Department of Conservation, Forests & Lands	VDCFL	5 FT admin/planning 2 FT field interpreters	seasonals + % ranger time	$535,000 (85/6)	0.3
Melbourne & Metropolitan Board of Works	MMBW	6 FT visitor services (3 central, 3 regional)	26 seasonals + % ranger time	$732,000 (87/8)	4.8
Tasmania, Department of Lands, Parks & Wildlife	TDLPW	4 FT + 1 PT admin/ planning	seasonals + % ranger time	$60,000 (86/7)	φ
Tasmanian Forestry Commission	TFC	4 FT admin/planning in information unit	9 PT field interpreters	$130,000 (86/7)	φ
South Australian National Parks & Wildlife Service	SANPWS	1.5 FT admin/planning 3 FT production	seasonals + casual guides + % ranger time	$320,000 + $40,000 information budget (87)	φ
South Australia, Department of Woods & Forests	SADWF	No FT specialists	20% ranger (×4) time	$21,500 (87/8)	8.6

Table 15.1 contd.

Organization	Acronym	No. of specialist Interpretive Services Staff	Other staff Involvement	Specific Interpretive Funding*	% of Total Funding
Western Australia, Department of Conservation & Land Management	WACALM	2 FT admin/planning 2 FT field interpreters	% ranger time	$69,000 (86/7)	φ
Conservation Commission of the Northern Territory	NTCC	3 FT admin/planning plus support from information unit	% ranger time	$260,000 (86/7)	φ
Queensland National Parks & Wildlife Service	QNPWS	8 FT admin/planning	% ranger time	$250,000 (86/7)	4.2
Queensland Department of Forestry	QDF	No specialist interpretive staff	% recreation staff time	$228,000 (86/7)	φ
Great Barrier Reef Marine Park Authority	GBRMPA	15 FT in Education Information unit 5 FT in Aquarium Interpretation Unit		$435,000 (86/7)	φ
Brisbane Forest Park	BFP	5 involved in admin/planning, (3 FT)	% Bush volunteer time + % other staff	$192,193 (85/6)	32.6

Source: Beckmann (1987a)
Notes: * excludes salaries in most cases.
   φ information not provided.
   FT – full-time, PT – part-time.

1985), explicit interpretation policies or draft policies are not universal, and most are relatively recent, having been produced as the result of organizational restructuring. Where there is no explicit policy (e.g. Australian National Parks and Wildlife Service, Northern Territory Conservation Commission), operational policies are determined on the basis of the experience and intuition of senior staff, and the perceived needs and opportunities of their management areas.

The existing policies demonstrate that Australian interpretation is directed towards encouraging the informed use, and enhanced management, of national parks and similar bushland reserves, with a particular emphasis on interpretation as a facet of environmental education (O'Brien, 1987). For example, the Great Barrier Reef Marine Park Authority aims to 'engender the public appreciation of, and responsibility towards, the Great Barrier Marine Park' while the Australian Capital Territory (ACT) Parks and Conservation Service wants interpretation to help people to 'contribute to environmental conservation and sound land management practices in the ACT'. Interpretation should 'encourage public attitudes and behaviour more compatible with conservation of flora and fauna and management of the forest, park and reserve ecosystems' in the view of the Western Australian Department of Conservation and Land Management, and 'broaden visitors' perspectives of park recreation' for the Melbourne and Metropolitan Board of Works.

Planning

Whereas other countries have often developed interpretive planning in terms of hierarchical systems, this has not occurred in Australia, primarily because no single government agency has had sufficient control over heritage resources to warrant a total systemic overview (Evans, 1985). To some extent this situation is currently changing, as smaller state land management agencies are amalgamated and restructured with greater responsibilities (e.g. Department of Conservation and Land Management in Western Australia: Department of Conservation, Forests and Lands in Victoria).

Management plans are now becoming commonplace in most states, with Queensland and South Australia appearing to have the most rigorous requirements and compliances. However, interpretation is usually relegated to a short section within a management plan, and interpretive plans for individual parks, or groups of parks, are still rare, although becoming less so.

Funding

Interpretive services funding in the various agencies is often difficult to isolate from other visitor service expenditure: salaries for full-time interpretation staff are generally excluded, and isolating the salary component devoted to inter-pretive services among rangers is impossible. Saleable publications are rarely usable sources of extra funds (for reasons of government accounting procedures). However, 'user pays' activities, such as the 'Go Bush' programme at Brisbane Forest Park, and charities, such as the New South Wales National Parks Foundation, which fund seasonal ranger programmes, sometimes stretch the allocated budgets. Unfortunately, examples of apparently misapplied interpretive funds are not uncommon, particularly in the case of capital-intensive structures such as visitor centres, some of which have become well-known interpretive white elephants.

Specific allocations for the 'nuts and bolts' of interpretation (signage, publications, etc.) are generally less than 5 per cent of total organizational budgets. On a national level, minimum annual expenditure by major resource management agencies in 1986 – 7 can be estimated as approximately $ 8 million ($ 3.7 million on specific interpretive projects – excluding major capital works such as visitor centres – $ 2.3 million on interpretive specialist staff, and $ 2 million on seasonal/ranger interpretive duties).

Staff and Staff Training

Total staff involvement in interpretive services is difficult to quantify because, apart from a small number of full-time staff involved in central interpretive planning and administration, most on-site interpretation planning and implementation is carried out by rangers, although the actual proportion of time spent varies significantly with organization, site, and the individual ranger's duties and interests. In several states, seasonal staff are important in providing most, if not all, the ranger-guided interpretive programmes during school holiday periods.

Training in interpretation for staff is restricted in most agencies, and most rely on appointing staff with appropriate backgrounds. Examples of specialized formal in-service training include the attachment of rangers to the visitor services officer for three four-month periods at Melbourne and Metropolitan Board of Works, an annual five-day interpretive workshop in the Queensland National Parks and Wildlife Service, and interpretive skills development courses at Brisbane Forest Park. Seasonal staff are more likely to be given simple pre-service training, and are often reselected in successive seasons.

The Queensland National Parks and Wildlife Service has produced an interpretive manual which provides some operational guidelines on inter-pretation philosophy, objectives, planning, techniques, and evaluation. Correspondence Park Ranger Certificate courses (e.g. University of Tasmania) include interpretation topics, as do many tertiary resource/environmental management courses, and the *Australian Ranger Bulletin* (published by the federal Australian National Parks and Wildlife

Service) has regular features on communicating with visitors.

Most agencies have a strong commitment to providing educational/interpretive services for schools. Several agencies have a teacher on secondment from the relevant Department of Education who is involved wholly with efforts directed at school-group visitors (school liaison; production of written material for schools; training teachers to run field trips in national parks; training rangers to manage school groups). Occasionally involvement may stretch to non-school visitors, and material originally produced for schools is often made available to other visitors as well.

Interpretive Strategies

O'Brien (1985) described the range of interpretive approaches used in Australia: self-guided trails, signage, outdoor exhibits, and guided walks are used extensively, while living interpretation, site museums, audio devices, short-range radio transmission, taped commentaries, and camp site amphitheatres are rare. Visitor centres are still a relatively recent addition to the repertoire and, although a popular response to a perceived interpretive need, the large capital investment required has been a disincentive for many agencies. One common strategy has been that demonstrated by the Tasmanian Department of Lands, Parks and Wildlife which, in its stated policy on the provision of visitor facilities, emphasized that they would be provided only where a need was clearly demonstrated, that simplicity of design and maintenance was important to reduce associated costs, and that 'the elementary nature of facilities and the Service philosophy should be liberally publicized in order that visitors' expectations be realistic' (Tasmanian National Parks, 1982).

Most Australian interpreters believe that interpretation has a real role to play in the management of parks (e.g. by reducing the need for regulation and enforcement, increasing visitor awareness of appropriate behaviour, enabling careful distribution of visitor pressure to minimize environmental impacts on fragile natural resources (Sharpe, 1982; Roggenbuck, 1987). In Victoria, a planned function of visitor centres is 'to direct visitors to areas which can withstand visitor pressure without unacceptable environmental damage' (Crocker, 1982). Interpretation has been used to prevent damage to Aboriginal rock art, and to improve regeneration possibilities for eroded heathland (O'Brien, 1986). Unfortunately, very few applications of interpretation to management in Australia are fully documented, and the full potential of interpretation as 'the public face of management' (Beckmann, 1987b) has still to be realized.

Evaluation

Few agencies produce detailed written aims for interpretive programmes, although most are now incorporating general interpretation objectives and strategies into any management plans, and evaluation of programme effectiveness therefore tends to be subjective. Queensland National Parks and Wildlife Service and the Great Barrier Reef Marine Park Authority have the most formalized approach to goal-orientated interpretive planning. Very rarely are interpretive objectives sufficiently explicit to be used for direct evaluation as described by Putney and Wagar (1973). Indeed, many agencies have, until now, relied solely on intuitive evaluation and very informal feedback, reasoning that the limited funds should be spent on providing new, rather than evaluating old, interpretation.

The occasional attempts at formal evaluations have been summative rather than formative, and generally very limited in scope, applicability, and dissemination (rarely reported externally). Formal evaluation most commonly involves visitor surveys (often multi-purpose in function and primarily aimed at collecting visitor profile data) and simple analyses of media cost-effectiveness. Techniques such as visitor observation, questioning visitors in terms of knowledge and/or attitudes, or assessing management successes from interpretation, have been rare to date in Australia.

Prospects

Many Australian interpretive specialists are somewhat frustrated that financial and staffing resources for interpretive services are rather limited and often the first to suffer in a difficult economic climate, partly because senior administrators often fail to understand the full potential management and educational benefits of interpretation. Comments included 'interpretation is extremely expensive with intangible benefits and therefore has difficulty (not only in this department) obtaining sufficient "clout" to warrant a public policy and funds', and 'interpretation is still not viewed as a tool but rather as "the finishing touches" – despite some good projects over the past ten years no real change in attitudes within the department appears evident' (cited in Beckmann, 1987a). The recent drafting and statement of interpretation policies by restructured agencies is an encouraging sign of possible change.

Many Australian interpreters believe that interpretation can make a fundamental contribution to the environmental education of the public (Beckmann, 1987b; O'Brien, 1987) which is such a central feature of holistic approaches such as the World Conservation Strategy (Boote, 1981). Potential audiences may be large, as approximately 4.5 million adult Australians, 38 per cent of the population, visited our national parks and/or world heritage areas between April 1985 and April 1986 (Australian Bureau of Statistics,

1986). Co-operation among agencies in choosing appropriate objectives and effective means of achieving them is essential if interpretation is to reach these visitors.

The Community Education and Information working group of the Council of Nature Conservation Ministers (CONCOM) is a potential vehicle for greater and more widespread co-operation and interaction between senior interpretation staff. The latter have stressed the great need for national inter-action at a practitioner level, with particular emphasis on 'regular meetings, skills workshops, and resource exchange . . . more information disseminated in specialist related areas, rather than general across-the-board environmental education . . . formal training for face-to-face interpreters', and 'a need to collate research and practical experience' (cited in Beckmann, 1987a).

Unlike the UK, USA and Canada, Australia does not have a professional association for interpreters of natural and cultural heritage. Although in the past Australian interpreters have probably been too few to warrant such an association, it may be that the increasing number and range of public and private agencies employing interpretation, and the needs expressed earlier, may hasten the formation of one.

Although almost all the agencies now recognize a need for more detailed and formalized evaluation, they believe that such approaches are necessarily complex and expensive, and therefore somewhat of a luxury. Nevertheless, most intend to use formal evaluation more often in the future, with an emphasis on finding out more about visitors, the use of visitor centres, the effectiveness of audio-visual, print and display media, and the attitudes of participants in interpretive programmes.

Summary – Preparing for the 1990s

The 1990s will hopefully bring increased status to interpretation in Australian national parks, conservation reserves, and other heritage areas. Specific developments are likely to include

- interpretation policies in all management agencies;
- increased inter-agency co-operation;
- improved training schemes and facilities;
- greater networking among interpreters and others, with the possible formation of a national professional organization;
- exchange of information and greater co-operation between management agencies and research institutions;
- increased evaluation and publication of results;
- increased use of interpretation as a management tool;
- more interpretation of management rationale and techniques;
- increased public participation in management decisions and interpretive planning;

- continued links with the environmental education movement;
- increased interpretation for non-English-speaking visitors (especially migrants);
- increased sponsorship and 'user pays' activities.

References

Aldridge, D. (1974) 'Upgrading park interpretation and communication with the public', pp. 300-11 in Elliott, H. (ed.) *Second World Conference on National Parks*, pp. 300-11. International Union for the Conservation of Nature, Morges, Switzerland.

Aldridge, D. (1975) *Guide to Countryside Interpretation, Part I: Principles of Countryside Interpretation and Interpretive Planning*, HMSO for Countryside Commission and Countryside Commission for Scotland, Perth.

Australian Bureau of Statistics (1986) *Environmental Issues and Usage of National Parks, Australia, April 1986*, Australian Bureau of Statistics, Canberra (Catalogue No. 4115.0).

Beckmann, E.A. (1987a) 'Interpretation in Australia – current status and future prospects', *Australian Parks and Recreation*, 23 (6), 6–14.

Beckmann, E.A. (1987b) 'Interpretation and heritage area management: an Australian perspective', *Heritage Communicator*, 1 (2), 5–8.

Boote, R.A. (1981) 'The World Conservation Strategy – some educational implications', *Environmental Education and Information*, 1 (1), 11–20.

Carter, (1979) *Interpretation: an Approach to the Conservation of the Natural and Cultural Heritage of Australia*, Queensland National Parks and Wildlife Service, Brisbane.

Crocker, C.R. (1982) 'Information centres in Victoria's national parks', *Australian Ranger Bulletin*, 1 (4), 86–7.

Evans, C. (1985) 'Heritage interpretation: philosophy and approach', in Australia Capital Territory Heritage Committee, (eds), *ACT Heritage Seminars 1985, vol. 3*, pp. 1–10. Australian Capital Territory Heritage Committee, Canberra.

Fox, A. (1980) 'National parks as educational resources', in Messer, J. and Mosley, G. (eds), *The Value of National Parks to the Community: Values and Ways of Improving the Contribution of Australian National Parks to the Community, Proceedings of the Second National Wilderness Conference*, pp. 107–23. Australian Conservation Foundation, Hawthorn, Victoria.

King, P. (1985) *Trends in National Parks Interpretation*, Conservation Commission of the Northern Territory, Alice Springs. Technical Memorandum 85/16.

McMichael, D.F. (1972) 'Management of people and facilities for recreation', in Australian Conservation Foundation, *Management of Conservation Reserves*, pp. 9–12. Australian Conservation Foundation, Parkville, Victoria.

New Zealand National Parks and Reserves Authority (1983) *General Policy for National Parks*, Department of Lands and Survey, Wellington.

O'Brien, C. (1985) 'Current status of interpretation in Australia', in *Proceedings of the First World Congress on Heritage Interpretation and Presentation, Canada*.

O'Brien, C. (1986) 'Interpretation for park management', in Department of Arts, Heritage and Environment, *Getting to People – Strategies for Community Educators: Proceedings of a Seminar and Workshops*, Australian Government Publishing Service, Canberra.

O'Brien, C. (1987) 'On the trail – interpreting the environment', in Department of Arts, Heritage and Environment, *Environmental Education – Past, Present and Future: Proceedings of a Seminar and Workshops*, pp. 44–80. Australian Government Publishing Service, Canberra.

Paskowsky, M. (1982) *Interpretive Planning Handbook*, US National Parks Service, Harpers Ferry, West Virginia.

Pennyfather, K. (1975) *Guide to Countryside Interpretation. Part 2: Interpretive Media and Facilities*, HMSO, for Countryside Commission and Countryside Commission for Scotland, Perth.

Putney, A.D. and Wagar, J.A. (1973) 'Objectives and evaluation in interpretive planning', *Journal of Environmental Education*, 5 (1), 43–4.

Roggenbuck, J.W. (1987) 'Park interpretation as a visitor management strategy', in *Metropolitan Prospectives in Parks and Recreation: Proceedings of the 60th National Conference of the Royal Australian Institute of Parks and Recreation*, pp. 24-1–24-14. Royal Australian Institute of Parks and Recreation, Canberra.

Sharpe, G.W. (1982) 'An overview of interpretation', in Sharpe, G.W. (ed.) *Interpreting the Environment*, pp. 3–26. Wiley, New York.

Tasmanian National Parks and Wildlife Service (1982) 'Tasmanian NPWS policy on the provision of visitor facilities', *Australian Ranger Bulletin*, 1 (4), 88.

Tilden, F. (1957) *Interpreting Our Heritage*, University of North Carolina Press, Chapel Hill.

Turner, J. (1980) *Scientific Research in National Parks and Nature Reserves*, Australian Academy of Science, Canberra.

United States Department of the Interior (1970) *Compilation of the Administrative Policies for the National Parks and National Monuments of Scientific Significance (Natural Area Category)*, United States Government Printing Office, Washington, DC.

16

Interpreting Cross-Cultural Sites

Astrida Upitis

This paper is about cross-cultural interpretation in national parks, and explores principles and issues when people of different cultures come into contact with one another. Cross-cultural sites – places where encounters between cultures occur, can provide a focus for interpreting different cultural perspectives.

From a world perspective, Australian cultural heritage is often associated with Aboriginal cultural sites. These are areas of significance according to Aboriginal traditional law or of significance to Aboriginal archaeology, anthropology or history. World Heritage properties such as Kakadu National Park and Uluru (Ayers Rock – Mount Olga) National Park in the Northern Territory, Western Tasmania wilderness national parks and the Willandra Lakes Region in New South Wales protect Aboriginal sites which are considered to be of universal value. In Kakadu these include some of the oldest sites of Aboriginal occupation on the continent and an outstanding array of Aboriginal rock art. The Kutikina Cave in south-west Tasmania is one of the archaeologically richest limestone cave sites in the western Pacific while the world's earliest evidence of human cremation is found in the arid Willandra Lakes Region.

In Australia, a greater awareness and interest in Aboriginal culture, coupled with tourism promotion, has contributed to large numbers of people visiting Aboriginal sites particularly in national parks and reserves. Interpreting these sites can be a sensitive issue among Aboriginal people, the tourist industry and organizations who manage natural and cultural resources. The choice of whether to interpret Aboriginal sites and why to do so, is an expression of control over those sites and so determines what level of visitor access will be permitted, what messages may be conveyed and what techniques may be most appropriate for interpretation.

Given that interpreting Aboriginal sites is an issue of choice and control, some ideas and practices are suggested which blend Aboriginal needs and values with visitor expectations whilst achieving long-term protection of Aboriginal sites. Though I concentrate on Aboriginal cross-cultural sites as a way of interpreting Aboriginal society and culture, similar ideas may apply in other parts of the world where different cultures meet. Some examples from Hawaii are also given.

Cross-cultural Awareness

When interpreting cross-cultural sites or carrying out cross-cultural inter-pretive programmes, interpreters require sensitivity to differing cultural perspectives, an ideological commitment to working together and good liaison skills. Similar principles apply to cross-cultural interpretive programmes and to educational programmes designed for improving inter-group relations. Lippmann (1977) suggests that these programmes should have three basic aims:

(1) Recognition of human dignity and the right of others to hold beliefs and values different from one's own.
(2) The achievement of attitudes towards people from other groups, including fair-mindedness, respect for feelings, and some measure of empathy and friendliness.
(3) Learning to accept differences with interest and pleasure, as an enrich-ment of one's own life and understanding rather than as an assumption of inferiority on the part of the different culture.

When interpreting cross-cultural sites, these basic aims should be part of our thoughts and actions. For me, interpreting cross-cultural sites is about understanding people – their needs, values and aspirations, and understand-ing how people see their place within the environment. It is a 'sense of place' and its significance that one tries to capture when interpreting a cultural site. A 'sense of place' is more than a physical location. Created over time, it is an attitude related to people's personalities, cultural backgrounds and experiences which gives people a sense of identity. This view may not necessarily be shared by Aboriginal people or people from other cultures as their needs and values may be very different from mine.

Aboriginal People and Visitors to Aboriginal Sites

In Australia a diversity of Aboriginal people are associated with cultural sites in national parks, ranging from those living on or near land to which they are spiritually and traditionally connected, to urban Aboriginal people who share an Aboriginal identity and maintain strong interests in their cultural heritage. In contrast, most park visitors to Aboriginal sites are from Anglo-Saxon or European cultural backgrounds and usually live in large cities or towns (85 per cent of Australia's population lives in cities). They visit Aboriginal sites in national parks as part of their holidays and show varying levels of awareness and interest in Aboriginal culture. When interpreting cross-cultural sites in natural areas, it is important to recognize differences between Aboriginal people and visitors, in attitudes towards the land.

To appreciate an Aboriginal 'sense of place' and attitude towards the land, one listens to the words of people who are responsible, in traditional Aboriginal law, for managing cultural sites found within national parks.

Leo Williams, Anangu from Central Australia stated: 'Our life revolves around the land. Without land there is no life, certainly no future. Our land is the key to a harmonious life, it is central to everything' (Morgan, 1986).

Bill Neidjie, traditional custodian, Kakadu National Park, Northern Territory put it this way:

'This law . . .	'Rock stays
this country . . .	Earth stays
this people . . .	I die and put my bones in cave or earth
No matter what people . . .	Soon my bones become earth . . . .
red, yellow, black or white . . .	All the same
the blood is the same.	My spirit has gone back to my country.
Lingo little bit different . . .	My mother.'
but no matter.	
Country . . .	'Our story is in the land . . . .
you in other place	It is written [painted] in those sacred places.'
But same feeling.	
Blood . . .	
bone . . .	
all the same.' (Neidjie et al., 1986)	

David Daniels, Ngalama person, Roebourne, Western Australia stated: 'We are the special people and you know we believe in the spirits, spirit of the land of ours' (Daniels, 1986).

Yilbie Warrie, Roebourne Community, Western Australia stated: 'This is my life – teaching the people about this land, Millstream land' (Warrie, 1986).

These quotes express the strong spiritual and personal links between Aboriginal people and land. Visitors' perceptions of land, however, are primarily aesthetic as they focus on observable features in the landscape. As Tuan (1974) states:

Visitors (and particularly tourists) only have a viewpoint; their perceptions are often a matter of using their eyes to compose pictures. Natives by contrast have complex attitudes derived from their immersion in the totality of their environment. Visitors' viewpoints being simple, are easily stated. Confrontation with novelty may also prompt them to express themselves. The complex attitudes of natives on the other hand, can be expressed by them only with difficulty and indirectly through behaviour, local tradition, lore and myth.

Aboriginal people's detailed knowledge of the land and the significance it holds for them has come about from a lifetime of learning. Visitors to Aboriginal sites are there for a very short time, yet many still want to learn something of Aboriginal culture. Interpreters need to be sensitive to the expectations and attitudes of Aboriginal people and visitors if they are to succeed in finding the 'cross-cultural common ground'.

Issues in Cross-cultural Interpretation

The key issue in interpreting Aboriginal sites is close co-operation with those having the responsibility for protecting and managing cultural sites. This determines the level of visitor access to sites, the cultural knowledge which can be shared, the messages to be conveyed and how this can most appropriately be done. On Aboriginal land such as at Uluru National Park, the interpretation of cultural sites is controlled by the traditional owners whereas in other areas where Aboriginal people do not have legislative title to land (and therefore control over cultural sites) the interpretation of sites can be a complex and sensitive issue.

In such areas working together with Aboriginal people is essential. How this is done depends on the situation. In some areas it may be through the local land council, or with representatives of an Aboriginal community or individuals who are responsible, in traditional Aboriginal law, for looking after a piece of land. Even though there may be no people directly identified with a site, advice should be sought from organizations responsible for Aboriginal heritage matters. There is a commonly held misconception in Australia that if Aboriginal people are not easily and directly identified with a place, then their collective view doesn't matter. There is much to learn from Aboriginal people and this is an opportunity for community involvement in the broadest sense. Discussions with Aboriginal people should include all aspects of site interpretation – the suitability of a site for public visitation, the site's significance and how this may most effectively be interpreted to the public.

In Australia, a whole range of Aboriginal and non-Aboriginal people interpret cross-cultural sites for visitors. As Vince Coulthard, an Aboriginal ranger from South Australia puts it: 'It's good that the man's heart is in the right place, by wanting to promote Aboriginal culture, but pity he can't put feeling into his interpretive work. The feelings are the feelings the public get when the talk is given by an Aboriginal person' (Coulthard and Johnson, 1986).

At times it may seem easier to interpret natural phenomena such as landscapes, habitats, plants and animals because these features are often based on scientific knowledge and information. The interpretation of cultural sites is more complex in that it relates to people living within an environment and as such human perceptions and expectations affect the way a site is interpreted and perceived. Aboriginal people have highly personal, spiritual connections with the landscape whereas Anglo-Saxon/Europeans are trained to be objective, empirical and scientific. As Gale and Jacobs (1987) put it: 'Potential conflict between European scientific and Aboriginal traditional interpretation may exist. Parallel interpretation is possible without denigrating either culture.' The difficulty is that Aboriginal knowledge will not be readily acceptable to non-Aboriginal people with a scientific system of ordering knowledge.

For example the origins of the two dominant landscape features in Uluru National Park – Uluru (Ayers Rock) and Kata Tjuta (The Olgas) – can be explained in two ways. Aboriginal people believe that Uluru and Kata Tjuta were created and shaped into their unique forms during the *Tjukurpa* or creation period. Geologically, Uluru and Kata Tjuta are believed to be the relics of an immense bed of sedimentary rock now almost entirely covered by windblown sand. Both explanations are given in the Uluru National Park information brochure.

Similar examples of melding cross-cultural perspectives are evident in the interpretation of volcano formation in the Jagger Museum in Hawaii Volcanoes National Park. A dramatic mural which tells the Hawaiian story of how Pele, the fire goddess, created the island's volcanoes, is complemented by several scientific displays which interpret volcanic eruptions and earthquakes. Appropriate and accurate information is presented in traditional cultural terms, together with scientific views. One is not added to the other; together they form the basis of how to interpret cross-culturally.

Another important issue is that of sharing knowledge. Interpreters need to be aware of the differences between 'public' and 'private' knowledge. Often for Aboriginal people there are rules about who can give which information to whom, when and under what circumstances. Visitors assume that all information is equally available to everyone, whether it be about plants and animals or sacred religious activities and beliefs. This is often not the case.

For example, for Anangu (Aboriginal people from the Western Desert area) restricted information or private knowledge cannot be shared with visitors. Information about sacred places is restricted to certain categories of Aboriginal people. 'Some information is appropriately known and managed only by senior men and women; some of this information is restricted to men, some to women' (Anon, 1987). At times it is difficult for visitors to accept these limitations as their expectations are to learn as much as possible about the site or Aboriginal cultural. Constant visitor questions may be inappropriate in that the knowledge or experience will not readily be shared. It is up to the interpreter to explain these cultural differences without offending either culture.

The 'time' dimension is an important point that interpreters must consider. Relating information in past tense, i.e. as history, is inappropriate when there are Aboriginal people living in an area or who have associations with a place even if they don't live there. For example, in the top end of the Northern

Territory, 'traditional ownership of most of the rock art and other sites of Aboriginal significance is either known or can be established. The rock art sites continue to be in a sense "living" sites . . . To them [Aboriginal people], some of the paintings represent objects or personages of still current beliefs' (Muir, 1987).

Often interpreters use analogies to convey meanings relevant to the audience. It is a technique which helps visitors understand concepts relevant to them. When interpreting cross-cultural sites this can be particularly difficult as language, lifestyles and perceptions are quite different. A classic example in Aboriginal cultural interpretation is trying to explain concepts which have no direct European language equivalents, and vice versa. The 'dreamtime' is one case in point. This term is loosely used to explain the creation time when Aboriginal people believe that ancestral beings created the landscape and all life within it. To non-Aborigines, the word 'dreamtime' conjures up images associated with sleep, dreams, fantasy, illusion and therefore, in a European sense, not real. The depth of meaning related to events that created the land is potentially diminished. As I recently heard on a radio programme, a visitor to Australia wanted to visit the 'dreamtime', as if it were a tourist destination. That example shows the difficulty in how complex concepts can become trivialized because of a lack of understanding. Less complex ideas, such as describing Aboriginal living places, can be more easily interpreted because basic human needs are a common link – the need for shade and shelter (a roof over your head), food and water are common to all cultures.

Aboriginal people have expressed concern about sites that are manipulated for interpretive effect (Sullivan, 1984). Sensitive site interpretation should include structures (such as boardwalks, signs and displays) that are appropriately designed for the site and in keeping with Aboriginal wishes. In Kakadu National Park, visitor access to the main rock art site at Ubirr was originally difficult because of the irregularly shaped boulders that surrounded the area. It was not simply a matter of building a large platform so that visitors could more easily see and photograph the rock art. A better alternative was to create a stone walkway which naturally led visitors to the site without disturbing the ambience of the site and at the same time protecting the art.

Another example of sensitive site interpretation is at Pu'uhonua O Honaunau, the Place of Refuge of Honaunau, on the big island of Hawaii. Managed as a historic site by the US National Park Service, the aim is to restore the area to how it appeared in the late 1700s, before white settlement. Here, visitors can find images of ancient gods which once warned people against intrusion on sacred ground. They can also see Hawaiians demonstrating skills of their ancestors – weaving mats, making nets and fishing. A sensitive, non-intrusive balance between Hawaiian people and visitors to the site has been achieved.

Photographing Aboriginal people or sacred sites can cause anxiety, frustration and anger among groups of Aboriginal people who have close traditional links with the land. Apart from an invasion of privacy, photos taken by strangers (park visitors) may include places or features which are inappropriate (from an Aboriginal point of view) for public viewing. As a matter of courtesy and respect, people should seek permission from their Aboriginal hosts before taking photographs.

Cross-cultural interpretation needs to be holistic in its approach. To display and explain culture in a fragmented way without providing an appropriate context, deprives visitors of that 'sense of place' and significance which is so important in interpreting across cultures.

As Marie McDonald (1985), a product of two bloods, two cultures, so poignantly puts it:

I wish now that when I first saw this awesome lei niho palaoa [a hook-shaped pendant carved from a sperm whale's tooth and attached to coils of finely braided human hair] it would have been tied about the neck of a resolute, proud, regal, tight muscled Hawaiian male of thirty years or so, but this was not, and never to be. I first saw this lei in a poorly lighted, cold, impersonal, museum show case. I was fourteen years old and my immediate reaction to it after reading the label was 'ugh'. I had formed a prejudice. I did not know it. I did not understand its reason for being and at the time, I did not care.

Interpreting Rock Art Sites

When interpreting Aboriginal art sites, the significance of the art must be based on accurate and appropriate public information. From a visitor's point of view the most often asked questions about Aboriginal art sites and engravings include:

What does it mean?
How old is it? (particularly for paintings and engraving sites)
Is it real? (authentic)
How did it get there?
How was it made?

These questions should be addressed, though often there are no clear-cut, precise answers. Some ambiguity is acknowledged. In the case of rock art for example, often we don't know exactly how old it is or exactly what the motifs mean. This in itself should be explained to visitors in a way which does not confuse or frustrate their understanding of the site. It is important for the message to be 'culturally honest' and to avoid making up stories which may appeal to people but lessen the site's significance. For example in Kakadu National park, at one of the Ubirr rock art sites, there is a painting of what looks like a *thylacine* (Tasmanian tiger) some ten metres above the ground. Aboriginal people say that the figure has always been there and was put there by the Mimi, the rock spirits. Researchers have found that the *thylacine* was living in northern Australia about 12,000 years ago. We cannot say exactly how old the painting is – the ambiguity remains. Guesses about the meaning of cave art which touches on secret and sacred topics are offensive to many Aboriginal people. Initiation, procreation and childbirth are never appropriate topics for public discussion (Anon, 1987).

The Australian National Parks and Wildlife Service manages two national parks of great Aboriginal significance – Kakadu and Uluṟu (Ayers Rock-Mt Olga). The management of these parks is based on joint management agreements between the traditional Aboriginal owners and the Service. As a result a range of interpretive techniques sensitive to cross-cultural interpretation have been developed. These included guided walks such as the Llru Walk of Uluṟu, special on-site signs, developed walkways and pamplets based on comprehensive cultural and scientific studies.

Acknowledgements

I would like to thank Professor J.D. Ovington and Con Boekel from the Australian National Parks and Wildlife Service for their constructive comments and ideas about this paper. I would also like to thank Lyn Baker and the Aṉangu women at Uluṟu (Ayers Rocker-Mt Olga) National park, for their story about the development of the Liru interpretive walk.

References

Anon (1987) *Uluṟu National Park Tour Operator's Manual*, Park Notes Collection, ANPWS, Uluṟu National Park, Northern Territory.

Coulthard, V. and Johnson, R. (1986) 'Aboriginal ranger training in the Gammon Ranges, South Australia', in D. Smyth et al., *Aboriginal Ranger Training and Employment in Australia*, ANPWS, Canberra.

Daniels, D. (1986) 'Aboriginal rangers for Millstream National Park', in D. Smyth et al., *Aboriginal Ranger Training and Employment in Australia*, ANPWS, Canberra.

Gale, F. and Jacobs, J. (1987) *Tourists and the National Estate*, Special Australian Heritage Publication (Series No. 6) AGPS, Canberra.

Lippmann, L. (1977) *The Aim is Understanding*, Australia and New Zealand Book Co., Brookvale, NSW.

McDonald, M.A. (1985) *Ka Lei*, Topgallant, Hawaii.

Morgan, C. (1986) 'Aboriginal involvement in Kings Canyon National Park', in D. Smyth et al., *Aboriginal Ranger Training and Employment in Australia*, ANPWS, Canberra.

Muir, M. (1987) *Rock Art and its Conservation in the 'Top End'*, Paper presented at the 8th Triennial Meeting of the International Council of Museums – Committee for Conservation, Sydney, (6–11 September).

Neidjie, B., Davis, S. and Fox, A. (1986) *Australia's Kakadu Man – Bill Neidjie*, Resource Managers, Darwin.

Sullivan, H. (1984) *Visitors to Aboriginal Sites: Access, Control and Management*, ANPWS, Canberra.

Tuan, Y. (1974) *Topophilia – A Study of Environmental Perception, Attitudes and Values*, Prentice-Hall, NJ., USA.

Warrie, Y. (1986) 'Aboriginal attachment to Millstream National Park', in D. Smyth et al., *Aboriginal Ranger Training and Employment in Australia*, ANPWS, Canberra.

17

The Birth of Interpretation in Spain

Jorge Morales

Nine national parks and more than fifty natural parks – similar to the 'regional parks' in France – today constitute an extraordinary potential for interpretation of the cultural and natural heritage of Spain. Traditionally, the natural aspects have been emphasized when the value of these parks is stated. However, in many protected areas in Spain, there is a cultural wealth that cannot be ignored: customs, traditions, land usage, archaeological sites, and so on.

The Value of Interpretation

The central administration and the regional governments have not yet recognized the importance of the discipline called environmental interpretation. Some administrators ignore its existence.

In different park management plans there are allusions to interpretation, and in some laws interpretation is mentioned as one of the objectives for such areas. In short, administration accepts the word, but not its meaning from a professional point of view. In many cases, however, there is intuitive knowledge of what it is, and some very interesting activities have developed, by mere chance.

There is great confusion in most of the parks when putting interpretive programmes into practice. This confusion is evident not only in identifying the kind of people to whom these programmes are addressed, but also in the methodology applied in the parks. Interpretive activities are often designed for school parties that visit the parks and considerable efforts are made for such groups. There is great demand from schools to visit the parks. These activities are called 'interpretive', but the methodology is usually traditional, not differing a great deal from what a natural science teacher would do with his or her pupils in the countryside on a fieldwork day.

Services for the general public or occasional visitors (the appropriate target group for interpretation) appear in a great variety of ways: automatic slide programmes, addressed to an audience with a medium to high cultural level; boring or over-informative two-dimensional exhibitions; varied brochures, of which there are some very good ones; exterior signs, (rather over-informative and brimming with prohibitions); poorly indicated and unkept trails, for example.

On the other hand, there has been a trend towards creating visitor centres, here called 'interpretation centres' as soon as a new park is established. Unfortunately these centres lack any real interpretation programmes and it is not unusual to find them insufficiently attended to provide even the basic information. Other countries are beginning to consider the pros and cons of the centres, and are viewing them in a new light. In Spain, however, we are suffering the beginning of the 'visitor centre fever'.

Usually the visitor does not feel welcome upon arrival at any Spanish park. Contributing to this feeling is the absence of information about what to see or what to do while there. No services exist for handicapped users. Not only are they left out in general programmes, but also with regard to the design of facilities that would aid their visit to the parks.

Regrettably, there are still administrators who do not see the necessity for planning interpretive services. It is a luxury wherever a plan exists, and there is a tendency to ask 'what is it for? It is clear what has to be done.' As a result there has been much improvisation, and up to now we only find a few references to interpretation in management plans. Or, at best, we find a plan of 'public use', a generic term which embraces everything from didactic activities for schools to tourism routes in the park.

Staff Training

The staff, although having acquired a medium or high level of education, often to degree level, have not received proper training to work with the public, so initiatives for the improvement of interpretation services are very scarce. At many sites staff undertake valuable work, but most achievements are due to their goodwill rather than to support received from their superiors or the organization for which they work. Finally, discouragement and disillusion arise, and consequently staff end up taking on routine tasks without getting involved in complicated matters, so as not to risk their jobs.

There are exceptions but, at the present time, protected areas are not endowed with the appropriate facilities and interpretive programmes, and even less with adequate and trained personnel for dealing with the public.

The Future

In order that this paper does not appear to be a continuous list of problems there follows a review of some positive points which seem to constitute the beginning of interpretation in Spain.

The second Spanish Congress of Environmental Education took place in November 1987. On this occasion there was a work team devoted to the subject 'educative use of natural protected areas'. Three points were clearly established: that environmental interpretation is an essential function for the management of protected areas; that its audience is the general public; and that this function has to be developed by a specific management unit for interpretation in the park organization.

At the above congress, almost all the participants in that team had some kind of relation to parks (either national or regional), but not all of them knew about interpretation. For some the occasion was the first time they had heard the term. A 'self-training seminar' was created, starting from the congress in November, and destined to unify criteria and sow the seeds of professionalism not only in interpretation, but also in other matters related to visitor reception in protected areas.

I wish to point out that in the first Spanish Congress of Environmental Education, in 1983, there was only one article related to interpretation. In the second congress, however, four years later, there were nine, and on countless occasions the word 'interpretation' was cited in other papers.

This does not mean that there is consensus on the subject. The word 'interpretation' has several meanings in Spanish, and it is not strange that there is confusion, even among the staff in the parks. Although identified with parks, there is a great need for definition or, even better, for diffusion, of the concept throughout Spain.

Another positive fact is the emergence of short courses for training interpreters. These activities are very sporadic and irregular, but a certain amount of training exists for the staff of parks in the Canary Islands and in the region of Andalucia. However, these courses have more to do with the development of facilities and techniques than with the doctrine and philosophy of interpretation, both basic elements in understanding the essence and meaning of this discipline.

I have to point out the absolute dearth of literature on interpretation in the Spanish language, something that has contributed to isolating the Spanish-speaking countries. Almost all knowledge has been produced and kept in the English-speaking world. A few papers in French circulated in Spain after some officials visited Canada and France, French being the foreign language learned by the 'generation of sixty-eight', now the administrators and politicians of the Spanish administration.

An important step was taken with the first edition of the quarterly magazine *Education Ambiental* at the beginning of 1987. Since it first publication it has included a permanent section called 'Interpretation'. In this section, many different definitions have been given to this science, and also its meaning, the principles, the philosophy, the techniques and interpretive media have been discussed.

Having seen the level of interpretation in natural protected areas in Spain, a situation that leaves much to be desired, and having reviewed the few but important individual efforts to increase provision and knowledge, I will now comment on the future.

If political policies permit, interpretation has immense and attractive potential in Spain. I am sure that in the third Spanish Congress of Environmental Education there will be more concern about this issue. I also have faith that the park administration will introduce more interpretive planning.

With respect to literature, articles and books on interpretation may be found in Spanish in the near future, either in professional translations or in works written in Spanish. However, literature alone is not sufficient. There is a need to organize specific courses on environmental interpretation: and some of us have already begun. Personal contact is essential for training. If I may give a personal example, in qualitative terms, I have learned much more interpretation talking for half a day with Don Aldridge in Scotland than reading all the books and magazines I receive.

Neither do I think a Socratic method is necessary, but rather an exchange of experiences among colleagues, which in fact is happening in the aforementioned 'seminar for park staff'; and along with this, the development of courses is required.

It may also be possible that with the impulse given to environmental issues since our entry into the European Community, the work in parks and other protected areas will become professionalized. Being a biologist, geographer or forest engineer is not enough. A serious and academic period of training is necessary to work in conservation of our heritage, especially concerning communication with the public.

Interpretation has been born in Spain but is still very much in its infancy.

18

Interpretation: A Key to Tourism and Conservation Expansion in Developing Countries

David Sayers

In just two decades interpretation in Britain has achieved extraordinary sophistication with such exhibitions as Viking York and Victorian Wigan. As a botanist and tour operator offering special interest holidays, and therefore a user rather than a provider of interpretation services, it seems to me all the world's interpreters are comfortably based in the developed world, far from where planet Earth now needs them, in the front line of the ravaged environments of the Third World. To a slightly lesser extent I get the same feeling, too, about conservationists.

Interdependence of Tourism and Conservation

Tourism, initially mostly foreign, domestic later, aids Third World conservation in many ways. Tourism brings money, and tourists come to see wildlife, so conservation of wildlife indirectly generates foreign exchange and thereby gains an immediate tangible and political significance. Wildlife tourism can create local employment and thereby enlist local self-interest to see that conservation programmes work. It stimulates investment so that services increase, which add to a resource's status, and benefits home tourists. Interested visitors give much-needed reinforcement to conservation staff. Satisfaction levels rise, the resource's status further increases. Greater understanding creates support that can convert into political pressure to assist long-term protection, often in the face of local corruption, abuse of privilege and short-term political expediency.

Where nature is spectacular, for example Africa's game animals, wildlife tourism is recognized. But the Third World has many natural riches that are not spectacular in the easily recognized sense, such as rain forest habitats that shelter shy or secretive animals, or vegetation that is unique. It is here that conservation is often most urgently needed and the problems are greatest in terms of marketing, of selling conservation to a nation's government and administration, of selling conservation to the population at large, and projecting it as a viewable commodity to the West's tourists.

But beaches, cities and architectural splendours dominate images and tourism, so tourism goes its own way, conservation struggles on and interpretation at best is left to local guides, albeit sometimes excellent, and touts.

Due to lack of experience, local visitor expectations and demands from a wildlife recreational activity are much lower than could be achieved. Consequently the stimulation for improved interpretation and visitor services must come from outside. To increase tourism to earn foreign exchange is a common objective for economic growth. I therefore argue that it is through foreign tourism that interpretation as we know it in the West can penetrate the Third World.

Problems of Third World Reserve Management

There are many relatively minor problems afflicting reserve management where help could be offered and which could be tackled as a modest beginning. Examples that must be familiar to everyone the world over include the following:

– Where there is easy visitor access to a reserve, information about the reserve is absent – no literature, no guidance, no maps.

– Wardens are inadequately trained and do not fully comprehend their role.

– Because reserves have no educational programme, visitors have no code of behaviour.

Many staff in the front line managing reserves and dealing with visitors say how much they would welcome accessible literature about their forests and wildlife. All too often what is available is too academic and too expensive for employees ever to afford. Even simple wall charts identifying groups of plants, animals and habitats would be appreciated.

Aid from overseas stops at securing protection. 'Project Tiger' for example is successful in protecting tigers in India, and the government's Department of Tourism has promoted certain reserves on the back of this success. Nowhere is there any educational programme, yet some reserves are crowded with foreign tourists, Indian city folk and busloads of schoolchildren. The potential benefits are not realized; there are lots of Instamatics for family photos, but no binoculars. There are noisy picnics, transistor radios, and wild orchid flowers in every young girl's hair.

A greater difficulty, and particularly frustrating, are those many reserves which are inaccessible to tourism because they have no visitor services.

Misdirected Resources in the Developed World

Conservation bodies, certainly in Britain, are understandably concerned at the way increasing recreation is having an impact on the environment. And while we must keep our own back yard in order, Britain's concern about its manmade landscape and remaining natural habitats is a misdirected concentration of resources in the urgent context of global conservation. There is a need for wider practical horizons and involvement. Small ways in which we might begin to contribute to Third World conservation could include:

– exchanges between our staff and Third World personnel – of benefit to both parties.
– promotion of the skills of interpretation services through the various voluntary overseas work schemes.
– twinning with a comparable reserve in the Third World, just as towns in Europe are commonly twinned.
– sponsorship of specific interpretation projects by conservation bodies.

To interpret nature in the Third World will mean a major new learning process for us in the West. Different backgrounds, cultures, education levels, environments and perceptions will present a great challenge requiring adaptability if our own expertise is to be acceptable and effective.

I also see the need for a greater role for interpretation in world conservation, and offer four experiences which have prompted my thinking.

Madagascar – a Role for Interpretation

Television has done more than any other medium to put Madagascar's wildlife on the map. There are over thirty natural reserves, some established in the 1920s. Special interest tourism is slowly increasing. Consultants preparing a tourism development strategy are favouring beach developments packaged with neighbouring Indian Ocean islands. But Madagascar is a unique place. Over 80 per cent of its wildlife species are endemic; there are many different forest types, altitudes and habitats, islands of evolution on the world's fourth largest island. And Madagascar is top priority for international conservation efforts. How wonderful it would be to see tourism there based on its wildlife. No high-cost luxury investment followed by tourist pollution; instead a network of simple basic amenities at reserves with much improved reserve management. Essential to the concept would be interpretation; indeed, it should be the lead discipline, and would bring together the story for marketing. With the right investment Madagascar could become the Galapagos of the Indian Ocean, and being over 1,000 miles long has room to take more than the restricted 30,000 tourists annually allowed in the Galapagos. It is surely the most filmed and most successful reserve for visitors, and access is privately owned and managed.

The Andaman Islands

The Andaman Islands are an archipelago of some 200 mostly uninhabited islands belonging to India and located off the south coast of Burma. Living on some are tribes who shoot arrows at anyone trying to land, and foreign tourists are currently restricted to some half-dozen islands. For the tourist they are unspoiled, many are covered in primary rain forest and can be reached by small boat. One may spend a day on an island playing Robinson Crusoe. There are proposals for tourism development. First there was to be a duty-free port, but now substantial developments for water-based recreation are favoured. What a tragedy to intrude the roar of power boats into what may be the finest forest havens left in Asia. Instead, forest access, marine nature trails over the coral; with the islands' history, fascinating anthropology and 'away from it all' atmosphere it could be a unique holiday experience as an end to a tour in India, or in its own right. There is even support among local businessmen for this alternative.

Nepal

Nepal tourism needs to entice its considerable short stay visitors to remain longer, and to get them away from the Kathmandu valley. A consultant colleague proposed in 1982 to create a year-round scenic and wildflower motor tour taking at least three days in an area few tourists see. The scenery is dramatic and the forests so rich in orchids to be of potential world heritage status. The proposal had two principal objectives; orchid conservation and tourism development. Interpretation of the landscape and vegetation were key elements. But sadly it takes time to convince politicians and investors. My company very successfully operated the holiday this year. However, in the twelve months we have known the area, already an oak forest supporting thousands of Pleione orchids had been decimated and all the other forests cut into by uncontrolled firewood traders. We shall be able to offer the holiday again in 1989 and hopefully 1990, but after that the forests and flowers will have gone for ever.

South Korea

The newly industrialized country of South Korea has an impressive well-managed network of national parks, all with excellent accommodation and remarkably easy access. The countryside is exquisitely beautiful and the thousands of buses filled with students and families that pour out of the cities in spring and autumn are a recreational phenomenon. But the image abroad is of a war-torn landscape which TV's soap *M.A.S.H.* can only reinforce. My Korean colleagues were astonished by our understanding of their countryside and, until interpretation services are provided, home tourism in the parks will remain almost exclusively physical recreation, and the understanding needed to promote their countryside abroad will continue to be elusive. Interestingly, a programme was announced in May 1988 to provide visitor centres in all eighteen national parks by 1991.

Conclusions

I see the need to establish an interdisciplinary unit to work with the Third World countries. A unit to interpret and develop conservation and train local management for tourism expansion; to create marketable wildlife tourism based upon conservation management for economic growth. Such a unit could seek funding and commissions from government aid programmes and world organizations, and general charitable fund raising.

Whatever our misgivings, world tourism is here to stay, and the potential demand to experience wildlife exceeds current opportunities. Conservationists who ignore the opportunities tourism brings imperil the environments they seek to conserve. Observation on site tells me interpretation could be the means to bring conservation and tourism together for economic development. Conservation may then cease to be seen as the luxury only the West can afford. Interpretation has come of age in the West; the time has now come to go global.

19

Interpreting the United Kingdom's Marine Environment

Susan Gubbay

Introduction

Marine interpretation provides us with an interesting challenge. This is particularly true in the UK with its relatively cold and turbid waters. A certain amount of lateral thinking about ways in which in the marine environment can be brought into the direct experience of the public is therefore required.

Until recently there has been very little emphasis on marine interpretation in the UK. However, the growing number of voluntary marine conservation areas around our coastline, and the declaration of the UK's first Marine Nature Reserve in 1986 are changing this situation (Hiscock and Bunker, 1987). In order to develop our expertise in this field the Countryside Commission and the World Wide Fund for Nature commissioned the Marine Conservation Society to identify the messages and mechanisms which could be used for marine interpretation. A logical point was to look at site-based techniques, as these could be implemented by the network of coastal wardens already in place but who, as yet, were not greatly involved in marine interpretation.

Site-based Marine Interpretation

Although techniques for marine interpretation may differ from those used on land, the planning and process of selection remains the same. The various stages are summarized in Figure 19.1, and these were the basis on which a marine interpretation programme for coastal wardens was investigated.

The target audience are the people whom coastal wardens deal with as part of their work and, as such, they fall into four main categories:

(1) those with a managerial interest in the coast;
(2) those with a recreational interest in the coast;
(3) those with a commercial interest in the coast;
(4) those with an educational interest in the coast.

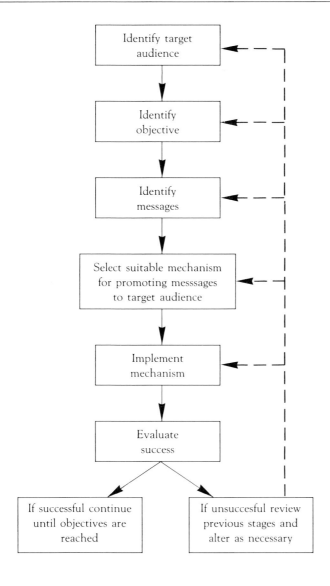

Figure 19.1 Stages in promoting marine conservation at coastal sites

The Marine Conservation Society sees one of the roles of marine wardens as the promotion of marine conservation. To achieve this, wardens need to foster awareness, appreciation and concern for the marine environment and, with this in mind, specific objectives can be identified for the four types of target audiences (Figure 19.2).

The next stage in developing a programme is to identify the 'messages' which need to be conveyed to achieve these objectives. These can essentially

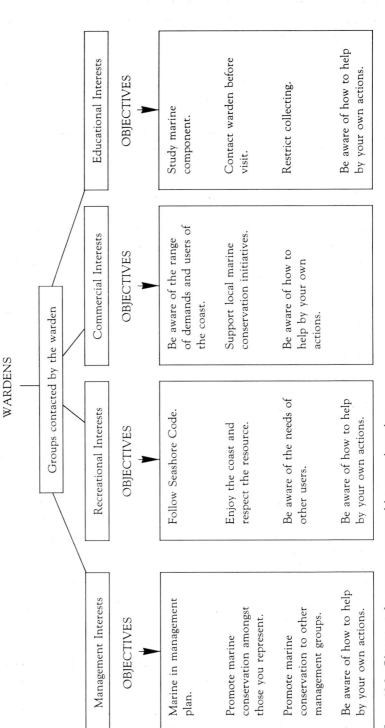

Figure 19.2 Objectives for groups contacted by coastal wardens.

be thought of as a focus for the programme and may usefully be described under a number of themes:

(a) Theme 1: Appreciation.
(b) Theme 2: The need for concern.
(c) Theme 3: How you can help.

The specific messages for each category of target audience which can be used under these themes are summarized in Figure 19.3.

Techniques for Marine Interpretation

A great range of techniques have been employed for interpretation (Pennyfather, 1975; Grater, 1976; Sharpe, 1982) and many of these tried and tested approaches are equally valid where the topic is the sea. Nevertheless there are also some specialist techniques which are particularly helpful when trying to bring the sea and the life it contains into the direct experience of visitors. Although wardens may be required to carry out marine interpretation away from their site, the emphasis of their work will be site based. This section therefore describes a range of shore-based and sea-based techniques which can be used (see Table 19.1).

Shore-based Techniques

There is rarely any shortage of topics to interpret on the seashore. Human influence is widespread around the UK coastline, providing issues and themes that can be used, and both rocky and sandy shores contain plants and animals that can be a focus for interpretation. Many visitors enjoy a leisurely exploration of the seashore, dabbling in rockpools and walking down to the water's edge to see what the tide has brought in. This activity can be developed into a very successful technique for interpreting the marine environment – a guided shore walk. This approach works in much the same way as guided walks on land but it can present many more opportunities for visitors to get involved with the environment if props are used to encourage direct viewing. Some examples include clear perspex-bottomed trays for looking into deep rockpools, a reverse periscope for examining marine life under ledges, and white formica boards on which delicate seaweeds can be laid out for display.

Other techniques can be used to show visitors what lives permanently submerged in the zone beyond low water, without the need for them even to get their feet wet. Live underwater video, relayed to a suitably shaded screen on the shore can not only show a new environment to visitors but also give them some idea of what it is like to explore the sea. By using a diver

---

THEME ONE: *Appreciation*

Key Message
Exploring the marine environment can be fun and there are lots of interesting and attractive things to see.

Specific Messages
(a) Inshore waters are particularly important.
(b) The marine environment is constantly changing.
(c) UK marine life is just as interesting and often as colourful as tropical marine life.
(d) Get in close to see the detail.
(e) A lot of the marine world is unexplored and exciting.
(f) The marine environment and the life it contains is of value, interest and special importance to humans.
(g) The marine environment is a complex system sustained by many interactions.

THEME TWO: *The need for concern*

Key Messages
Individual and group actions are having an impact on the marine environment.

We can live in harmony with the marine environment if we manage our activities.

Specific Messages
(a) Inshore waters are the most productive areas of the sea and the most threatened.
(b) Most of the damage comes from shore-based activities which can be controlled.
(c) Many substances are released into the marine environment without proof that they will not damage marine life or the environment.
(d) There is inadequate liaison between shore-based and sea-based users.
(e) The pressures on the marine environment from human activity are increasing all the time.

THEME THREE: *How you can help*

Key Message
Your actions as an individual can make a difference.

Specific Messages
(a) Bring problems to the attention of conservation bodies as well as those responsible for their occurrence.
(b) Approach conservation bodies for advice.
(c) Support marine conservation organizations.

Figure 19.3 Messages wardens should try to promote

Table 19.1 Suitability of various techniques for promoting themes

Technique	Appreciation	Concern	Help	Audience
Shore-based				
Seashore walks	3	2	2	2
Self-guided walks/trails	2	1	–	3
Viewpoints	2	–	–	3
Display boards	2	2	2	3
Leaflets	1	2	3	3
Impromptu events	3	3	3	2
Information duty	1	3	3	3
Interpretation centre	3	3	3	3
Touch tanks	3	2	1	2
Touch box	2	2	1	2
Games	2	2	1	2
Projects	2	3	3	2
Bulletin boards	1	–	–	3
Video	2	–	–	2
Sea-based				
Underwater nature trail	3	1	–	1
Boat trips	3	2	1	2
Plankton trawls	3	2	1	2
Viewing tunnels	2	–	–	3
Underwater cable car	2	–	–	3
Glass-bottomed boats	3	1	1	2
Direct viewing tubes	2	–	–	1
Waterproof leaflets	3	–	–	3
Submerged objects	3	2	1	2
Remote				
Displays	2	3	3	3
Slide shows	2	2	2	3
Aquarium	3	–	–	3
Films	2	2	2	3
Drama	2	2	2	3
Games/projects	2	2	1	2
Publications	2	3	3	3
Formal education	2	3	3	3
Computer games/interactive	1	3	3	1
Demonstrations	2	2	2	2
Media – radio/TV	3	2	1	3

Note: Each technique is scored for its suitability to promote the three theme areas; appreciation, concern and how you can help (3 = good, 2 = fair, 1 = poor, – = none). There is also an indication of the number of people each technique could reach on a single occasion (3 = > 30, 2 = 10–30, 1 = < 10).

to take the video film the visitors can see the diver getting prepared and, whilst in the water, follow his route by watching the bubbles reach the surface. This technique is particularly suitable in areas where the water is not especially clear as it can still give a good impression of the underwater world.

More standard techniques that can be used from the shore include outdoor display boards, leaflets and viewpoints. A small marine aquarium can also be set up on the shore, to be used as a touch tank for visitors, although a warden does need to be present at all times when such a technique is being used, to ensure that the animals remain in good health. An extension of this idea is to use a touch box where no living material is required. Shells and items collected from the strand line make up the contents and little super-vision is required by the warden for this to operate.

Most wardens are familiar with the idea of being on 'information duty' – present at a site to answer the queries of visitors and to encourage them to take an interest in the area. The challenge of such a technique is for wardens to make themselves approachable. One idea put forward by Foster-Smith and Foster-Smith (1987) is the 'impromptu-event'. This involves doing something which looks interesting so that visitors are attracted to the warden. Techniques which have worked particularly well on the shore include simply carrying a clip-board or perhaps laying out a tape measure across the beach. Children in particular soon approach the warden, becoming a ready audience for an impromptu interpretation event.

Sea-based Techniques

The second area from which wardens can carry out marine interpretation is the sea, as many techniques can be run from a boat whilst under way. One example is a plankton trawl, a novel idea as few people have looked at the smaller forms of marine life that make up the plankton. This technique is particularly appropriate for promoting marine conservation as the importance of good water quality and the interrelations of food chains can be brought into the discussions. Another technique is the raising of small pre-placed submerged objects colonized by marine life. Visitors can examine these as one of the activities on a boat tour after which the objects can be returned to the sea bed. The live underwater video technique described earlier can also be run from a boat, particularly if there are no suitable locations from which to attempt this technique on land.

For visitors who are happy to enter the water, snorkeling and diving along underwater nature trails are a possibility. This has been tried in tropical waters and now a number have been set up in the UK. This technique will reach a limited audience and all indications are that it might become very popular with this group.

SEA-BASED UNDERWATER NATURE TRAIL			
Advantages	*Limitations*		
Encourages observation.	Limited audience.		
Active involvement.	Site limited.		
Accompanying material	Expertise to set up.		
provides guidance.	Site damage potential.		
	Good	Fair	Poor
Appropriateness for messages			
Theme 1: Appreciation.	*		
Theme 2: Reason for concern.			*
Theme 3: How you can help.			*
Opportunities for presentation technique			
Active involvement.	*		
Enjoyment.	*		
Generate curiosity and interest.		*	
Show relevance.			*
Personal contact.			*
	> 30	10–30	< 10
Number of people reached			*

Figure 19.4 Pro-forma for considering aspects of using a particular technique (in this case, an underwater nature trail)

Deciding on the Technique To Use

Despite the relatively new field of marine interpretation there are clearly many techniques available. This makes it important to give careful consideration to all the choices before deciding on the techniques to be used for a particular programme. The decisions should rest on two main aspects:

(1) Will it promote your message to the target audience?
(2) What are the practical requirements of the technique?

The earlier part of this paper described the types of audience and messages which are appropriate to promoting marine conservation. Using this example it is possible to construct a table to show the relevance of each technique for your site (Table 19. 1). Expanding on this further, people are more likely to retain information if it is presented in a way which has the following characteristics:

(a) uses *active involvement*;
(b) shows the *relevance* of the information;
(c) makes the experience *enjoyable*;

(d) generates *curiosity and interest*;
(e) uses *personal contact*.

A pro-forma designed to take all these aspects into account is shown in Figure 19.4 using the examples of an underwater nature trail (Gubbay, 1988).

Conclusions

The marine environment of the UK is increasingly becoming a focus for interpretation. This presents a valuable opportunity for promoting marine conservation in an enjoyable and positive way. The techniques available include those developed for interpretation on land but also some specialist ideas which are geared for use on the seashore or at sea. By giving careful consideration to the reason for carrying out such interpretation, and to the selection of particular techniques, a new field of experience can be opened up for the visitor. Marine interpretation, despite the difficulties which this particular environment presents, can become as valuable a focus for interpretation as areas of land.

References

Foster-Smith, J. and Foster-Smith, B. (1987) *Marine Wardening in Northumberland, 1987*, Marine Conservation Society, Ross-on-Wye.

Grater, R.K. (1976) *The Interpretive Handbook*, South West Parks and Monuments Association, Globe, Arizona.

Gubbay, S. (1988) *Wardening the Shore; a Practical Guide to Furthering Marine Conservation*, Marine Conservation Society, Ross-on-Wye.

Hiscock, S. and Bunker, F.P.D. (1987) *Requirements for the Interpretation of the Skomer Marine Nature Reserve*, Nature Conservancy Council, Peterborough, Cambridgeshire.

Pennyfather, K. (1975) *Guide to Countryside Interpretation. Part 2: Interpretive Media and Facilities*, HSMO, for Countryside Commission for Scotland, Perth.

Sharpe, G.W. (ed.) (1982) *Interpreting the Environment*, Wiley, Chichester and New York.

20

Interpretation, Participation and National Park Planning

Timothy O'Riordan, Ann Shadrake and Christopher Wood

Introduction

In any country, national park landscapes are very special. In Britain such landscapes are planned to protect natural beauty, provide a link with the past through maintenance of culturally characteristic features, and allow for public access and enjoyment. Landscape templates have never been static. UK national park landscapes are currently undergoing profound changes due to dramatic shifts in the economics of agriculture and forestry. It may prove prohibitively expensive to maintain the 'traditional' countryside features so cherished in British national parks. Future national park planning will have to take into account the links between policy change, the aspirations of landowners and occupiers and the expectations of the local and visiting public. Interpretation can play a vital role in laying out various landscape futures so as to enable those most interested, involved and motivated to participate in the design of the national park landscapes of tomorrow. This paper covers the objectives, method and early achievements of action research in innovative countryside interpretation in the Yorkshire Dales National Park.

Nowadays exciting opportunities exist to extend the role of interpretation in original ways for imaginative purposes. To date few have responded, particularly with regard to planning the countryside or managing natural resources. True, several planners have called for interpreters to become more fully integrated into management and for interpretation to be directed more positively in assisting the resolution of specific ecological and land use problems. We recognize an even greater challenge for interpreters, namely to explain to the public possible management options so as to assist decision-makers to reach debated and agreed choices about how best to plan and care for the land.

This paper describes the background to an experimental interpretation programme recently begun in the Yorkshire Dales National Park, aimed at extending the influence of interpretation and resource management and landscape planning. The issue the project tackles is landscape change, currently in need of urgent consideration in the UK because of the sweeping policy changes influencing agriculture and forestry.

The three-year experiment is a co-operative venture between the University of East Anglia and the Yorkshire Dales National Park Authority, funded by the UK Economic and Social Research Council and the National Park Authority.

An Evolving Role for Countryside Interpretation

Most interpreters seem to accept the model of the educational process of interpretation produced by Freeman Tilden (1957), as illustrated in Figure 20.1.

Interpretation

to create *understanding*
of the site

leading to an *appreciation*
of its value

creating a desire for its *protection*

Figure 20.1   Tilden's model of interpretation

Since in this experiment we are looking at the issue of landscape change, we can rewrite Tilden's model, as shown in Figure 20.2.

Interpretation

to create understanding
of *landscape evolution and genesis*

leading to appreciation
of *landscape changes in the past
and potentially into the future*

creating a desire for its protection

Figure 20.2   Tilden's model applied to the research project

Many also agree with Tilden's assertion that site conservation is the result of, and the reason for, countryside interpretation: 'Not the least of the fruits of adequate interpretation is the certainty that it leads directly to the preservation of the resource itself' (Tilden, 1957, p. 57).

Similarly, many interpreters agree on the route by which interpretation contributes to resource conservation and to more appropriate and sympathetic visitor behaviour, arising from a better understanding of the value and sensitivity of the site. Indeed, since the beginnings of the national park movement in the United States, park managers have recognized that interpretation can be an effective process for promoting park values, thereby providing vital support for park protection (Conservation Foundation, 1972).

Interpretation and Landscape Management

This is not the only route by which interpretation can assist site protection. Through the generation of a concern for the site, based not only upon personal appreciation of its value but also upon a perception of the wider pressures threatening its future, interpretation can stimulate more people to become involved in decisions concerning the best way to manage a site or a whole landscape. Certainly some park managers have argued that interpretation and park management should be more closely linked in their objectives as well as their practices (Conservation Foundation, 1972). But many countryside planning authorities see interpretation as having a mainly subservient function in park management, being confined to presentation of politically determined park plans and explanation of already committed choices.

Interpretation and Planning Landscape Futures

In this project we take the use of interpretation one stage further by looking at it as a means of reaching a more assured and publicly supported future for cherished areas, through encouraging informed participation in the planning of whole landscape futures. That involves fundamental economic decisions which extend well beyond park management.

The research outlined here addresses the analysis of and response to major landscape management choices. These decisions will involve substantial sums of public money, considerable changes in agricultural practice, and a degree of sensitive appreciation of what all this means to the individual landowner and the public purse. This must take place involving a public not previously concerned with this depth of participation in determining landscape futures. Such a widening of public involvement in landscape management planning is particularly vital in the present era of major and widespread change in the British landscape, and is seen by some as an integral part of the planning process (Skeffington, 1969).

Interpretation

to develop *understanding* of the special
qualities of the site

leading to an *appreciation*
of its value

leading to improved *awareness of threats* and
concern for its future

stimulating a desire to *participate*

through modifying personal   through active expression
behaviour   of support

leading to
enduring landscape protection and appropriate management

Figure 20.3   Tilden's model extended as the basis of the current interpretive
experiment

Figure 20.3 summarizes the way in which we believe that interpretation can
assume a more participatory, stimulative role, assisting the planning of landscape futures based on informed consensus.

We believe that the interpretive tool can assist in this widening of interpretation in landscape decision-making by linking the feelings of the main
groups of people concerned with influencing and directing landscape change,
as outlined in Figure 20.4.

Note that the burden of responsibility falls ultimately on the land
occupiers, whose co-operation is essential if landscapes are to be adequately
safeguarded.

By 'linkage' we essentially mean carrying the Tilden triad of understanding,
appreciation and concern into the voids in communication that tend to exist
between these three processes. The act of interpretation then becomes a kind
of communicative lubricant of feelings and aspirations between the three
groups of interests illustrated in Figure 20.4.

Background to the Research

Forces Behind Landscape Change in UK National Parks

The Yorkshire Dales National Park, (hereafter referred to as 'the Dales')
situated in northern England, is the study area for the research. It covers
1,760 square kilometres of upland moor and rough grassland, intersected by

Those who are responsible for carrying out landscape management policies in national parks and for advising ministers on policy options *the policy managers*	Those who live in and visit national park landscapes and who ultimately pay for public investment in landscape care *residents and visitors*

Those responsible for working in, maintaining and creating national park landscapes

landowners and tenants

Figure 20.4   Principal interests involved in the Yorkshire Dales National Park interpretive project

a number of glacier- and river-cut valleys (known as dales), where the lower grazing land is suitable for fodder production as hay or silage. The study area is characteristic of most of the upland national park landscapes in Britain in that the dominant land use is agriculture based on sheep. True, afforestation of exotic conifers has increased of late, but in national parks land prices are high enough and amenity interests sufficiently strong to restrict new planting to a manageable proportion.

Nowadays, the prospects for the agricultural economy of upland parks are not so reassuring. Since 1983 British agriculture has begun to feel the effects of a tightening of price support and a reduction of official grant aid that in the past have fuelled increased productivity. There is no doubt that the trend of policy is towards a further reduction of price support, an extension of compensatory measures to enable farmers to set aside land from surplus cereal and livestock production, together with even tougher restrictions on grant aid or intensifying production. It is not government policy in the UK to increase public controls over decisions by individual farmers to alter landscape features. For the most part landscape decisions operate through consent and conciliation, not compulsion. Only for a small number of special areas do positive controls exist over landscape decisions, but always with full financial compensation for lost potential income.

At present the hill sheep economy is protected by special support payments operating through the European Community Agricultural Policy. Under the Less Favoured Areas Directive of 1975, hill farmers in areas troubled by topographic and climatic adversity are eligible for various payments per ewe to maintain income, so as to retain unprofitable sheep farming on tough terrain. Indeed, the 'real' income for many of these farmers, in terms of actual contribution to the economy, is almost zero. But the 'social' income is vital to maintain both the agricultural economies upon which upland landscape features depend, and the village communities which support the farming families.

As cereal prices fall in the more profitable lands of southern Britain, so farmers there are turning to sheep production to diversify their incomes. This could have a major effect on upland economies over the next decade, pushing smaller farms with high debt to asset ratios out of business. Larger, longer established farms with low mortgage repayments are likely either to intensify to maintain market share in upland livestock, or to diversify into non-agricultural income businesses. A few will benefit from an increased lowland demand for high quality breeding stock, but these will tend to be the more adventurous and profitable farms.

Either way, intensification or neglect, the landscape features of the upland Dales, notably the dry-stone walls and barns and unfertilized hay meadows, so intrinsically associated with the region, could change due to economic forces beyond the control of local farmers and national park planners. Hence the need for policy intervention. What new policy measures may be required depend, of course, on what landscapes people want to enjoy and whose maintenance they are prepared to finance with the consent and support of the farming communities. There is no doubt that it will cost as much as £150 per hectare per year to retain the fabric of existing landscapes in the Dales. Such landscapes cannot evolve through compulsion. Hence the vital need for this experiment in participatory interpretation. Whatever is finally determined, the future landscapes of the Dales cannot evolve without new public money or redirected agricultural payments or some combination of both. So every landscape future will have an economic tag attached to it. This will require public understanding and support if landscapes are to evolve through informed consent. The social and financial cost of each landscape option will have to be determined and illustrated.

Defining Landscape

Perhaps it would be useful at this point to explain what we mean by the term 'landscape'. Landscapes are not just collections of physical and ecological features, whether natural or human modified. To stop there would give the countryside no sense of life, culture or history. Landscapes are the collection of physical and ecological features given meaning through a sense of beauty, a perspective of the past and an understanding of the economic and cultural forces that shape the present. The dry-stone walls and barns that grace the dales of North Yorkshire are not just the outcome of history and immense human toil. They are the repositories of a particular form of agriculture and community life that created and maintained their existence. Such landscapes are the physical manifestation of people – land relationships that have evolved over many centuries.

So the landscape is as much a psychological phenomenon as it is a physical scene. It evokes feelings and preferences, hopes and anxieties, pleasure and inspiration in the owner and visitor. Because modern landscapes are very much the outcome of deliberate policies and particular political decisions through financial assistance to agriculture and forestry and via publicly directed planning controls, the job of the policy manager is also very important in determining landscape futures.

Research Methodology

Four objectives, of equal priority, have been set for the interpretation experiment:

1. To generate new interpretive material through the establishment of a network of participants who represent the range of farmers and policy managers, i.e. those people whose personal and professional reactions to public expectations and policy determine the landscapes of the Dales.

2. To explore the use of interpretation as an interactive tool by presenting the public (both Dales residents and visitors) with opportunities to consider and comment upon a range of possible landscape futures.

3. To develop interpretation as a communicative lubricant aimed at enhancing understanding and effective communication between policy managers, farmers and the public.

4. To extend the use of interpretation to widen participation by providing reactions from each group which may help the Yorkshire Dales National Park Authority in the development of its interpretation and policy guidance programmes.

Four main phases of work are involved:

1. Interview policy managers and farmers to establish their perceptions and aspirations with respect to landscape change in the Dales, and to determine some measure of the costs of policy implementation.

2. Analyse these responses to create 'images' in words and pictures of the possible future shapes of the the Dales countryside.

3. Present this material as a major public interpretation programme based on imaginative use of interpretive techniques designed to provoke a desire to participate in the landscape decision-making processes.

4. Analyse and review this use of interpretation to widen understanding and debate on landscape futures, and assess public responses and preferences elicited, noting particularly reactions to economic and social implications.

The project began in October 1988 and will run until early 1990. The main interpretive experiment is being conducted during 1989.

Stage 1: Interviews. The purpose of these interviews is to establish a cross-section of views, representative of the spread of opinion and attitude towards landscape changes in the Dales. Interviewees are carefully selected on the basis of their special knowledge and involvement in the Dales, and their willingness to play a substantial and long-term role in the research.

Five statutory countryside management and planning organizations have been identified as playing a major part in implementing and developing landscape policy in the Yorkshire Dales National Park. Staff at a comparable middle management or regional officer level have been selected for participation and all have assisted in the project.

Various voluntary groups are active in the study area. Some of their work involves operating policies affecting the landscape, or lobbying for changes in policies of the statutory bodies. Representatives from this 'satellite' group of policy managers include staff from farming unions, voluntary conservation bodies, rural community groups and recreation organizations.

Farmers are at the base of the countryside pyramid of landscape policy. It is their individual and collective response to the policy 'levers' wielded by the policy managers that to a large extent determines the shape of the Dales landscapes. For this study, a sample of farmers (numbering about 100) has been identified to represent the range of land holdings, farming patterns, available agricultural support options and personal circumstances of the Dales farming community.

Stage 2: Creating images of future landscapes. Converting the verbal responses of the interviewees into a visual image that is both representative and accurate is one of the challenging and original tasks of this research. Various approaches are being considered, including the use of ranking and averaging schemes to indicate how respondents place weight on particular characteristics of landscape dynamics. It is probable that the method chosen will necessarily be a mix of quantitative and qualitative analysis. What is most important is to identify what each group sees as the most probable extent, distribution and quality of each feature, and this will form various future landscape scenarios.

Trial versions of various landscape future images will be constructed and presented to a sample of the original interviewees to see how closely these pictures represent their views. This will not only help refine the images, but also reinforce the involvement of these key participants. In a sense this part of the experiment is also interpretive, since it gives these people the chance to react and to modify their own ideas about landscape change.

Stage 3: The public interpretation programme. Using the resources and skills of the national park interpretation and design team, the basic images of possible future landscapes for the Dales will be worked upon to produce new and imaginative interpretation. A range of interpretive techniques will be used, some fairly well established (such as displays and audio-visuals), and others more unusual (for example role playing games, mazes and board games). Since the intention is to reach those members of the public who perhaps would not ordinarily participate in countryside interpretation, it will be particularly important to produce material or opportunities which are inviting, enjoyable and intelligible.

The interpretation will be presented in a variety of packages, using different combinations of techniques and aimed at different sorts of audiences. But the theme will be the same for all the interpretive packages and can be divided up in the following way:

Generating understanding and appreciation

* introductory stage – describing the way the landscapes of the Dales have changed in the past, through natural forces and human use, especially traditional farming.
* gateway stage – explaining the complex web of policy, land management and public preferences which influence landscape change today, and the role of our research project.

Promoting participation and feedback

* choices stage – illustrating in words and pictures how Dales landscapes may look in the future, depending on different mixes of change, in a way that encourages people to make personal choices about the sort of future they want for the Dales.

Linked in this way, the three stages in each package will offer the public the chance to use their new understanding of landscape change (gained from the introductory and gateway stages) to choose a route to the future by making decisions in the choices stage. In effect, people will follow their own chosen pathway to the future, making choices on the basis of financial costs, implications for farm management and relevance for correct and future policy. They will end up at one of the possible futures, and be confronted with a painted or drawn image illustrating the landscape implications of their choices.

Although the chosen technique for the choices stage might be a role playing game, a physical or computer 'maze', or a story book, the sets of choices and the pictures used will be common to all. The basic format is shown in Figure 20.5.

Examples of interpretive packages

One sort of interpretive package could be an evening for a community group. The introductory stage could take the form of a small display, the gateway stage could be explained by an audio-visual presentation, and finally people could join in with a role playing game for the choices stage.

Another package could involve a travelling 'roadshow' for use at village halls, agricultural shows or schools. A display, with recordings, artefacts, pictures and models could explain the introductory stage. Then people could pass through a symbolic gateway into an indoor maze, for the choices phase. This could also include a 'design-a-landscape' game, using adhesive shapes or models.

(Introductory stage)
↓
(Gateway stage)
↓
Choices stage
↓
A Dales landscape today
(based on a composite of
actual dales views)

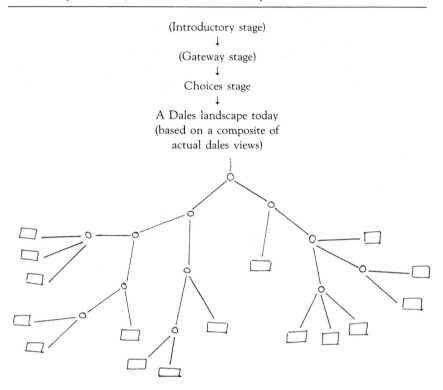

Notes: Boxes represent a range of images which illustrate several possible future forms of the composite Dales landscape.

Circles indicate points where choices must be made. Number of choice points can vary between pathways. Information will be provided along pathways to help people understand the implications of each choice they make.

Figure 20.5   Basic format for third (choices) stage of the interpretive packages

Evaluating the interpretation experiments

Each interpretive package will be evaluated to assess to what extent people have gained a deeper understanding of landscape change, and have been motivated to make decisions about the future. The choices they make, and the basis for their decisions, will also be studied. Interviews, self-completed questionnaires, observation and automatic recording devices will be used as appropriate for different interpretive packages.

Stage 4: Project review. Throughout the project, a variety of research papers will be produced which will be of interest to professional interpreters, academics and landscape managers. Some of this material will be presented at conferences and seminars. In the final stages, a comprehensive review document will be produced. The Yorkshire Dales National Park Authority intends to incorporate the research findings into its interpretation programme. Currently the Authority is also investigating the possibility of developing the participatory element of interpretation to help it determine its future management policies. This process could provide a method of increasing the degree of community-based involvement in the review and development of national park plans.

References

Conservation Foundation, (1972) *National Parks for the Future*, Conservation Foundation, Washington DC.
Skeffington, A. (1969) *Public Participation in Planning*, HMSO, London.
Tilden, F. (1957) *Interpreting Our Heritage*, University of North Carolina Press, Chapel Hill.

21

Interpreters in the Community:
A Discussion Paper
Gillian Binks

Introduction

The first stated priority of the London-based Community Arts group 'Free Form' is 'to be responsive to the specific requirements of an area, and match a programme of work to the social needs of a given community by close consultation and creative action with people living and working in that area'.

It is a philosophy which is expressed in a similar form by many groups committed to community action.

I should like to explore in this paper the extent to which interpreters might be encouraged to adopt a similar philosophy and approach to their work and to look at the implications of that for their training needs.

My basic premise is that whilst much of the interpreter's work is related to provision for tourists and day visitors to specific sites, there is much to be gained from working closely with the local communities who live in and around the sites where they operate – urban fringe, country parks, inner city, historic towns, city parks, heritage coasts and national parks and the commonplace countryside. However, many of the people charged with the job of providing interpretation, in Britain at least, are essentially resource managers of land or buildings or museum collections and are trained as such, and few have the necessary skills for working with local communities.

There is now, however, an established expertise in working with communities amongst urban and rural development workers and community arts groups, for example, and training in the required skills is available either formally or in service. Whilst the area of concern of community action workers is much broader than environment, their skills and approaches can be readily applied in dealing with environmental issues and in interpretation.

It is my belief that we should include training in community development skills in the programmes offered to countryside rangers, social and local history curators in museums, wardens in national parks and urban-based parks and recreation officers. The purpose should not be to turn out comprehensively skilled community development workers but to raise awareness of the approaches and skills used and provide competence in some of them; to raise awareness of the existing organizations working in community development and the training and support they offer, as well as awareness of those areas of common ground where both interpreter and community action workers might work together.

Interpreters in the Community – the Common Ground

The common ground where interpretation and community development meets is in a concern to create or enhance a sense of place, to establish what is significant and valued in the environment or heritage of a particular community, and to provoke action for its wider appreciation and conservation.

Community, Environment and Heritage

The term community usually relates to people with something in common, traditionally a territory or a community of interest. 'Community of attachment' as a definition encompasses the relationship among people and with the place in which they live and work. Community action is defined as those activities which people undertake themselves to improve the quality of their own lives within their community, and community development as the strategy used by community workers and to encourage community action (Roome, 1988).

In the past, community action has tended to concern itself with social and economic issues – housing, education and social welfare. More recently the quality of the environment has become an important element in the quality of life of a community. Environment is one of *the* issues of the 1980s, and community action is being encouraged as a way of addressing environmental problems locally.

Environmental issues are also increasingly recognized as valuable and effective vehicles for promoting community action. People care about the environment, it is often an issue that is a spur to action; small improvements are readily achieved, and small successes are important in sustaining community action; the 'act locally, think globally' connection is readily made in relation to environmental issues; and the links between economic, social and environmental issues are often highlighted in an immediate way at community level (Roome, 1988).

Many of the projects which have emerged from community action programmes relating to environmental issues involve interpretation and presentation of the local environment or a particular community's heritage. Community Action in the Rural Environment (CARE) is one such project, operating in the countryside west of Barnsley in South Yorkshire. It is jointly sponsored by eight parish councils, the District Council, the Countryside Commission and the Peak National Park, who fund an advisory officer whose brief is to foster community confidence and responsibility for the environment through community action. Projects which have emerged include landscape improvements, ecological surveys, and management of community recreational areas, together with the production of village maps, oral histories and the revival of local customs – all of which arose from a wish to celebrate and enhance the sense of place felt by the people in the area.

The desire to promote and facilitate community action is also the basis of the Rural Tourism Development project set up in 1987, sponsored by the Rural Development Commission and the Countryside Commission and run by the Extra Mural Department of Bristol University (Lane, 1988). Using an educationalist as an animateur, the project aims to help communities understand and capitalize on their tourism potential, and to facilitate small-scale tourism initiatives. Three village communities are taking part in the pilot phase of the project and each has a rural Tourism Forum, where the issues, implications and opportunities for tourism can be discussed and understood. Various projects have been implemented, including provision of small-scale enterprises such as tourist accommodation; farm diversification, devising marketing strategies, and the production of publicity leaflets. Several interpretation projects have also been developed, including setting up a local heritage centre, making an audio-visual programme about one village and developing and promoting a series of circular walks with interpretive leaflets.

Most of the work linking communities, heritage and environment has been undertaken in rural areas, is relatively recent and has yet to be evaluated. Work with urban communities and their environment has tended to relate primarily to environmental improvement and to community technical aid centres designed to help local people influence the planning system. Some projects relating the environment, sense of place and the heritage of an area have been developed in community arts programmes, and more specifically in relation to ethnic communities.

Development work with ethnic minorities recognizes the value of interpreting the ethnic community's heritage and 'sense of place', both for the members themselves and for the wider community in which they live. Susan Place, Director of the Mersey Heritage Trust, is working with the black community in Liverpool and writes:

only through mature awareness of the history of our communities can our society as a whole grow in wisdom. Every historian has compelling social responsibilities to all strata of society, to give dignity and substance to every day lives as well as dealing with the high points of history . . . Clearly a need exists to document the Black heritage of Britain side by side with that which is traditionally seen to be the British identity and to integrate the two. If their story is not made part of the national narrative by historians then every reinforcement of national identity through the media, publishing and cultural institutions like museums can be perceived by a black person as a reinforcement of white identity at their expense. (Place, 1988)

Processes and Products in Community Development

The philosophy behind most community development projects is that it is the *process* of involving people in community action which is of prime importance – not the product of that action. Whilst a successful product – a good leaflet, a tree-planting scheme, an oral history archive – is desirable, the real objective is a strong sense of community. One of the objectives for example of the Rural Tourism Development project referred to earlier is 'to set up self-renewing local groups and development trusts to help the progress of rural tourism at the grass roots, thus ensuring that the social, economic and cultural benefits of development and the control of those developments stay within the community'. The initiatives are seen as vehicles for building co-operative working, understanding issues, developing confidence and responsibility for dealing with local authorities and other controlling agencies, drawing on local skills and knowledge, creating opportunities for people to feel valued, developing confidence and responsibility for dealing with local issues, recognizing and asserting community values.

Whilst the process is an inward-looking, community strengthening activity, the 'product' when it relates to interpreting that community's environment or heritage is very much an outward-looking presentation. It is a statement of 'this is our heritage, this is what we value in our environment, this is part of us, this is what we want to share and how we want you to know us'.

Michael Dower (1988), National Park Officer for the Peak National Park, concluded his paper to a major conference of rural tourism in London in November 1988:

rural tourism is (*par excellence* among sectors of the rural economy) an activity which will most truly help local economies and offer the visitor the truest recreation and freshest contact with 'his roots' if it is based in the character of the place and the life of the rural community. I rejoice at a development which reflects the spirit of the place, which reveals its special character and history, which by the accents of the staff, the local food, the names, even the quirky pronunciation, breathes a sense of localness.

Interpreting that local heritage and environment in all its forms and expressions is a key aspect of the process of community development. It has a significant role to play in identifying and maintaining the richness of diversity of communities both urban and rural. A tourism product so well grounded in a community's heritage and environment is (much more) likely to be self-sustaining long after the fashion for a more ephemeral tourist activity has passed.

Interpreters clearly have a contribution to make. Their skills in researching, and understanding the environment or history of a place; drawing together the threads of a story; and presenting it in the most appropriate form, are valuable tools in the process, to be shared with and used by the community.

Given some new skills, they have the potential to work more effectively with the community as enablers, and animateurs on environmental issues.

The Need for Interpreters to Work with Communities

Interpreters have always been concerned to communicate a 'sense of place'. This is often established within a framework of 'intellectual' values of ecological importance, historical, geographical, archaeological or architectural significance, which reflects for the most part their initial academic training as scientists, land managers, planners, geographers, historians, and in particular their own cultural perspective. This framework might be appropriate for the 'star' attraction of, for example, national nature reserves, wilderness parks, major national historic monuments, national collections in museums, and the grand buildings of a capital city. It is less so for the more commonplace countryside and urban environment where communities live, work and take their recreation; or for the local or ethnic heritage of an area.

Writing about interpreting Aboriginal sites in national parks and reserves in Australia, Upitis stresses the sensitivity of the issues which this raises. 'The Aboriginal people have a personalized spiritual connection with their landscape which is difficult for Anglo-Saxon Europeans trained to be objective, empirical and scientific to grasp' (Chapter 16). What is interpreted about these sites and how they are interpreted to visitors requires sensitive understanding and delicate negotiation with the people who 'own' them in a cultural context of which visitors have little or no conception.

This is perhaps an extreme example which illustrates that sense of place is more than just a physical location – it is an attitude, created over time which relates to people's personalities, cultural backgrounds and experiences and which gives people a sense of identity. That sense of identity may be difficult or impossible to articulate in any conventional form of guidebook, verbal presentation or exhibition. It may be more properly and unselfconsciously expressed in local tradition, in myths, in poetry and music, in a person's love of a place, in their behaviour within and towards it.

Interpreters are often the interface between the resource and the public. Where the public arrives as 'visitors' or 'tourists' to a particular site, or to view a museum collection, then the interpreter is more or less skilled to communicate with them effectively. Where the public, however, comprises local residents of the inner city, or of a national park, or those people living around an urban fringe countryside management area or an archaeological dig, then interpreters will need to assume more of an 'outreach' role, and that involves skills in working with communities which traditionally trained, resource-based interpreters often lack.

If interpreters want accurately to reflect, encourage and harness a community's sense of place and pride in their heritage and local environment, then they also need the skills to be responsive to local community feeling, to get alongside local community groups and to work with them. Where it is unrealistic to expect interpreters to acquire all of these skills, then they should be encouraged to enlist the support of those agencies already involved in community action – community art groups and community development workers for example.

East Durham Heritage Trails and Walkways is a guide to the local countryside of East Durham which

encourages more than a discovery of East Durham's heritage. It is the result of a true community commitment, the work of local people concerned with the preservation of a unique heritage. It represents an important contribution to the overall character of an area which is often misrepresented by outsiders.

Interestingly, it has been produced as the result of a collaborative effort between local community volunteers and East Durham Community Arts.

Perks (1988), of the Bradford Heritage Recording Unit, describes the 'crisis of confidence' amongst museum curators concerned to make their museum and its activities relevant to 'an ethnic minority constituency which rarely enters museums at all and whose interests are represented by only the embarrassing remnants of imperial Victorian collecting policies'. His oral heritage and archive recording project set out to consult, involve and represent the communities themselves in museum activities. In recording over 700 life story interviews with members of the many different ethnic groups the purpose 'has not been to plunder people's memories for good interpretive display material; but rather to work with the communities themselves . . . to "write" their own history in their own words'. The result is 'a powerfully emotive archive of personal life stories . . . a unique history of migration to Bradford'. The collection is now available to the communities themselves through the library service, and to a wider public in the form of tape collections of extracts and a touring exhibition of archive and contemporary photographs with an oral history soundtrack. Having established access to and the confidence of the ethnic communities through this outreach programme, the unit is now responding to groups who initiate their own projects and is also bringing their work into the museum itself.

Common Ground, a small catalyst agency established in Britain in 1983, has used community action and community arts approaches to promote projects which celebrate the local and commonplace environment and heritage of rural communities. Their handbook *Holding your Ground* is a practical, comprehensive action guide to local conservation, embodying the group's two main objectives:

to promote the importance of our common cultural heritage – familiar and local places, local distinctiveness and links with the past: and to explore the emotional value these things have for us by forging practical and philosophical links between the arts and the conservation of nature and landscapes.

Exploring the relationship between people and environment through arts, through emotional responses, is the basis of much of Common Ground's philosophy:

Very often we do not appreciate our everyday surroundings until we learn that someone else values them. Paintings, photographs, descriptive writing and poetry can all help us to see familiar things in a new light and give us courage to take pride in what may appear at first glance to be a very ordinary place, and in turn to take more care of it. (King and Clifford, 1987)

Festivals, crafts, drama, poetry, film, photography, painting and music are all suggested as vehicles for celebrating a sense of place. More specifically their 'Parish Maps' project provoked not only conventional maps which identified features which local communities valued in their environment but many other imaginative and artistic expressions of valued localities in the form of collages, paintings, word pictures, embroideries, and models and sculpture.

We can identify many reasons, as I hope the case studies have shown, for involving local people in our interpretation programmes, and for being more carefully attuned to their interests and wishes. At one level those reasons are philosophical, cultural, social and political, at another they are more pragmatic. Failure to 'think community' can result in under-used resources, irrelevant provision, difficulties in harnessing voluntary effort, missed opportunities to get your agenda of conservation on to your local community's agenda for involvement and action and, above all, a lack of faith that interpretation has any real role in raising awareness or affecting change at grass roots.

Typically in the urban fringe, country park planners, architects and rangers set up a visitor centre and want a permanent exhibition to go into it. They see this as an ongoing attraction for visitors which they, the managers, no longer have to think about – a diversion for school groups, and a feature with which they can promote the park. What is really needed is a centre which is attractive to local people – humming with events and changing activities/exhibitions that they can visit regularly; a meeting place for staff and visitors and a venue for appropriate community-based activities. But, if they are to be well done, and if they are to involve local people, all these activities require significant and regular input of time and creativity by park staff who are primarily concerned with land management. If the Ranger Service had community arts/development skills in its team then it would be much more successful in creating an 'outreach' centre of the kind that is needed.

Interpretive programmes in national parks, for example, which do not reflect the interests of the local people or relate to their perceptions of what is significant in the landscape and the area's heritage, miss out on the opportunity to harness much good will, expertise, and practical support. Pippa Woolf (1988) in her paper 'Revitalisation of national parks: the human resource', identifies local people who have contact with visitors in shops, accommodation, pubs, cafes and other areas of public services as the key to providing personal interpretation of real quality and meaning for visitors.

An investment of community development skills and of time is required from park managers and interpreters to encourage them to become involved, to feel that their views have value and interest, and to give them confidence in their ability as informal interpreters. They need ongoing support in terms of skills training, information, and the maintenance of morale and enthusiasm – all of which are familiar features of community action programmes, but rarely of interpretation programmes established by park managers and interpreters.

Economic regeneration programmes, particularly for old industrial areas which include tourism based on the interpretation of that area's 'heritage', need to be firmly grounded in what that community sees and accepts as its 'heritage' and need to show tangible benefits for that community. If they do not, interpretation programmes and tourism developments based on heritage are likely to be resented by local people, rejected as irrelevant to their community and their needs, and may become politically unacceptable.

The Calderdale Inheritance Project, a major scheme for the regeneration of a traditional textile area in the north of England which includes a significant element of interpretation of that area's 'heritage' to visitors, has had success in improving the environment, attracting new development and raising the profile of this area in tourism terms. Local politicians, however, have insisted that the project add a new community development arm to direct the resources attracted into the area to communities in need, and be renamed 'Calderdale Fairshares Inheritance'.

There is the need to conserve and protect the commonplace in the local environment in Britain. Many such areas are unspectacular in landscape or ecological or conservation area terms and as such are unprotected by planning legislation; undervalued in those terms, they are vulnerable to development or other forms of degradation. One way of protecting them is to raise the awareness of local people of the value to them of their local environment, to encourage them to celebrate what they value and to conserve it. The effectiveness of community action, already well demonstrated through the work of Common Ground, offers many opportunities for interpreters to get their message across and to add their skills to the process.

Interpreters who are first and foremost conservationists, countryside managers, community architects or social historians, often have an agenda of raising awareness, of changing attitudes, and of 'getting the community involved'. Putting environment, heritage interpretation and conservation on the community's agenda may involve taking a much more direct role. Interpreters may have more success in this if they use the approaches used by campaigning community activities: getting to know the local community and how it works, who the local leaders are, who are the groups who will help, being sensitive to local interests and feelings, getting people involved and managing volunteers, and making sure that benefits are fed back into the local community. Equally the work of community arts groups exemplifies many effective and imaginative approaches which interpreters can borrow as a means of raising awareness.

Finally, perhaps the most pragmatic reason of all for broadening the range of skills available to interpreters of the traditional kind is that they need to have their own creativity stimulated. The value of having other views on and understanding other approaches to their work is immense. Good community artists are trained to tackle issues and to create a 'sense of place' in ways that stimulate and communicate through many of the senses. Community development workers are trained to respond to community needs and feelings, and to help people become involved in and express their 'sense of place' in their own way. These artistic, emotional and cultural responses to environment are essential extra dimensions to the scientific and intellectual approaches more commonly used by interpreters.

Encouraging Community Involvement – the Implications for Training of Interpreters

In conclusion, what are the implications for the training of interpreters if they are to work effectively with local communities? What sort of skill is it realistic to add to the repertoire of traditionally resource-based and resource management trained staff?

Training should primarily aim to raise awareness of what communities are, how they work and what approaches are needed to operate effectively within them. An understanding of those organizations already involved in community action over a wide range of issues will enable interpreters to draw on their skills and support services and to initiate joint projects, where appropriate.

Training which will enable interpreters to be responsive to community needs, contribute to community development and get the community involved, will need to relate to:

- understanding communities and the social, economic and cultural factors that affect them;
- understanding the many dimensions to a sense of place and heritage and the role that interpretation can play in exploring, developing and presenting a community's relationship with its environment and heritage;
- understanding how communities work, how they are structured, how groups relate to one another, recognizing leaders, key individuals and policy formers;
- understanding the various approaches to promoting community action; the role of the enabler/facilitator, catalyst/animateur and campaigner; the scope of directive and non-directive involvement;
- appreciating the emphasis on processes rather than product;
- appreciating the value of their skills as interpreters and how they can effectively contribute them;
- understanding their own limitations and knowing when and where to go for specialist advice and support.

Specialist skills are required which will enable interpreters to identify what is significant about the local environment and heritage to the people who live there. These might include

- research skills in local history, in ecology and landscape;
- group and depth interview skills to establish attitudes and interests;
- networking skills to identify people with a specific knowledge or expertise;
- skills in oral history recording, reminiscence work;
- skills in provoking artistic and other expressions of the relationship between people and place;
- skills in selecting and structuring the mass of information into acceptable themes and stories for interpretation.

Skills which will enable interpreters to promote and support community action include:

- networking to identify key groups and individuals and potential support systems;
- group working and confidence building skills, getting the best out of people and handling them carefully;
- training skills and the ability to manage volunteers;
- practical skills in dealing with local politics, fund raising, marketing, promotion and working with the media;
- specialist presentational skills, particularly in relation to low-cost media – exhibitions, oral history recording, desk-top publishing;

and finally,

- 'impressario' skills – the ability to draw in others, particularly community arts workers, to put on an appropriate mix of activities and events which will celebrate and sustain a sense of place and heritage.

Employers of countryside rangers and national parks wardens, of city park keepers, social history curators, archaeologists, historic site custodians, interpreters and interpretive planners could well be much bolder in the roles they encourage their staff to play in relation to local communities; more relaxed in the approaches considered appropriate to the 'serious' business of interpretation and nature conservation, heritage, archaeology and landscape; and more adventurous in the skills they encourage staff to acquire and which they look for when drafting job descriptions. Perhaps the time will come when every interpretation programme has trained community development workers and community artists included in the team.

References

Dower, M. (1988) 'The changing rural scene', Paper to *Visitors in the Countryside: Rural Tourism Conference*, London, 17 November 1988.

King, A. and Clifford, S. (1985) *Holding Your Ground*, Maurice Temple Smith, London.

King, A. and Clifford, S. (1987) *Holding Your Ground*, Wildwood House, Aldershot, Hampshire.

Lane, B. (1988) 'Rural communities and tourism', Paper to *Visitors in the Countryside: Rural Tourism Conference*, London, 17 November 1988.

Perks, R. (1988) 'Interpreting community history through oral history', in *Environmental Interpretation*, May, p. 14.

Place, S. (1988) 'Snake dancer interviews African prince', in *Environmental Interpretation*, May, p. 8.

Roome, N. (1988) Background paper to *Making Community Action Work in the Environment*, Conference, Losehill Hall, England, 7–9 November 1988.

Woolf, P. (1988) 'Revitalisation of national parks: the human resource', Paper at the *Second World Congress on Heritage Presentation and Interpretation*, University of Warwick, England, 30 August – 5 September 1988.

22

Towards a Co-ordinated Approach to Interpretation Training in Britain

Geoffrey Lord and Graham Barrow

Interpretation and presentation are above all about communication. Communication involves people, and we all know that however much we spend on hardware, at the end of the day it is the people who matter. This paper attempts to review the whole field of the education and training of interpreters and interpretive planners in Britain. It is a developing field and we still persist in undervaluing training. We expect a whole host of professionals educated in disciplines ranging from geography and planning to museums studies and history to pick up the philosophy and practice of interpretation as they go along. It is not surprising that the standards of heritage and environmental interpretation in Britain are variable.

Training is of equal value to employers as well as employees

Most environmental and heritage bodies (public, private and voluntary) in Britain have woefully small training budgets and little or no policy as to how these are spent. For employers, appropriate in-service training can:

- increase the motivation and morale of staff;
- introduce new and better skills to the organization;
- be used to build team spirit and co-operative working between members of staff;
- give more versatility and a chance to redirect and adapt staff to new or changing roles.

We suggest that for most organizations a budget of between 2 per cent and 4 per cent of salaries should be allocated to training activity, and some policy for its use should be evolved.

For the individual, training offers the opportunity to gain an outside perspective on the job, to have contact and exchange of ideas with fellow professionals, and can lead to greater job satisfaction through increased confidence and morale, improved skills and better job prospects.

In many situations in Britain there is no dialogue between employer and employee about the type of in-service training that is required or available. More often than not it is left up to the individual to seek out a course and persuade the manager that it is value for money. As for the manager, he or she may not think 'training' at all relevant to themselves. There are welcome signs that things are changing and some employers are now calling in specialist interpretation training organizations to organize on-the-job training.

What balance is required between types of education and training in interpretation?

There is a need to recognize the relative roles of five areas of education and training: full-time education where the philosophy and practice of interpretation is taught at postgraduate level as the main focus of the course; as an option in undergraduate and postgraduate courses in other relevant subjects; in-service training on short courses off the job; programmes of on-the-job training in-house; and distance learning courses.

A pattern of education and training in interpretation in Britain is now emerging. The first full-time Diploma Course on Heritage Interpretation has begun at Strawberry Hill College, London. The modular Masters and Diploma Course just launched at the Ironbridge Institute includes a unit on interpretation as do the Countryside and Landscape Management Courses at Manchester Polytechnic and Manchester University respectively.

For those involved in planning, managing and delivering interpretation programmes in Britain, access to training is primarily through in-service and on-the-job courses and, whilst the number and scope of these is growing, more recognition of their value by employers is required if they are to be effective in meeting needs. Distance learning materials are beginning to emerge through the work of the Open Tech. Unit and these have a valuable role to play in on-the-job training of non-graduate staff.

Who requires training and what are their priorities?

Field staff, those people responsible for communicating directly with the public, are clearly a priority for training but there are others who also would benefit from training and education opportunities. There are five groups of professionals who play a part in planning, managing and delivering interpretive programmes. These are:

- field interpretation staff;
- middle managers, planners, consultants;
- senior managers and politicians;
- specialist designers, communicators;
- conservationists, resource managers.

Table 22.1 Suggested areas of training required by different groups of staff involved in planning, managing and delivering interpretive services

Category of staff	*Training requirements*
1. FIELD STAFF E.g. rangers, wardens, volunteers, tourist guides, museum and information staff, historic site custodians.	• understanding visitor needs and interests • personal communication skills • personal presentation and confidence • ability to analyse the resource and devise themes and messages • use of support media eg AV

2. MIDDLE MANAGERS, PLANNERS
E.g. visitor services officers, park and centre managers, (public and private sector) local authority planners, consultants,
	• philosophy of interpretation
	• interpretive planning
	• facility planning:
	  – finance, budgeting.
	  – marketing.
	  – evaluation.
	  – staff management.

3. SENIOR MANAGERS, POLITICIANS
E.g. officers, members of local authorities and government agencies, directors, trustees of voluntary trusts, landowners and site owners.
	• awareness raising on:
	  – what interpretation is.
	  – costs and benefits.
	  – policy framework for tourism, recreation, conservation.
	  – value of interpretive planning.

4. SPECIALIST DESIGNERS AND COMMUNICATORS E.g. graphic and exhibitions designers, audio-visual programme makers, architects, copy and scriptwriters, performers.	• philosophy of interpretation, recreation, tourism. • heritage and conservation context. • interpretive planning process.
5. CONSERVATIONISTS AND RESOURCE MANAGERS E.g. ecologists, historians, museum curators, farmers, foresters, historic house owners, archaeologists.	• value of interpretation as aid to enjoyment and support for conservation. • understanding the needs of visitors. • value of interpretive planning.

Providing training solely for field staff, important as this is, could lead to frustration if managers and planners and the professionals with whom they must interact are not also made aware of the value of effective interpretation. Those providing training and those organizations developing training policies should recognize the need for understanding and commitment to interpretation to spread across the whole organization.

We have identified some of the training priorities of various groups of professionals involved in presenting heritage sites to the public; these are outlined in Table 22.1.

A syllabus for education and training in interpretation

We recognize six main subject areas which constitute a syllabus for interpretation training and education. These are:

(1) The philosophy and historical development of interpretation
(2) Understanding the audience
(3) Understanding the resource
(4) Interpretive planning
(5) Communication techniques and media
(6) Management and evaluation

Topics which might be covered within each of these broad categories are shown in Table 22.2. This syllabus offers a thorough grounding in the philosophy, planning and practice of interpretation, backed up of course with case studies of good practice and the development of appropriate practical skills. A comprehensive programme of in-service training should aim to address each of these areas, although the weight given to them will vary according to the training requirements of the staff concerned. The syllabus is offered here as a 'shopping list' for anyone planning courses either as full-time, in-service or distance learning training.

An example of co-operation and co-ordination in in-service short course training

Progress towards establishing a comprehensive in-service short course training programme across the broad field of interpretation in Britain has been aided by one national initiative which is an encouraging sign of inter-agency co-operation in the training field. It is a model which we believe is readily transferrable to other countries and can be extended to other forms of training.

Recognizing their common interest in heritage site presentation and interpretation six central government agencies are jointly funding a programme of short courses which are delivered by some seven training organizations

Table 22.2 A suggested syllabus for training in the philosophy and practice of interpretation

1. *Philosophy and Purpose of Interpretation*
   - the history, and development of interpretation in Britain (from its North American origins).
   - objectives of interpretation: why interpret and when not to.
   - relationship to information services, museums, recreation facilities etc.
   - benefits for the audience, the resource, the providers, the economy.
   - relationship to local community development, the voluntary sector and development of participatory concern for the environment/heritage.

2. *Understanding the Audience*
   - leisure and recreation patterns and trends.
   - tourism in Britain.
   - leisure motives and activity patterns.
   - recreation survey techniques and analysis.
   - perception studies and psychological survey techniques.
   - educational psychology and methods of learning.
   - community initiatives and sociology of 'community'.
   - expanding patterns of visitors and residents.

3. *Understanding the Resource*
   Resource appraisal techniques
   - ecological survey.
   - landscape and land use appraisal.
   - urban land use.
   - rural land use and agriculture.
   - archaeology and industrial archaeology.
   - research methods in social history and present culture.
   - who to ask: research organizations, government agencies.
   - identifying key themes and stories.

4. *Interpretive Planning*
   Introduction to planning theory and setting objectives
   (a) Strategic plans for interpretation:
   - relationship to town and country planning.
   - recreation and tourism planning.
   - museums and library services.
   - educational services.
   - regional interpretive plans.
   (b) Site plans:
   - survey of human and physical resources.
   - understanding the audience.
   - management objectives.
   - media selection.
   - predicting use and capacity.
   - financial considerations and staffing.
   - relationship of interpretive plan to the master plan.

Table 22.2 contd.

(c) Facility and service planning
- selecting the site.
- identifying themes.
- media selection.
- predicting use and capacity.
- capital and revenue costs.
- staffing.
- review and evaluation.

5. *Communication Techniques and Media*
- selecting the right media.
- copywriting and scriptwriting.
- basic design principles (exhibitions, leaflets and boards).
- printing and publishing.
- drama and theatre.
- events, open days, demonstrations.
- audio-visual techniques.
- tactile and olfactory techniques.
- public speaking.
- trails and guided walks.
- visitor centre design principles.

6. *Managing and Evaluating Facilities*
- business management.
- financial management and budgeting.
- fund raising.
- charging policies.
- market research.
- marketing and promotion.
- managing volunteers.
- educational use of interpretive programmes.
- monitoring interpretive services.
- maintenance of facilities.
- staffing structures, management, training.
- running a shop and sales.
- customer care.

throughout England and Wales. A form of training brokerage is being operated through the Centre for Environmental Interpretation at Manchester Polytechnic.

The agencies are the Countryside Commission, English Heritage, English Tourist Board, Nature Conservancy Council, Forestry Commission and the Training Commission. All of them share concerns for the conservation of the natural and manmade environment and heritage, its appreciation by visitors and its value as a tourist resource.

The basis of the co-operation is that the skills required for planning and delivering interpretive programmes are common to sites whether urban or rural, natural or manmade, contemporary or historical. Economies of scale operate with a programme of short courses planned to meet the common needs of staff from a variety of employers.

Delivering the training at a variety of venues around the country, many with different skills and approaches, encourages: a geographical spread of courses; the transfer of training skills between training organizations; co-operation in course planning and delivery; a co-ordinated approach to evaluation; and joint marketing.

In this initiative 8,000 copies of the annual programme of thirty short courses is distributed by direct mail throughout the country. Over a three-year period there has been a trebling in the quantity of short courses available, both supply and demand led, and the profile of training in interpretation has been raised considerably. No single government agency could have afforded to fund and promote such a programme of training, but through this consortium approach significant progress has been made.

The future challenge

It is widely recognized that good personal interpretation is a most effective means of communicating with visitors, and yet many of the organizations involved in presenting sites to the public still put insufficient emphasis on personal interpreters and their training. There is a need to raise the profile of the training requirements of interpreters and to reflect this in increased provision of appropriate training programmes.

If training standards are to continue to improve it is important that the support and finance for training development is made available by central government agencies and by employees. The experience gained from co-operation on the in-service training programme shows that co-ordination of effort between agencies concerned with conservation, recreation and tourism yields valuable results. Whilst some agencies appear not to have formulated a training policy for interpretation, others such as the Countryside Commission have done much to stimulate training through subsidizing the fees of participants. A consortium approach to other training initiatives could support the development of full-time courses and distance learning materials.

More interaction and sharing of experience between the providers of training would help improve standards. The Centre for Environmental Interpretation has been encouraging this dialogue, discussing a range of issues from the content of courses to their marketing and promotion and encouraging training for the trainers, for example through links with the United States National Park Service training centres at Harpers Ferry and Albright.

We need to encourage more involvement by practitioners in developing and delivering training programmes. Knowledgeable interpreters and interpretive planners who are confident and interested in training others are a vital ingredient in providing up to date and realistic training. If they are in the private sector, however, there are seldom the funds to pay for their involvement in training.

The funding of training remains a problem. With so many and varied employers of staff concerned with presenting heritage to the public in Britain, few organizations can afford their own training staff or programmes. The funds for training can come from three main sources:

(a) fees paid by employers or individuals for course attendance;
(b) subsidies on course places from central government agencies;
(c) block grant support to training organizations so that below market price training can be offered.

We believe that support to training providers should be given more priority by government agencies. The need is to concentrate expertise and commitment to the provision of interpretation training in a small number of organizations.

They need the resources to innovate and establish new courses, pay for specialist professional expertise and to market more effectively.

Conclusion

The challenge therefore in Britain in the next decade for those concerned with educating and training interpreters and those responsible for planning and managing the programmes revolves around four main areas: how to maintain and improve the quality and relevance of training programmes; how to evaluate the impact of training on employees and their organizations; how to market courses and training events so that employers allocate the time and finance to them; and how to fund the training organizations so that they can afford to develop courses, promote them and involve specialist expertise. Some of these objectives could be achieved through more accreditation of training and education courses and the establishment of a professional institute for interpreters. This is presently being investigated by the Centre for Environmental Interpretation and the Society for the Interpretation of Britains Heritage.

23

Training Interpreters
William J. Lewis

Developing effective personal communication skills is obviously a vital component in any training programme. I suggest that within such a programme there are two important principles to consider when training interpreters.

(1) That trainees should be provoked to discover principles of interpretation for themselves;
and
(2) Positive critiquing in a supportive climate secures the most effective response in trainees.

Provoking the Self-discovery of Principles of Interpretation

While trainers of interpreters have generally accepted Tilden's idea that site visitors should be provoked to discover the meaning of things and that visitors to a facility should be involved, they seldom practise these principles in their own training. I believe that provocation to discovery is equally important to both interpretation and the training of interpreters. Outlined below are three exercises I use to help interpreters discover important principles of communication for themselves.

In the first exercise, trainees are asked to follow my instructions without asking questions. They are asked to draw a circle on their paper and put a dot in it, then to draw another circle and put a triangle in it. A poll is then taken of the trainees to see what they have drawn. Most of them will usually put their dots in the centre of their circles. What is the meaning of what has been drawn? I often refer to this part of the exercise as the 'so what?' stage. When doing training, I have the trainees tell me the meanings they have discovered and add any additional ones that have come to mind.

During this exercise trainees discover that most people centre their dots and triangles and that the triangles are equilateral. But what does this mean? Among other things, it suggests that we have been acculturated to be centred and balanced, that off-beat thinkers can be quite scarce in our society. Does this prevent us from thinking of new ways of doing interpretation? How does it affect the ways in which visitors respond to stimuli?

In the second exercise trainees are asked to listen to about three minutes of music and to write down their reactions to it; what they feel, what images they see, or the name of the selection or composer, or anything else they experience during the listening process. These writings are gathered, shuffled and redistributed. Trainees are asked to read along what others have written. The music I use is a modern tune (e.g. by the Beatles) generally known by everyone, but played in a baroque style. When trainees hear this music, they almost always fail to hear the theme of the modern tune. When I tell them where the theme is in what they have heard and play a little of the original theme, most can hear 'the real thing' when it is played for a second time. Why the difference? The 'problem' of not hearing it the first time arises from the speed with which we label things. Hearing the first few notes is usually enough for most listeners to label the music 'classical' or 'baroque', and from then on to hear the music only with that context. Do our labels, instantly applied, prevent us from seeing what is really there?

Do the labels we put on visitors prevent us from seeing who they really are? Do the labels on our interpretive sites limit our perception of them? Is one of the purposes of interpretation to help people see what is really there? How important are the beginnings of messages? What labels do people attach to interpreters within the first few seconds of contact? What role does non-verbal communication play in this judgement? Does *style* often prevent one from being aware of *content*? These and many more questions can be raised from this exercise for a meaningful discussion with trainees.

A third exercise involves 'watching' slides with the eyes closed. All of a training group, except for one volunteer, is asked to close their eyes while a slide is projected on to the screen. The volunteer describes what he or she sees, allowing the hearer to form a mental image. When the single viewer has given as much information as he or she wishes, the others are invited to look. It is remarkable how different the mental images are from the image on the screen. Again, the trainees are asked, 'so what? . . . What does it mean?' Primarily, it illustrates that people have different meanings for the same words, that lakes does not equal lakes, which leads to the generalized principle that A does not equal A.

At this point I usually introduce for discussion an addendum of two lists of concepts and principles which relate to the experiences of the exercise.

Concepts

(1) We all bring our pasts to the present.
(2) Categories can blind us.
(3) First impressions are specially important.

(4) Unless helped, we often fail to find, see, comprehend.
(5) Meanings are in people, not words. *A* does not equal *A*.
(6) My perception is not your perception.
(7) Circuit overload causes distortion and fatigue.
(8) Feedback is essential.
(9) Simplicity and organization clarify messages.
(10) A picture is worth a thousand words.

Learning Principles

(1) People learn better when they're actively involved in the learning process.
(2) People learn better when they're using as many senses as appropriate.
(3) People prefer to learn that which is of most value to them at the present.
(4) That which people discover for themselves generates a special and vital excitement and satisfaction.
(5) Learning requires activity on the part of the learner.
(6) Friendly competition stimulates learning.
(7) Knowing the usefulness of the knowledge being acquired makes learning more effective.
(8) People learn best from hands-on experience.
(9) People learn best when the experience is close to them in time and space.
(10) Questions can be effectively used to help people derive meanings.
(11) Giving people expectations at the beginning of an activity will focus attention and thus improve learning.
(12) The ways in which people are responded to affects their learning.

Practising Positive Critiquing

When trainees have absorbed the concepts and learning principles on the addendum, they are ready to be exposed to some real, live examples of interpretation. As they join a regularly schedule interpretive event, they try to experience the event as if they were visitors. Afterwards, they examine the event, applying and deriving concepts of interpretation. The resultant discussion involves the trainees in the learning process, giving them the opportunity to examine a 'real life' experience. Thus they inductively complete this phase of their training, just as they started it.

As the trainees move on to making their own interpretive presentations, they should be assisted on a one-to-one basis by a supervisor or other knowledgeable person. This process is often called 'critiquing', and involves observation and feedback. If the critique is to be successful, trainees must not be defensive, or they will then resist hearing the feedback which is given to them. This is best accomplished by establishing a supportive climate.

Of all the research that has been done on this subject, the most helpful model was developed by Jack Gibb. This model shows behaviour that arouses defensiveness and that which makes a supportive climate possible. Note that the types of behaviour in the two columns are opposites. For example, if one is 'provisional', that is suggestions are made that *might* work, instead of being dogmatic or *certain* that the way to do something is . . . then a supportive climate is likely. Again, if one is 'descriptive' instead of being 'judgemental', a supportive climate is more probable.

I use a segment from the 'Fine Art of Interpretive Critiquing', a videotape distributed by the US National Park Service, as a good illustration of Gibb's model. It shows an interpreter at the Independence Hall National Historic Park giving part of a presentation at one of the buildings, Carpenter's Hall. It is interpretation that needs a great deal of improvement. In the critique session following the presentation, the interpreter moves from a defensive posture to a receptive mood because the person doing the critiquing follows Gibb's model demonstrating 'provisionalism', 'description', 'empathy' etc. Thus the second principle, that trainees respond more effectively when critiquing is done within a supporting climate, is illustrated.

Below are extracts from two key texts on interpersonal communication. The principles they outline should both underpin the trainer's relationship with the trainee and, above all, form the foundation of the interpreter's relationship with the visitor.

Interpersonal Communication

'Characteristics of a Helping Relationship', from Rogers (1967):

(1) Can I *be* in some way which will be perceived by the other person as trustworthy, as dependable or consistent in some deep sense?

(2) Can I be expressive enough as a person that what I am will be communicated unambiguously? Accepting of my own feelings and sensitive to them.

(3) Can I let myself experience positive attitudes (warmth, caring, liking, interest) towards this other person?

(4) Can I permit separateness?

(5) Can I enter the other person's world – see it as he sees it?

(6) Can I free him from the threat of external evaluation?

(7) Can I meet this individual as a person who is in the process of *becoming* or will I be bound by his past and my past?

Characteristics of constructive communication relationships according to Dean Barnlund (1968):

(1) A constructive communicative relationship is likely when there is willingness to become involved with the other person. This means willingness to take time, to avoid distraction, to be communicatively accessible, to risk attachment to others.

(2) A constructive communicate relationship is likely when one or both persons convey positive regard for the other. The other is valued as a human being, not as an object to be coerced, manipulated, or used.

(3) A constructive communicate relationship is likely when a permissive psychological climate develops. An atmosphere laden with positive or negative interpersonal judgements would seem to prevent a sensitive exchange of experience.

(4) A constructive communicate relationship is likely when there is the desire and the capacity to listen. This means listening without anticipating, without interfering, without competing, without refuting, and without forcing meanings into preconceived channels of interpretation.

(5) A constructive communicate relationship is likely when empathic understanding is communicated. It appears to be more satisfying and helpful when the listener can participate fully in the experience of the speaker, sharing his assumptions, his values, his motivations – seeing events as he sees them.

(6) A constructive communicate relationship is likely when there is accurate reflection and clarification of feeling. Of all the verbal techniques of the therapist, this seems the most appropriate to apply more widely in the ordinary interactions of men.

(7) A constructive communicate relationship is likely when the communicators are genuine and congruent. Each person should be open to his own experience so that no feeling relevant to the relationship is denied awareness.

References

Barnlund, D. (1968) *Interpersonal Communication: Survey and Studies*, Houghton Mifflin, Boston.

Gibb, J.R. (1978) *A New View of Personal and Organisational Development*, Omicron Press, London.

Rogers, C. (1967) *On Becoming a Person*, Constable, London.

24

Romantic Interpretation: A Look at Training Techniques

John Wagoner

Nearly all the training I have witnessed, over the last twenty-one years in the profession, has involved itself with mechanical techniques, of oral communication and written communication as well as 'how to conduct' methodology. Interpreters have been encouraged to fill their oral presentations and written media with a profusion of facts and scientific jargon. Yet, though visitors may seem to be impressed by all of the fact-based information, they are often genuinely overwhelmed by it. So often we fail to take into consideration two simple facts which tend to reinforce each other: that visitors to our sites are generally on holiday and intent on enjoying themselves; and that the memory curve indicates that we tend to forget much of what we see and hear, especially when we are not in a learning mode.

One of the best ways of ensuring high quality programmes designed to meet the needs of the site and fulfil the desires of the visitor is to provide good on-the-job training for new interpreters. Where training is given by supervisory staff, it is important that they learn and practise appropriate training methods and set the standards required for high quality performance in the trainees.

The approach to training new interpreters outlined below has evolved over long experience in a US national park, but is readily adapted to many other situations where interpreters are employed.

What every new interpreter should know

New interpreters must learn everything they can in order to become subject-matter experts. Their uniform, badge, patch, or whatever, makes the following statement for them – 'Hi! If you have questions, ask me; I'm the subject expert.' The visitor deserves and expects no less. It is the responsibility of the trainer to provide new interpreters with as complete a bibliography as possible and to encourage them to do their own research on the site.

Trainees should be provided with a detailed history and philosophy of their employing agency (such as the United States National Park Service) and of the site (for example Shiloh National Military Park). The significance of the site should be discussed: what event, process and/or scene is being protected and why it is important to the heritage of the nation? Every effort must be made to instil a sense of pride in the participants in the agency, the site, and in their jobs.

Understanding the visitors

An effective programme cannot be presented unless the interpreter has some understanding of the visitors including their average educational level, where they come from, and why they come to the site? It is obvious that the same programme should not be presented to a specialist group of scientists, historians or naturalists as would be presented to the general public or a children's group. Details of the visitor profile and pattern of visitation at the site are essential background information.

Trainees should be impressed with the idea that most visitors come to park areas to get away from their workaday world and are usually on holiday; the last thing they are expecting is to be educated. Therein lies the challenge; it is the duty of the interpreter to educate the visitor about the site without their knowing.

Putting a programme together

The following process is basic to all types of interpretive programmes – illustrated talks, walks, tours, demonstrations, camp fire talks and so on.

A *topic* concerning the site should be selected. At the Shiloh Military Park this might be 'the American Civil War, the Battle of Shiloh'. this is a good topic but, like most topics, it is far too broad to fit into a fifteen- or twenty-minute programme. It is necessary therefore to select a *theme*, which in this case might be 'Field Medicine at the Battle of Shiloh'. Once a theme is selected, the *theme statement* should be written in a concise single sentence. For example, 'The horror of war is never more graphic and explicit than in a battlefield hospital.'

The theme statement can then be referred to throughout the programme's development. It is the key to logical organization and is the single item that ties the programme together for the audience (Lewis, 1980).

The writing of an *objective(s)* is the key to discovering whether or not the programme is effective in meeting the needs of the visitor and the agency. The objective should be written as a clear and concise action statement – what you want the visitor to know, or what you want the visitor to do, or how you want the visitor to react (Mager, 1975).

There are usually two or three objectives for each programme. For example: 'at the conclusion of this programme, the visitor shall be able to *recite* the names of three surgical instruments used in a field hospital during the Battle of Shiloh'. An objective easily measured by asking questions at the end of the talk.

With the topic, theme, and objectives as guides, it is time for definitive research on the chosen topic. Again interpreters must be convinced that they are to be subject-matter experts.

Preparing an outline of your presentation

The three primary failings I have noticed in most interpretive programmes are: providing too many facts, poor organization, and poor or non-existent conclusions. The latter two can be easily overcome by convincing interpreters to prepare a proper *outline*.

First have the trainees write a *statement of purpose* using their theme statement as a base. The statement of purpose should be concise and to the point, for example: 'the purpose of the programme is to inform the visitor that war consists of individual action, pain and suffering; not just the glory of dead generals, troop movements, and skirmishes.'

Now, for a bit of heresy. The next task is to have them write the conclusion. It should be written exactly the way they will say it at the end of the programme. Many interpreters balk at this, but it makes good sense. The outline is nothing more than a road map. The statement of purpose is the reason for going somewhere; you look for the destination before leaving (conclusion); then you choose the route to get there (the outline). The conclusion should be three things: an obvious end to the programme without the use of such clichés as, 'that's all', or 'thank you for attending': the statement that ties the theme and essence of the programme together; and a powerful, memorable statement for the visitor – the take-home message.

The introduction too should be written exactly the way it will be spoken at the beginning of the programme. It informs the audience about the content, the theme, and why the subject is important to them and to the site. The most important sentence in the entire programme is the opening sentence. It must jolt the audience to attention and pique their curiosity. This sentence is sometimes called the *grabber*; for example, 'Ladies and Gentlemen, do you know that _____ died at the Battle of Shiloh because of poor medical attention and facilities?'

Writing the outline is an intensive and exacting process and essentially a brainstorming session. The trainees should start to write in short, curt sentences, every conceivable point that might help support the theme. Once they have exhausted their ideas it is likely each will have thirty or more supportive points. They must then look at each point and ask if it is absolutely necessary to the story and theme? A twenty- to thirty-minute programme may require a maximum of ten major points.

With outline in hand, it is time to write the script for the body of the outline, which is added to the introduction and conclusion. Many people, when they write, have a tendency to be more flowery and to use a construction that is too complicated to flow smoothly when spoken. The script must therefore be written as it would be spoken. It is not to be memorized but must be familiar enough for a brief reading of the outline to recall the essence. This will also promote confidence and lessen the inevitable nervousness that comes with the act of public speaking. All that is now left for the trainee to do is practise.

The mechanics for developing a well organized interpretive presentation are now in place. But how about the quality of a presentation? Do the mechanics of organization ensure quality? I think not.

Assessing the quality of the interpretive programme

In his book, *Zen and the Art of Motorcycle Maintenance* (1974), Robert Pirsig has a lengthy discussion on the subject of quality. In suggesting that quality as a cohesive theory does not exist in reality, he uses the age-old debate on the subject of Classicism versus Romanticism. In essence, this implies a continuum with those who feel that informational and technical design represents quality at one end and those who see aesthetics representing quality at the other. The rest of us fall somewhere between.

Classicism	*Romanticism*
Technicians	Poets
Mechanics	Artists
Engineers	Actors

Pirsig also makes the point that quality is relevant only to the individual: what one person considers quality, another may not.

A quality programme from a site manager's point of view is one where the visitor leaves with a memory of something pertinent to the significance of the site and its protection. Studies in the field of psychology over the years have consistently shown that lists of information presented orally are quickly forgotten, and that the mind has a tendency to remember a well told story more than a series of facts or ideas. There is also a tendency to remember activities which have been pleasant and positive over those activities that have been unpleasant and negative.

From the foregoing I have developed a concept for use in judging whether or not an interpretive presentation has quality. I have called the concept *Romantic Interpretation* and it consists of four elements – The Triadic Configuration of Interpretation, Wagoner's Hypothesis, Memory Coercion, and the Vivid Talk. The principles of each of these elements are outlined in Figure 24.1.

---

1. THE TRIADIC CONFIGURATION OF INTERPRETATION

The underlying form

The basic facts as they are presumed to be and set forth by a supposed authority.

The Classical Form ———————— *The Romantic Form*

Understanding and relating
basic facts in language(s)
comprehensible to the
uninformed.

Relating to the uninformed
the story intimated by
one's understanding of
the basic facts in an interesting and
entertaining manner.

2. WAGONER'S HYPOTHESIS

In any given interpretive task, it is the goal of the interpreter to provide the visitor with one valid and important point which relates to the visitor's daily life, in as interesting and entertaining way as possible.

3. MEMORY COERCION

1. Tell a thematic story.
2. Have only one point or idea to get across.
3. Use only those facts absolutely necessary to support the point or idea.
4. Relate to things familiar in everyone's daily life.
5. Paint word pictures.

4. THE VIVID TALK

A talk is vivid when the thing talked about can be seen, smelled, heard, touched or tasted.

A talk is vivid when it has the power to excite the emotions. This can be accomplished by using:

1. Elements of drama
2. Short simple sentences.
3. Image bearing words.
4. Action words.
5. Human interest stories.
6. Brief allusions to familiar experiences.
7. Personification – letting inanimate things come to life and speak.
8. Strong appeals to the basic wants of the audience.
9. Appeals to sentiments.

Figure 24.1 Romantic Interpretation

It is my experience that if these principles of quality and Romantic interpretation are discussed with trainee interpreters, and if they are encouraged to incorporate these ideas in their programmes, then the quality of interpretive programmes will improve greatly.

References

Lewis, William J. (1980) *Interpreting for Park Visitors*, Eastern Acorn Press, Philadelphia, PA.

Mager, Robert F. (1975) *Preparing Instructional Objectives*, Fearon Publishers, Belmont, Calif.

Pirsig, Robert M. (1974) *Zen and the Art of Motorcycle Maintenance*, William Morrow, New York.

25

For the Dedicated Interpreter of Many Years: Renewal, Invention and Creativity

John Brooks

The scene is all too familiar: the seasoned guide after many years of service yawns and fidgets before the start of yet another tour. Information, anecdotes, facts, humour, stories, and more information have been sculpted into an informative and interesting presentation to be delivered for the thousandth time to a never satiated public. We all know the type. He or she is a first-rate guide, but tired after years of touring, the enthusiasm gone, the edge dulled. Our professional responsibility, indeed challenge, is to reinfuse this interpreter with new life, direction, interest and vitality. How do we reinspire the seasoned guide?

Of many possible methods, I describe below two which I have used successfully in training guides for art gallery tours. Whilst the examples I quote relate to seeing paintings and sculpture afresh, the same methods can be applied equally effectively to reinspire interpreters in historic houses, in museums, in town parks and in wilderness.

The Enquiry Method

The enquiry method is something we all practise in dealing with children. We receive some delightful answers from youngsters, sometimes extraordinary perceptive, sometimes innocent and refreshing. When applied with adults, well planned questioning can generate from the floor new insights and observations, which the interpreter can respond to or, even better, can rephrase and discuss with the group. At least four different questioning levels have been identified, each labelled in heavy jargon: cognitive-memory questions (facts); convergent questions (comparisons and analysis); divergent questions (predicting, inferring); and evaluating questions (judging, choosing).

Well planned, inventive and leading questions which can be answered from the visual material directly available can generate a stimulating tour in which the participants feel involved and rewarded and the interpreter is challenged to keep the discussion continuous, relevant and provocative. No two tours are ever the same when this approach is practised successfully.

At my art museum, which displays primarily nineteenth-century French and American art, there is a portrait by the American John Singer Sargent with an inscription in French, 'To my dear master', from his 'affectionate pupil'. If a member of a tour group can read and translate the easy French, he or she might ask: how did Sargent feel about his teacher? What did Carolus-Duran teach his student, using a nearby painting by Carolus-Duran for comparison? Would the sitter (and the public) have liked his portrait? All of these questions can generate revealing answers, especially if the painting is compared to other portraits by various artists. This approach also gives the guide the opportunity to move to other works of art in a search for answers. And so the tour develops.

Practice sessions with guides acting as the public and discussing the merits of each type of question can be very stimulating and an effective training device. However, not everyone feels comfortable with this more demanding approach, and it should not be forced on interpreters.

Seeing Through Poetry

As a more creative method for infusing a tour leader with new insights we use a technique to stretch the imaginations and visual acuity of our guides. This allows them to develop a new dimension to their appreciation of a work of art, by seeing through poetry. The eighteenth-century critic Gotthold Lessing in a major treatise on the legendary priest Laocoön and the famous antique sculpture, tried to define the distinctions between art ('figures and colours in space') and poetry ('sounds in time'). More recently, others like Mario Praz have suggested a more harmonious relationship between the two arts. I always recall W.H. Auden's poem entitled 'Musée des Beaux Arts' for its moving response to Brueghel's painting *Icarus* when I encourage connecting the two art forms.

We use poetry in our training to inspire new viewpoints on works of art, to generate a special awareness and appreciation of a visual image. The interpreter's imagination is kindled and allowed to respond to an image that previously had been analysed, researched and critically evaluated. Now the guide is encouraged to be creative and react in a personal manner, with no pressure on him or her to feel right or wrong, only as Wordsworth remarked about poetry, 'the spontaneous overflow of powerful feelings'.

The poetry which is written is done during guide training sessions and the results are shared and discussed with the group in a positive way. The revealing, personal insights expand everyone's appreciation of a particular work of art; the poetry writing, however, does not become part of a tour nor is the public asked to create poetry. We have scheduled a series of workshops for children and on other occasions for senior citizens, but these are special programmes.

Encouraging new insights and appreciation of the familiar

We exhibit a dramatic painting by Turner, *Rockets and Blue Lights*, which was shown at the Royal Academy in 1840. You can just make out the smoke from two steamboats hidden in a mist behind the spray and rage of a wild but subsiding storm. But Turner is not really specific about what occurs, he only suggests and hints using rich colours and a dynamic composition full of spirals and diagonals. Adult guides were asked to respond to this dramatic scene in poetry.

One interpreter/poet pondered the theme of reality here, talking like Coleridge's Ancient Mariner about a 'ghost-like vessel surrounded by . . . drifting mist'. He concluded: 'The ship is real I know, but not appearing so'. Never mind that there are in fact two ships riding out the storm. The poetic dimension asks us to question the reality of the scene – is it fact or a vision? Turner does the same thing visually.

Degas's famous *Dancer Dressed* was a very controversial piece when shown in the sixth Impressionist exhibition of 1881. Many casts of it were made after Degas's death, and we have one in our collection. It inspired many imaginative and poetic responses from our guides. One verse developed a beautifully phrased parallel between the hard, black metal and the ballerina's firm, unyielding personality, even to suggesting a dark colour for her mood. Another poem responded to the statue's pose and facial expression. The poem asked, 'Are you dreaming, resting, . . . or is there a . . . sadness, a sadness too old for one so young?' Yet another imaginatively explored the feelings of this girl, suggested by her expressive posture.

These interpretations provide sensitive insights and elicit personal responses. Each poem enlarges the context in which the sculpture can be seen and elaborates on the meaning of the work of art. As has been expressed in a small book called *Poetry in the Gallery: Introducing Poetry through the Visual Arts* published by the Los Angeles Municipal Art Gallery, 'poetry is not intended to mirror visual images but . . . to evoke associations with . . . personal experiences'. It is a joy to share these verses among our guides and hear their responses. While discussing the poems of others, we often realize we have made discoveries ourselves.

The Muse as a trainer of guides

My role is as the Muse – to inspire the imagination and encourage creativity and invention with words and thoughts. How rewarding to see new personal meanings elicited from familiar works of art and in the end to note a deeper and more intimate appreciation, especially in the interpretation of the mood or emotion of a painting or sculpture. Guides can then draw on their experiences to enhance their tours.

We feel that by relaxing the blinkers of factual analysis and critical interpretation, important though they are, we encourage creativity and free associations through poetry, and thus nurture the internal and personal psyche of our guides. On the external and public side we advocate, to those who want more of a challenge, the use of multi-dimensional questioning and interactive conversations with the public.

The techniques I have mentioned have proved in our case to be beneficial in generating a new enthusiasm for old topics. I feel sure they will work for interpreters elsewhere looking for reinspiration and willing to embark on a little creativity and conversation in their own programmes.

26

Development Training and its Significance in Training Interpreters

James Carter

In this paper I aim to present some ideas and recommendations for development training which I believe are important both for individual interpreters and for the profession. Opportunities for making use of these ideas exist already in present training programmes but are rarely used to the full.

Skills-based Training v. Development

Training in interpretation at present, at least in the UK, is skills-based. That is, it is designed to train staff to be able to do a particular job. Sometimes the skills involved are very specific 'hard' skills such as the ability to use video equipment or knowing the principles of good graphic design. Sometimes they are more general, such as the skills of planning interpretive provision, or general communications skills: the subtleties of how to approach and deal with people which seem innate in some yet hard to learn for others. With these latter skills, training is dealing with more personal attributes, but the objectives of training remain firmly job based and definable in clear behavioural terms.

Training requires a wider approach than this. In the early decades of this century the standard training format was 'front-end' loaded: people were trained at the beginning of their lives for a job and often received no further training until retirement. The modern working environment, however, now changes much more rapidly than before. We need an ability to acquire new skills quickly, to adapt previous knowledge to new circumstances (Kenney and Reid, 1986). This is as necessary for individuals in an insecure job market as it is for employers coping with changing markets and priorities. It is worth noting that interpretation is a classic case of this: how many practising interpreters set out to enter this profession on leaving school? Most will have acquired various skills from several previous jobs, and now combine them in their present work.

This adaptability requires that people are more aware of their central

strengths and interests, of how they learn and adapt, and that they are confident in their own abilities. Training in these areas moves us away from
'front-end' models towards the notions of 'continuous development' which
see training as a process that takes place throughout life. These ideas
emphasize the 'development' part of the often linked but widely different
pair, 'training and development'.

Development is usefully defined by the Training Commission as: 'the
growth or realisation of a person's ability through conscious or unconscious
learning'. The Commission also comments: 'Development programmes
usually include elements of planned study and experience and are frequently
supported by a coaching or counselling facility' (see Kenney and Reid, 1986).

Development training provides the 'planned experience' part of this
programme and, as the definition implies, is concerned very much more with
the person being trained and with their fulfilment, than with strictly defined
job skills. It seeks to enable trainees to gain:

- a greater awareness of themselves and their strengths;
- a greater sense of their own power in choosing ways of behaviour and
  directions in their career;
- a greater fulfilment of their potential.

These aims have direct relevance to all working situations.

Development training frequently includes objectives which reflect this
relevance, such as:

- increasing trainees' knowledge of their effect on others;
- developing their ability to manage others or to work effectively in
  teams;
- increasing motivation;
- team building.

The Value of Development Training for Interpreters

To those with no experience of this type of training, these may seem difficult
objectives to achieve. My own experience comes from a centre which used
much outdoor activity as a vehicle for learning. Course participants worked
in groups of about eight on unfamiliar and sometimes physically challenging
tasks such as building rafts, hill walking, canoeing and camping. These
activities did not include being dumped in the middle of nowhere without
a map or being encouraged to 'push yourself to your limits' – a popular
image of such courses which I had to work hard at to dispel before any real
learning could take place. The intensive programme also included indoor
exercises which often produced some of the most valuable results.

The important elements in all the activities is that they are designed to lead
to a review and discussion of what happened. During this, the tutor working

with the group encourages participants to talk about their feelings and reactions, and to give other group members feedback on their contributions.
Through this, the participants learn about how they respond in particular
situations and about how others perceive them. They also learn about the
behaviours which encourage effective group working, or those which
contribute to good management. It is important to build into the programme
opportunities to try new ways of behaviour as a result of learning from
previous projects.

At present, development training is used primarily in management training, in programmes which introduce graduate or school leavers to work, and
in programmes for unemployed people to help them regain a sense of their
worth and direction. It is also used with groups of young offenders as a way
of enabling them to reassess their patterns of behaviour. So, is there a place
for this in interpretation training?

It is, to some extent, already happening or the ground is at least already
fertile for it. For example, on courses which give training in video production, participants are required to learn new and complex skills very rapidly:
a situation analogous to the intensive programme of challenging outdoor
activity outlined above. They also usually work very closely together with
other people in small project groups: an ideal situation in which to learn
about themselves and how they relate to others. On public speaking courses,
participants learn much in areas concerned with very personal skills and
abilities, and often overcome fears far greater than those which confront a
novice climber. Participants on such courses frequently comment that they
have found the experience of discovering their own capabilities, or of working with other people, as interesting as the skills the course actually set out
to teach. This is exactly the subject material of development training, but
without proper tutorial support any learning in these areas can at best be
partial. The advantages of building this type of training into the development
of interpretation staff are many. Principal among these are the following:

(1) Interpretation, whatever else it concerns, is about communication skills.
These are sharpened by a greater sensitivity towards and awareness of others:
a major element in development training.

(2) Development training increases participants' abilities to manage and
work with people: abilities which are essential in contact with the public and
in their working relationships with other staff.

(3) Development training can lead to greater motivation at work, and to a
sense of greater fulfilment. It could help to produce interpreters who are less
easily bored, and more able to make decisions about their own future as well
as that of the facility they work for. Apart from the beneficial effects this
would have on the interpretation they provide, it seems to me that any
responsible employer should have their staff's future development as an
altruistic objective.

Introducing Development Training into Courses for Interpreters

Having examined briefly the nature of development training and its relevance to interpretation training, four options can be suggested for its introduction:
  Firstly, opportunities for development learning exist already but are not being used. This is, at least in part, because development objectives are not on the agenda of the courses concerned: they are not a part of the contract between trainer and trainee. If development training is to be introduced it must be done openly and accepted by all participants. This will mean including aims such as 'to explore the factors which lead to effective team working and how you can best contribute to this' in the course outline. If this is not done, any discussion of issues such as these may well be seen as threatening, and so be rejected.
  This requires acceptance of these aims both by participants and by the employers who are paying the course fee. Within existing courses, it might be possible to set up one group with some development training objectives for participants who are interested.
  Secondly, trainers working with these objectives need to be aware of what they are doing and to be skilled and sensitive in using group work. The role of the trainer in development training is very definitely not that of an instructor. There are no specific learning goals or lists of facts which must be communicated. The trainer needs rather to facilitate discussion and to construct guidelines for participants. The Training Commission quoted earlier, referred to development programmes as being supported by a 'counselling facility', and indeed the role of the trainer in these programmes is far more akin to that of a counsellor than to an instructor.
  Thirdly, development training must have support back in the workplace. This is a necessity for all training if it is to be really effective, but especially for development training. Participants may well return with new insights into themselves and how they operate, and new ideas of how they would like to operate and interact with others. For them to gain maximum benefit, and for the development process to be truly continuous, this requires wise and supportive managers who are not afraid to relinquish control, to let their staff grow and try new ideas.
  Finally, those managers must not have unrealistic expectations of what development training can achieve. I believe it to be a very powerful and valuable tool, but a one-week course will not turn an overbearing and sulky ranger into everyone's favourite workmate, or a new and unconfident supervisor into a captain of industry. What it will do, however, is give them new insights into themselves and new ideas to try. Trying those ideas, revising them and trying new ones may well occupy the rest of their lives but they will be enriched and stimulated by the process. That is surely the meaning of continuous development.

References

Kenney, J. and Reid, M. (1986) *Training Interventions*, Institute of Personnel Management, London.

27

Where Arts, Imagination and Environment Meet

Jan Dungey

In this paper my intention is to explore the contribution which the arts can make to the practice of interpretation and the presentation of the environment. The training which artists receive is designed to encourage them to look for new ways of experiencing places and of expressing that experience through their particular artistic language. The value of adding artistic approaches to the repertoire of skills available to the interpreter is, in my view, immense.

The Contribution of Arts to Interpretation

Arts *approaches* offer new ways of experiencing places, arts *languages* offer new ways of *expressing* experience of places, arts *expressions* can contribute to life-affirming cultural values which seek to encourage understanding of our interdependence with place. These are values that celebrate a philosophy which recognizes that our understanding of organic life support systems, other species and other cultures is vital to our existence.

Arts Approaches

Arts approaches offer new ways of experiencing places using our *senses*, our *emotions* and our *imaginations*. Our physical instruments are highly sophisticated sensory receivers, but rarely do we switch on our senses and tune them in so that our receptors are picking up as much information about our surroundings as they are capable of. Arts approaches can help with sensory development.

Visual artists and visual art educators are trained in ways of looking, to analyse what they see and to use that analysis to further their and others' understanding of the visual information around them. Those working with music are trained to listen and to use their ears to distinguish sounds and the acoustics of places, and to make sense of aural information.

Tactile artists and educators are encouraged to touch, to explore with their hands and to allow what they touch to educate them about tactile properties and possibilities. They are trained to make sense of tactile information. Dancers are trained to explore space with their bodies and understand the interplay between their surroundings and themselves – to comprehend spatial information.

The enquiring body and the enquiring senses are as important as the enquiring mind, and the arts offer different ways of developing the enquiring senses; different approaches to looking, listening to, touching and knowing places. Arts approaches encourage different ways of 'sensing' places and understanding sensory information.

Understanding the Emotional Impact of Places

The arts are also known for the value they place on feelings, for the importance of being receptive to the emotional impact of a subject. They encourage people to become more conscious of how places affect them, how they make them feel.

The arts encourage empathy; understanding life from another perspective. If creative writing techniques are applied to places then, instead of finding words for fictional personalities, writers can give voice to actual places. If acting techniques are applied to understanding the character of a place, rather than a character in a play, powerful feelings about a place can be portrayed.

The arts value the importance of inspiration as a stimulant to the imagination, the forming of images in the mind. Inspiration is defined by the dictionary as being both 'a stimulus to creative activity' and 'the act of inhaling'. The act of inhaling or breathing in a place, allowing the smell and taste of a place to be drawn into you, can stimulate both the senses and the mind to creative activity. Places can be powerful stimulants to inspire and fire the imagination to form memorable images. However, if our physical instruments, our senses, emotions and imaginations can become more sophisticated receivers through arts approaches, if we increase our capacity to switch on, tune in and pick up the frequencies of places, how can that information be transmitted?

Arts Languages

As interpreters, what languages do we use to heighten people's awareness of the visual, aural, tactile, inspired and inhaled nature of a place? How do we intensify people's experience of the spatial and acoustic properties of a place that are part of its uniqueness? How do we deepen the emotional connections between people and places? How do we fire people's imaginations with a place so that their minds form and retain images so powerful that they live on in their memories?

Arts languages focus the process of sensing and feeling a place and offer structures so that the imagination can fill in the detail. Drawing, painting, print-making and other visual media; sculpture, weavings and other tactile media; dance, performance and other physical media; music and vocal media; poetry, story and other written and spoken media are all languages that can 'transmit' and communicate the 'information' we have received from places. Arts language gives form to sensory and emotional experience, as the imagination gives form to inspirations.

Arts languages can increase the range of on-site interpretation and presentation techniques. For example, music and dance composed and choreographed to express the images and emotions evoked by a place can be presented *in situ* in such a way as also to heighten awareness of the spatial and acoustic characteristics of a place. Static two- and three-dimensional images can reflect visual qualities of place, enhance details and meanings, and encourage physical and tactile discovery.

Theatre and performance can combine a number of expressive media and also offer interaction between the place, the interpreter and the public.

Arts Expressions

The arts can offer ways of approaching places and the means of articulating and communicating experience of place to others. It goes without saying that sensitivity, feelings, empathy, inspiration and imagination are vital qualities to foster in human beings, especially if we want our species to understand, care for and enhance the world in which we live.

If arts expressions can give cultural importance to these qualities and their application to places, if they can introduce new images, myths and celebrations of places into our cultural store, they will be of as great a practical value as the physical preservation of a particular historic building or an area of outstanding natural beauty.

Index

Aakjaer, J. 140
Abelson, R.P. 36
accuracy – historical 21, 108
Alderson, W.T. 31
Alden Biesen 93
Aldridge, D. 2, 35, 123, 142
Andaman Islands 168
antique (vb) 59
'Archeology meets Education' 119
Architectural Heritage Year 93
Association of Independent Museums 19
Australian National Parks 144–5
authenticity 44–5

Bagpipe Museum, Morpeth 59
Banagher 105
Barrows, H.H. 80
Bayley, S. 58
Beamish Open Air Museum 22
Boddington, J. 115
Bolivia 117
Blickling 49–53
Bradford Heritage Recording Unit 195
Branodunum Roman Fort 49
Brisbane Forest Park 147
British Museum Act 18
burials 98, 105
Burke, Edmond 70, 82
Butser Ancient Farm 62

Calderdale Inheritance Project 197
Capilano Indians 91
C.A.R.E. Community Action in the Rural
  Environment 191
Carrickfergus 101
Carson, C. 107
Castlerigg 49
ceremonial time 110
Centre for Environmental Interpretation 125,
  206–7
Chakrabarti, G. 116

Charteris, Lord 16
Chartres Cathedral 49
Cherryburn 59
Clifford, S. 196
Cliffords Tower 42, 43
Colonial Williamsburg 29, 122
Common Agricultural Policy 126
'common ground' 195, 197
Conservation Foundation 181
  global 167
  political significance 165
'conserve as found' 26, 101
Cothele 55
Coulthard, V. 156
Council of Europe 93
Countryside Act 123
Countryside Commission
  (for England and Wales) 123, 127, 206, 207
  (for Scotland) 123
creative conservation 3
critiquing (positive) 211
Crocker, C.R. 148
cultural decline 24, 90
  honesty 159
  identity 91, 92
  values 93, 94
Cyril, H. 53

Danebury Hill Fort 59
Daniels, D. 155
Darwin 72, 78, 80
Das Haus am Checkpoint Charlie 34
Davies, G.L. 67
Debord, G. 20
Degas 222
determinism 80
Dilthey, W. 83, 84
Disney 20, 59
Dower, M. 193
Down Cathedral 105
dreamtime 158

Dunluce Castle 106
Dunstanburgh Castle 50

East Anglia University 180
East Durham Community Arts 195
eclectism 58
Eco, U. 20
Economic and Social Research Council 180
economics 25, 73, 88, 197
Education Ambiental 163
Elgin Marbles 16
emotional response 46
English Heritage 4, 15, 18, 27, 43, 49, 59, 60, 125, 206
empiricism 68
English Tourist Board 19, 206
Erddig 54
ethnic minorities 97, 98, 192
Europa Nostra 93
European Community Regional Fund 19
evaluation 86, 128
Evans, C. 146
Everhart, W.C. 137

Festival of Britain 27
Florence 48, 49
Forestry Commission 125, 206
Foster, J. 123
Foster-Smith, J. 175
Foster-Smith, B. 175
Fountains Abbey 50, 59
'free form' 190
Freud 46
Fyson, A. 33, 43

Gadamer, H.G. 83, 85
Gettysburg Battlefield 107, 111
Gibb, G.R. 212
Gilpin, W. 70, 82
Glacken, C.J. 67
Goethe 83
Goose Green Battle 46
Graham, A.D. 138
Grand Canyon 49
Great Barrier Reef Marine Park 143, 146, 149
Greencastle 101
Grey Abbey 104
Grossman, L. 80
Groundwork Trusts 126
Gudbrandsdalen 80
guidebooks 50

Hawaii Volcanoes National Park 157
Hazelius, A. 79, 122
health – and conservation 73
Herder, J.G. 84
Heritage – defined 15, 16
Heritage industry 18
hermeneutics 83

Historical Association 116
historicism 21
Hivernaud, J. 38
Hogarth, W. 82
Horne, D. 22, 41
Huxley, A. 90
hyperreality 20

idealised past 21, 24
identity – sense of 154, 194
Ightham Mote 50
Imperial War Museum 40, 41
Independence Hall 111
inspiration 230
Italian Renaissance 24
interpretation – defined 64, 123
interpretation free zones 49, 129
Ironbridge Gorge Museum 22, 126
Ironbridge Institute 202

Jameson, F. 20, 21
Jencks, C. 58
Johnson, L.B. Library 20
Jorvik Viking Centre 19

Kakadu National Park 158, 159
Kehoe, A. 117
Kilvert, Rev F. 49
King, A. 196
Knockmany 102
Kutikina Cave 153

landscape defined 184
left brain – right brain 108
Leopold, A. 76
Leuven – University of 94
Levi-Strauss 5
Lindisfarne 59
Lippman, L. 154
living history 30, 44, 60, 62, 79, 111
Londonderry Walls 100, 101
Llanthony 49
Lovejoy, A.O. 137, 138
Low, S.P. 31
Lowenthal, D. 44, 78, 79, 108, 109, 135, 139

Machlis, G. 86
MacPherson, J. 82
Malthus 72, 73
Madagascar 167
Mammini, S. 116
Manchester Polytechnic 202
    University 202
Manpower Services Commission 19
Marine Conservation Society 170
Marine Nature Reserve – U.K. 170
Marsh, G.P. 77
Meli, F. 117
memory coercion 218

Mersey Heritage Trust 192
Military Museum, Lisbon 41
Mitchell, J.H. 110
Morgan, C. 155
Morris, W. 26
Mount Rushmore National Park 137
multi-period sites 103
Museum of the Year 59
Museums and Galleries Commission 19
museums – outdoor 18, 111
myths 17, 29, 45, 79, 83

Naess, A. 73
narrow water 100
National Heritage Acts 16
National Heritage Memorial Fund 16, 19
national identity 78, 117
National Maritime Museum 27, 55
National Parks Service, USA 2, 49, 81, 122, 207, 214, 215
National Parks of England and Wales 72, 180
National Trust 25, 50, 53, 54, 126
Nature Conservancy Councils 125, 206
nature – defined 136
Nepal 168
Newtonwards Priory 104
Nordiska Museum, Stockholm 79, 122
nostalgia 77, 78, 91, 130

objectivity 33, 34
O'Brien, C. 148, 149
Olsen, B. 79, 122
'only connect' 55
Oradour-sur-Glane 37–9
oral history 155, 195
Owen, R. 79

Passmore, J. 137
Peak District National Park 123
Penning-Rowsell, E.C. 139
Perks, R. 195
picturesque 82
Pirsig, R. 217
Place, S. 192
place
  emotional impact of 230
  sense of 6, 49, 111, 154, 194, 198
Plas Newydd 53, 54
plausibility (historical) 109
Podgorny, I. 119
poetry 221, 222
politicalisation of past 117
possibilism 73
post modernist hyperspace 21
professionalism 26, 125
Project Tiger (India) 166
provocation 46, 85, 209
Putney, A.D. 149
Pu'uhonua O Honaunau (Hawaii) 158

Quarry Bank Mill 55
Queensland National Park 147, 149
questioning levels 220
Quoile Castle 103

Rare Breeds Centre 55
Ray, J. 69
Regional Planning of Interpretation 128
Reich, W. 46
Rock Art sites 159
Rockefeller, J.D. 122
Rogers, C. 212
Roggenbuck, J.W. 148
romanticism 81, 82
Roome, N. 191
Royal National Park 142
Royal Society for the Protection of Birds 126
Runte, A. 2
Rural Development Commission 126
Rural Tourism Forum 192, 193
Ruskin, J. 26, 104

Sanctuary Wood, Belgium 42
Sande, T. 109, 112
Sandvig, A. 80
Scandinavian Folk Life Park 81
Scarborough Castle 61
scholarship 17, 27
selectivity 26, 89
sensory awareness 111
  development 239
  enjoyment 73
Sharp, G.W. 148
Shier, J. 42
Shiloh National Military Park 215
simulation 62
Sinclair, P. 114
Skansen Open Air Museum 79, 122
Skeffington, A. 181
Society for the Interpretation of Britain
  Heritage 2, 125
South Korea – National Parks 168
Spanish Armada 21, 27, 29
Spanish Congress of Environmental
  Education 163
Spencer, H. 78–80
Spinoza 68
stewardship 17, 68, 77
Stonehenge 25, 49, 118
Strawberry Hill College 202
Strong, Sir R. 20, 22

Tank Museum, Bovington 40
Tasmanian National Parks 148
Tate Gallery 58
teleology 68
Third World Reserve Management 166
Thomas, K. 67
Thomas, W.L. 67

Tilbury 27
Tilden, F. 35, 46, 85, 107, 123, 142, 180
time passed 108, 109
tourism and conservation 3, 165
Training Commission 206, 225, 227
truth 29, 43
Tully Castle, Co. Fermanagh 102
Turner, J. 142
Turner, J.M.W. 58, 222

Uluru National Park 156, 157
United Nations World Heritage Convention
    17, 22

Vasa, Stockholm 58
Victoria and Albert Museum 18, 20, 22

Wagar, J.A. 149
Wallace, M. 36
Warrie, Y. 155
Waterloo 88
Weightman, B.A. 8

Wigan Pier 19, 20
wilderness 71
Wildfowl Trust 126
Wildlife Tourism 165
Willandra Lakes 153
Williams, L. 155
Williamson, J. 5
Wimpole 55
Wincklemann, J. 78
Woolf, P. 196
Woomera 16
Wordsworth (William) 83
World Archaeological Congress 113
World Conservation Strategy 76, 149
World Heritage Site 50
World Wide Fund for Nature 92, 170
Wyperfield National Park 143

Yellowstone National Park 122, 137, 138
Yorkshire Dales National Park 179, 182
Young National Trust Theatre 54

Contents
Volume 2: The Visitor Experience

List of Figures   vii

List of Tables   viii

List of Contributors   ix

1 Introduction: The Visitor Experience   1
  David L. Uzzell

2 Plural Funding and the Heritage   16
  Neil Cossons

3 Funding our Heritage   23
  Stuart Smith

4 The Search for New Funds   29
  Richard Broadhurst

5 Can Heritage Charities be Profitable?   44
  Marc Mallam

6 Marketing in Visitor Centres: A Study   51
  Terry Robinson

7 Broadening the Market   58
  Antony Eastaugh and Nicholas Weiss

8 Implications of Special Interest Tourism for Interpretation and
  Resource Conservation   68
  Raymond Tabata

9 An Interpretive Challenge: The US National Park Service
  Approach to Meeting Visitor Needs   78
  Michael D. Watson

10 Warwick Castle: Safeguarding for the Future through Service   84
    Martin Westwood

11 Planning to Improve Service to Visitors in Canada's National Parks   96
    Jenny Feick

12 The Visitor – Who Cares? Interpretation and Consumer Relations   103
    Terry Stevens

13 Managing the Town and City for Visitors and Local People   108
    Ian Parkin, Peter Middleton and Val Beswick

14 Interpretive Planning for Regional Visitor Experiences: A Concept
    whose Time has Come   115
    Alan Capelle, John Veverka and Gary Moore

15 On-Site Real-Time Observational Techniques and Responses to
    Visitor Needs   120
    Paul Risk

16 Evaluation in Museums: A Short History of a Short History   129
    Harris Shettel

17 Heritage as Media: Some Implications for Research   138
    Roger Silverstone

18 The Social Helix: Visitor Interpretation as a Tool for Social
    Development   149
    Alan Machin

19 What People Say and How They Think in a Science Museum   156
    Paulette McManus

20 Outdoor Education for Rural Fifth-Graders: Analysis of Attitudes,
    Expectations, Knowledge and Perceptions   166
    Robert C. Wendling

21 Time-Lapse Photography: Advantages and Disadvantages of its
    Application as a Research and Visitor Behaviour Monitoring Tool   179
    Gail Vander Stoep

22 The Formative Evaluation of Interactive Science and Technology
    Centres: Some Lessons Learned   191
    Terry Russell

23 Truths and Untruths in Museum Exhibitions   203
    Jerzy Swiecimski

24 Heritage Revisited: A Concluding Address   212
    David Lowenthal

    Index   217

    Contents for Volume 1   221